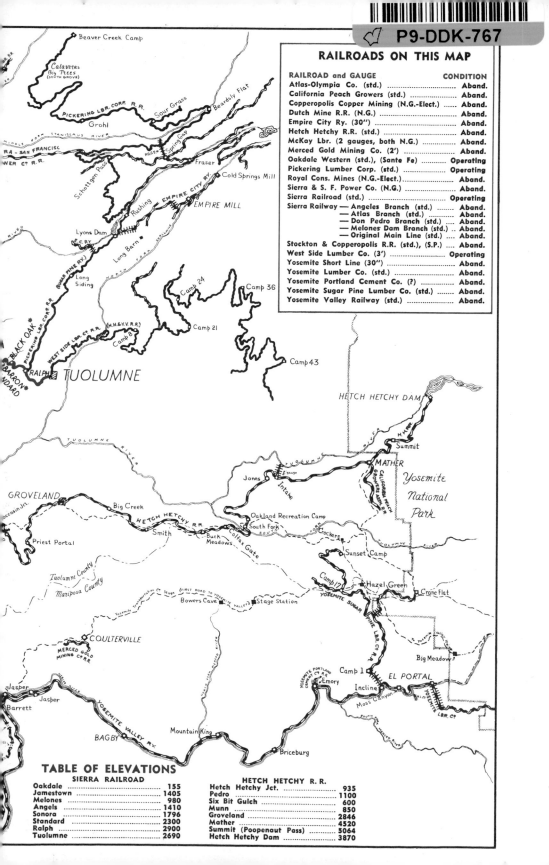

RAILROADS ON THIS MAP

RAILROAD and GAUGE	CONDITION
Atlas-Olympia Co. (std.)	Aband.
California Peach Growers (std.)	Aband.
Copperopolis Copper Mining (N.G.-Elect.)	Aband.
Dutch Mine R.R. (N.G.)	Aband.
Empire City Ry. (30")	Aband.
Hetch Hetchy R.R. (std.)	Aband.
McKay Lbr. (2 gauges, both N.G.)	Aband.
Merced Gold Mining Co. (2')	Aband.
Oakdale Western (std.), (Sante Fe)	Operating
Pickering Lumber Corp. (std.)	Operating
Royal Cons. Mines (N.G.-Elect.)	Aband.
Sierra & S. F. Power Co. (N.G.)	Aband.
Sierra Railroad (std.)	Operating
Sierra Railway — Angeles Branch (std.)	Aband.
— Atlas Branch (std.)	Aband.
— Don Pedro Branch (std.)	Aband.
— Melones Dam Branch (std.)	Aband.
— Original Main Line (std.)	Aband.
Stockton & Copperopolis R.R. (std.), (S.P.)	Aband.
West Side Lumber Co. (3')	Operating
Yosemite Short Line (30")	Aband.
Yosemite Lumber Co. (std.)	Aband.
Yosemite Portland Cement Co. (?)	Aband.
Yosemite Sugar Pine Lumber Co. (std.)	Aband.
Yosemite Valley Railway (std.)	Aband.

TABLE OF ELEVATIONS

SIERRA RAILROAD

Oakdale	155
Jamestown	1405
Melones	980
Angels	1410
Sonora	1796
Standard	2300
Ralph	2900
Tuolumne	2690

HETCH HETCHY R.R.

Hetch Hetchy Jct.	935
Pedro	1100
Six Bit Gulch	600
Munn	850
Groveland	2846
Mather	4520
Summit (Poopenaut Pass)	5064
Hetch Hetchy Dam	3870

SIERRA
RAILWAY

Sierra Railway station at Sonora.

SIERRA
RAILWAY

by
§ DOROTHY
NEWELL
DEANE

HOWELL-NORTH • Berkeley, California
1960

SIERRA RAILWAY

Printed and bound in the United States of America.

Library of Congress Catalogue Card No. 60-15643

Published by Howell-North Books
1050 Parker Street, Berkeley 10, California

DEDICATION

To my father, WILLIAM HAMILTON NEWELL, a New Jerseyite, who stopped in at Ann Arbor, Michigan, in 1885 to get himself a degree before moving West to build frontier railroads.

He had undaunted faith that these would be the prime agents in the growth and development of the country.

His keen humor and his forward thinking through sixty years spent mostly in Tuolumne County, inspired the writing of this book.

ACKNOWLEDGMENTS

For assistance in the compilation of this book the author wishes, firstly, to thank her brother, Paul C. Newell, Director of the Sierra Railroad, for patient checking of facts and figures. Also the following California friends and friendly companies for generously giving of their time, letters and pictures: Mr. John S. Anderson, Fresno; Mr. Joseph Azeveda, Tuttletown; Mr. James Baker, Jamestown; Mrs. F. H. (Louise Bullock) Beeston, San Francisco; Miss Della Butterfield, Jamestown; Mr. John Thomas Bullock, Berkeley; Mr. Joe Cavagnero, Jamestown; Mr. William Cheney, Manager and Vice President Sierra Railroad, Jamestown; Mr. F. Norman Clark, Felton; Mr. and Mrs. Wade Coffill, Oakdale; Mr. D. C. Demarest, Berkeley; Mr. Ferol Egan, Jamestown; Mr. Fred Ellis, Tuolumne City; Mr. and Mrs. Jesse Fowler, Jamestown; Mrs. John Keagy, Sonora; Mr. Ralph Kerchum, Oakland; Mr. Keith Kerr, Sonora; Mr. Hugh McLean, Sonora (for Jamestown *Mother Lode Magnet* files); Mr. F. F. Momeyer, Manager, and Mr. William Scott, Pickering Lumber Company, Standard City; Mr. and Mrs. R. W. (Alma Newell) Moran, Jamestown; Mr. Eugene M. Prince, Tuolumne City and San Francisco; Mayor W. B. Reynolds, Oakdale; Mr. Arthur Ronten, Manager of West Side Operation of Pickering Lumber Company, Tuolumne City; Mr. Alex Rosborough, Yreka; Mr. Donald I. Segerstrom, Sonora; Miss Irene Simpson, History Room, Wells Fargo Bank, San Francisco; Judge J. A. Smith, San Andreas; Mr. Stanley A. Snook, Del Rey; Mr. Archie Stevenot, Sonora; Mr. Fred Stevenot, Carson Hill and San Francisco; Mrs. J. (Lorraine Moran) Valente, Angels Camp; Mrs. William Wenneson, Jamestown; Miss Mary Wheeler,

Secretary, Sierra Railroad offices, Crocker Bank, San Francisco; Mrs. Ed (Vivian Burgess) Zimmerman, Oakdale; *The Oakdale Leader* and *Sonora Union Democrat* for access to their files.

This list could hardly be complete without mentioning the California Historical Society, San Francisco, and the Pacific Gas & Electric Company, San Francisco. For permission to use the roster of locomotives compiled by D. S. Richter and G. M. Best, thanks go to *The Western Railroader* who granted, too, the use of maps from Alfred Rose, Jr., of Modesto. Mr. Rose also furnished pictures and negatives.

Less tangible, perhaps, than pictures and facts, has been the kindly cooperation of people whose enthusiasm for the completion of this work made the years of preparation pleasurable. I thank them all.

DOROTHY NEWELL DEANE

Oakland, California
1960

TABLE OF CONTENTS

CHAPTER ONE

This is the story of a little, old short-line railroad that said: "I think I can," in 1896 and did. And still does in 1960. The story of the Sierra Railroad would be black and white without the color of its setting in California's foothills and some of the people who built it, nurtured it and almost killed it; people who loved it, people who hated it and people who keep it operating today. Shorter and longer standard-gauge short lines have existed in California but none with longer continuous operation, or with shorter columns in the red. None whose long and short whistles have echoed through more historic country or during more spectacular days. None whose ups and downs, not only in grades but in booms and depressions, have been more unique on a roadbed presently fifty-seven miles short of having been one hundred and forty miles long. Nor powered by gayer, shorter little wood-burning locomotives followed by bigger and bigger oil-burning steam engines finally replaced by diesels whose long mournful blasts sounded the death knell of steam.

The Sierra Railroad, having been unique since its conception, has had its share of publicity through the years in news, photography and moving pictures. This book then is a compilation of known data with the addition of some little-known facts about it and the people who kept it full steam ahead. It is the long and the short of it with a fourth dimensional slant at its ups and downs and the sadness and fun of it.

The setting of the Sierra Railroad has been immortalized by the exciting drama that took place fifty years before its rails were laid in that section of California known as the Mother Lode country. The free gold found there turned the green eyes of the world on those fabulous foothills for ten ripsnorting years. The saga of that rags-to-riches placer and pocket mining era will live forever, dramatized in books and memories, but the story of this little railroad begins in the less glamorous quartz mining era that followed and continues, alive, into the present. Even into the future, so far as we can see, looking down its shining, working tracks.

That peculiar geological structure called the Mother Lode extends north and south one hundred and fifty miles along the western slopes of the central portion of the Sierra Nevada Mountains in California. On it, and on gold bearing ledges branching out three to seven miles from it, are located nearly all the fabulous placer and quartz gold mining areas that attracted hundreds of thousands of men to it over a period of sixty years. By means of picks, washing pans, rockers, hydraulic rams, sluices, crude and modern machinery, men extracted two billion dollars worth of gold. Before the days of astronomical national debts, this was a noteworthy amount of money, and this gold industry was still a big one in 1897 when the Sierra Railroad came to the then operating quartz mines in the southern section of the Mother Lode. Most of the mines reached by these rails were in Tuolumne which was then California's leading gold producing county, having produced over $2,000,000 worth in that year. Also there were uncounted square miles of virgin forests in Tuolumne County as well as other heavy hauling potentials worthy of rail transportation.

In the early 1800's, before Mr. Marshall found his nugget, Tuolumne County was an undeveloped little-known region of some two thousand square miles bounded by five counties and crossed by three rivers. With rolling hills at its lower three hundred and fifty foot elevations, to towering forested mountains and bleak crags over thirteen thousand feet high, the county had seven hundred thousand acres of unentered government land, much of which was above the winter snow line and accessible only in summer by immigrant trails crossing the Sierra Nevada Mountains in this perilous vicinity. The county's lower lands, too rocky for good farming and often too dry for year around feeding of cattle, was spotted with the homes of some fifty settlers for whom travel to a city meant days spent behind horses on barely discernible roads.

But then, in January 1848, that famous first California nugget was picked up by James Marshall in a sawmill race in the north central part of the Mother Lode country. From this spark, the pioneering race for riches caught fire resulting in the migration to California of countless gold seekers who poked and picked into every nook and corner of the state. One of these Forty-Niners, as they came to be called, turned up a nugget in Tuolumne County which made Marshall's look like a grass seed. It brought him $3,000 and fifteen thousand fortune hunters to his area. These first Forty-Niners took an estimated 4,350,000 ounces of loose gold worth $55,000,000 out from under one bullpine-shaded town and its environs which is now Columbia State Park. In the following ten years the county was host to thousands of gold seekers who almost brought the state capital from Monterey to Columbia. But when the placer gold petered out, most of these early boys followed the new gold and silver strikes, leaving the craggy upper reaches of Tuolumne County untouched and the placer-pitted foothills staked out in mining claims, many of them questionable.

The once famous placer town of Columbia remained a rough but settled community of some four hundred hangers-on, living among its graveyard-like, white limestone, washed clean of dirt and branch by millions of gallons of water which had been hosed through each crevice to purge the gold. This and other "boom" towns of the county had all but become "ghost" towns by 1865. In the next thirty years of doldrums and hard times, after the Civil War, local industries were kept alive by Tuolumne County's population of some six thousand people in meager contact with the outside world.

Before and during the Gold Rush, ox-team carts and mule pack trains meandered over hundreds of elusive trails in Tuolumne County, some of which, however rough, became recognized and actively traveled roads such as the Sonora road running without toll from Stockton, in California's central San Joaquin Valley, to Sonora, the county seat. This road, and a half dozen others crossing and joining it, was traveled by private mule and horse teams, and then those praiseworthy public conveyances, Wells Fargo stagecoaches. These ran, daily, in 1853, from Columbia and Sonora all the way to San Francisco with overnight stops in such valley towns as Oakdale, Stockton, Tracy and Livermore. When this service was discontinued about 1878, locally owned stage lines took over to wind up hill and down among the settlements of Tuolumne County, clinging to the edges of cliffs, mired by the muds of winter, over the hubs with water during spring thaws and choked with dust through the rainless seven or eight months of an average California foothill summer. Later this road was traveled from mining towns in the Sonora area to nearer rail connections like Milton and Oakdale, where Southern Pacific spurs attracted enough passenger traffic to warrant as many as four stages a day in 1875. Some notable roads in Tuolumne County at that time were usable in their higher altitudes only in summer. One, the Big Oak Flat road, was a free road, except for toll bridges, on its route from Milton via Chinese Camp to Jamestown, Sonora and Tuolumne in one direction and to Groveland and Big Oak Flat in the other. Beyond Big Oak Flat this road was opened primarily as a tourist route in 1878 by the Yosemite Turn-Pike Company, and continued southeastward through the Tuolumne grove of Big Trees where W. C. Priest, one of the Yosemite commissioners, had a hole twelve feet wide and ten feet high bored through a stump thirty-three feet in diameter for stages to pass through.* Reaching the North Rim this toll road descended steeply and spectacularly to the floor of Yosemite Valley. Another notable road was the tremendous undertaking begun in 1861 by three counties, Tuolumne, Calaveras and Mariposa, and intended as a free road from Sonora in Tuolumne County to Bridgeport, on the eastern slope of the Sierra Nevada Mountains where new California gold strikes had made "boom" towns such as Bodie. This Mono road, one hundred and fourteen miles long, crossed the summit at over nine thousand feet elevation. After $400,000 was spent carving the upper portion, alone, out of solid granite cliffs, the road became a turnpike with varying charges per vehicle, animal, man and so forth. In the '70's and '80's this steep, narrow and dangerous road was traveled considerably by private traffic as well as one regular stage a day, taking as much as three weeks for the trip.

Since placer-mining days, two of Tuolumne County's larger water companies had owned and fought over hundreds of miles of ditches, diversions and flumes which spread "mining" water

---

*Tuolumne *Independent,* June 1, 1878: "A needle going through a camel's eye might have been a wonderful thing in the old days but to drive a six horse stage through the stump of a tree is reserved for the 10 inst."

around central Tuolumne County without much regard for other industries requiring power or to stockmen, who, in the spring, drove fifteen thousand head of cattle through towns and country-side in mile-long clouds of dust to mountain grazing. Since animal power transported everyone and all human necessities in and out of the county, barns overshadowed ranchers' homes and town streets were lined with stables, blacksmith shops and feed yards. The tremendous hauling done by teamsters in 1885 made not only mining, but also lumber, marble and other heavy industries possible in Tuolumne County.

The original Palace Hotel in San Francisco had been supplied with marble, mule-freighted from Columbia to rail connections forty miles away. Lime rock was hauled to a lime kiln settling the white dust of its operation on rural Sonora. Mine timbers were hauled to the increasing number of gold mines boring into the Mother Lode's quartz veins, and ores from them were hauled all the way down to the valley as well as to local reduction works. And, next to mining, the biggest business with the heaviest transportation problem was the newer one, lumber.

Mr. John Muir made an issue of the fact that millions of acres of government forests were being stolen, or passed into private hands and destroyed by extravagant woodsmen. This action contributed to the establishment by Congress in 1891 of Yosemite Park and the South and Tuolumne groves of *Sequoia gigantea*, as National Forest reserves. The largest portion of these parks was in Tuolumne County. Prior to this the forests of the county had seemed limitless and lumbermen were merely hacking and devastating their lower fringes. But there were still uncounted acreages of forests left to lumbering interests in the county which cut as high as fifty thousand board feet of lumber to the acre. Sugar and ponderosa pine, fir and cedar lumber in that market was worth from thirty to fifty dollars a thousand. Forty thousand feet of such lumber was cut and hauled out daily on twelve-horse freight wagons with trailers which rumbled down the tortuous mountain grades to the crack of teamsters' bull whips. Logs two to ten feet in diameter were hauled to small mountain sawmills or all the way down to the San Joaquin Valley.

At the first snowfall, lumberjacks, swampers, teamsters and teams pulled into Sonora or Oakdale to "live it up" for the winter when logging was shut down and mountain sawmills closed. With lumberjacks swelling the ranks of teamsters, blacksmiths, cowboys and miners, the activity in local saloons in 1890 almost equaled that of the past high, wide and handsome Gold Rush days.

This might be called the climax of the second act of the Mother Lode's gold drama. Instead of the theme song sung to pick, shovel and hydraulic activities, as in the first, or placer-mining act, the music of this second quartz-mining act was set to the clang of hard rock miners' powder and mills. This act lasted more than twice as long as the first and now, in the middle of it, the southern Mother Lode stage was set with hundreds of established quartz mines methodically stamping out fabulous amounts of gold and profitably reworking the previously discarded tailings by the use of improved methods. Pocket mines, for the most part, had been worked out and many promising quartz veins had petered out but the scene's activity had not become humdrum. Among miners, owners, experts, failures and gamblers, it was too often the shyster promoter who maintained the element of suspense. By selling any location where a "stringer" met a "cutter" to "suckers" and "greenhorns," these villains caused many serious, but not too well informed money interests to shy away from legitimate mining speculation. Fortunately, however, undaunted speculators maintained a lively scene of good and bad claims being bought, sold, hijacked and exploited by reputable and disreputable promoters. As soon as a new or reopened mine proved richly lucrative, the news traveled down rutted roads to rail and waterways and thence to mining interests around the world, bringing back an ever new supply of hopeful investors.

And so, with gold still the chief publicity agent and magnet, financiers, speculators and tourists from all over the world were drawn to Tuolumne County in the 1890's. Most of these travelers came by rail or river steamer to Stockton, then by Southern Pacific rails to Oakdale, thence eastward, by coach and six horses operated by the Sierra Stage Company or Shine's Stage Service, over the Sonora road running up the south side of the Stanislaus River. Another stage service ran from the S.P. rail terminus at Milton in Calaveras County, taking the north side of the river to Copperopolis which was the principal copper producing town of the United States in Civil War days and was still a community of actively operating copper mines. About eight miles out of Copper-opolis this stage road crossed the Stanislaus River at O'Byrnes Ferry by toll bridge to join the Sonora road and continue eastward or turn southward via Chinese Camp and the Big Oak Flat road. A less used road followed up the Stanislaus canyon, after crossing at O'Byrnes Ferry, and arrived at Tuttletown by what was known as Black Bart's Trail, due to that bandit's past activities on its twisting grades. From Tuttletown, stages ran northward along the Mother Lode crossing the Stanislaus River by flatboats at Robin-sons Ferry and continued along Calaveras County mines to and beyond Angels Camp. Also stage drivers whipped their teams eastward from Tuttletown to Columbia, Sonora and the East Belt mines, and southward, crossing Table Mountain to the more southern Mother Lode mines, passing Jamestown, Quartz Mountain and Chinese Camp.

From Chinese Camp the Big Oak Flat road crossed the Tuolumne River at Jacksonville and entered mines in the Big Oak Flat, Groveland and Second Garrote areas.*

By these main roads and lesser ones, crossing and crisscrossing lower Calaveras and Tuolumne Counties in the '90's, public and private conveyances brought people and supplies to the mining scene. By this time a stream of hardy tourists were passing through the now famous old mining towns with spectacular distant views of California's highest snow peaks and three recently world-famed groves of *Sequoia gigantea* just beyond, as well as that tourists' mecca, Yosemite Valley.

During the gay nineties most tourists saw more beauty than lumber in the forests, and more romance than profit in operating and abandoned mines in these hills strewn with rocks and poison oak. Cattle land there still sold for one dollar and a quarter an acre, but a cattleman's life seemed a grueling business when several acres were required to feed one cow, and cattlemen owning thousands of acres were still dependent on government-owned mountain forests for summer feeding. Fortunately, however, all travelers were not tourists. A few were men with capital looking

---

*With minor changes, reduced curves and considerable broadening, all of these roads except Black Bart Trail have remained state and county highways.

not so much at the present as at the future of California's undeveloped mountain area. Some of these saw deeper mining, some, greater lumber production, and some, huge power sources. One saw profit in a railroad in this particular area where heavy industries were operating with elementary transportation facilities.

This railroad-thinking man was an Eastern gentleman named Thomas S. Bullock who had made considerable money promoting varied projects in the United States, Europe and Mexico. Two such projects had been short line railroads, one in Arizona and one in Mexico. His profits in Mexico had been reduced by William Jennings Bryan's free silver, turning his railroad receipts into fifty-cent dollars, while bonds were payable in gold. His profits in Arizona were reduced by Santa Fe rails which paralleled his seventy-seven mile long railroad. It was to find a new location for the rails and equipment of this defunct Arizona railroad that he had come West. To further this plan he had attempted to promote a railroad from Stockton into the Central Mother Lode mines. When the project failed, due to the prohibitive cost of rights-of-way, he started negotiations to sell his rails to the representative of a proposed Yosemite Valley Railroad. But before the sale was consummated he made a trip which changed his mind.

On a tour through Calaveras and Tuolumne Counties he had watched ponderous freight wagons grinding along rutted roads with dust-blinded drivers on the off-mule, shouting "Gee" or "Haw" to the animals straining at chain and leather while the brakeman gripped or released wooden brakes screaming on iron-banded wheels. Also, he saw passengers clamoring for space in stagecoaches and springless buckboards in which to travel those primitive roads. These sights emphasized the need for rails in this area but it was the question of whether local economy warranted such costly expenditure that led Bullock to look twice at the letters "C.E.C." which were prominently marked on many inactive mining properties there, as well as in the Calaveras County Recorder's ledgers. Local humor had it that the letters stood for "Catching English Capital," and Bullock returned to San Francisco to investigate these indications that large capital was being invested there before making his own decision.

Among those men interested in promoting Mother Lode mines at this time were some who had seen mining on the African Rand

and who felt that mining methods used in California were outmoded and the mines unprofitable chiefly for that reason. One of these was a Frenchman of noble Polish descent named Prince Andre Poniatowski who was also, as Bullock learned, largely responsible for the lettering "C.E.C." placed on Mother Lode properties, since he was president of the California Exploration Company, for which the letters actually stood. In 1896 this company, formed for promotional purposes anywhere in California, was acquiring options and ownerships in mines up and down the Mother Lode, as well as in adjacent marble and timberland. Therefore, it was to Poniatowski that Bullock presented his proposition to build a railroad into the mining area where C.E.C. capital was invested.

Prince Poniatowski was in immediate agreement with Bullock's contention that such a railroad would be a mutually profitable venture, and he influenced Mr. William Crocker, San Francisco banker, and treasurer of the C.E.C., to provide Bullock with the financial backing he requested. Their projected railroad, in its first conception, was to contact the Calaveras County mines in which C.E.C. was interested, and the forests of the Calaveras Big Tree area owned by Mr. James B. Sperry, uncle to Prince Poniatowski's wife. Years before, a San Joaquin and Sierra Nevada Railroad had been promoted to run from the San Joaquin Valley to Sperry's resort at the Big Trees, primarily to increase tourist trade and the value of timber in that area. This narrow gauge line had, in fact, been built from Lodi to Valley Springs when its promoter, Mr. F. Birdsall, died in 1885, and the aborted line had passed into the hands of the Southern Pacific Company. Now, fifteen years later, Bullock and Poniatowski seriously considered the continuance of this line which would cross the Mother Lode mines of Calaveras County. The Southern Pacific, while not willing to sell the unfinished piece of narrow gauge, made a concession for its use which was agreeable to the Crocker interests now backing the proposed new line. But Bullock hesitated, preferring a more independent line, and preferably not one of narrow gauge. Also, he had previously been convinced that a route to the south was a more direct one to the most productive of the southern Mother Lode mines, and was still of that opinion.

Prince Poniatowski and Will Crocker willingly acceded to Bullock's suggestion to look further for a railroad location before building, but meanwhile, the original articles of a projected railroad named the Sierra Railway Company of California were drawn up and incorporated in 1897 by Mr. Sidney Freshman, brother-in-law of Bullock. Then Poniatowski and Bullock set out by horseback to make a detailed study of all the southern mines area, with the intention of finding the most accessible route to the most productive section. As a result of this trip the first plan was discarded and an entirely new projection drawn up. This projection was to start at Oakdale, in Stanislaus County. From there the Sierra Railway was to follow, more or less, the route of the Sonora road directly eastward into the gold-bearing hills of Tuolumne County.

The intention was first to lay rails to these rich mines, but secondly, the ambitious promoters intended their rails to also run northward along the Mother Lode, arriving from this direction into the Calaveras County mines and the Sperry-owned Calaveras grove of Big Trees above Angels Camp. A still further extension to the projected mainline was, in due time, expected to reach the Tuolumne and Mariposa groves of Big Trees where Bullock had acquired large timber interests.

Putting aside these future extensions for the present, the Sierra Railway started modestly with a franchise to lay their rails on a thirty-five mile roadbed from the Southern Pacific tracks at Oakdale to Jamestown in Tuolumne County. Due to long mutual affiliation, dating from Crocker money invested in the building of the S.P. Railroad, this new road, backed by Crocker money, could expect favorable freight and passenger feeding from the Southern Pacific although it was an entirely independent line. There was no assurance of such favorable treatment by the Santa Fe Railroad which a year before, in 1896, had come into Riverbank only six miles south of Oakdale. A spur track from that line to the Sierra's rails at Oakdale was suggested for the mutual transfer of business, but the Santa Fe did not immediately agree to such an arrangement. Therefore, the possibility existed that the Santa Fe might build eastward after its own gold and lumber freight. The threat of such a paralleling line may explain some of the haste with which the Sierra Railway began construction.

The Oakdale *Graphic* of February 3, 1897, states:

"The Sierra Railway Company proposes to build a railroad from Oakdale to the town of Angels in Calaveras County. The estimated length of this road is sixty-five miles. Intermediate roads are to be run to Modesto, Knights Ferry and La Grange in Stanislaus County, and to Coulterville in Mariposa County. The incorporators and directors of the company are Sidney D. Freshman, San Rafael; J. M. Bonner, Stockton; Charles Gross, Alameda; Ed E. Simpson and James Henry, the latter two from Stockton. Capital stock is five million dollars, of which fifty thousand has been subscribed by Freshman, and eighteen thousand five hundred by each of the other directors."

The above article was as accurate as might be expected at that premature date but the "intermediate roads" mentioned were never built; it is doubtful that they were then under consideration. The five million dollars of subscribed capital stock was divided into five thousand shares, of which a controlling number was in the hands of Poniatowski and Bullock when the first ties were laid. This fact spoke well for the Sierra Railway as an intendedly sound investment with a remunerative future, which could not be said of all the railroads projected by this time over most of California. Of these numberless railroads, those few which had emerged as great railroad powers were now symbols of progress and dependable American enterprise to most Californians, but to converts to the growing Socialism fad, successful railroads were writhing octopuses, sucking the whole state to their bosoms. Unfortunately according to local newspapers, this latter opinion predominated in Tuolumne County. Sonora papers, while proudly claiming theirs to be the home of Bonanza Kings, decried the evils of corporations, including those controlled by that selfsame royal gold. The ire of these local papers turned on that little corporate monster, the Sierra Railway Company, whose intention was to bring the "Iron Horse" into their presently backward locale. "We do not care for your railroad, gentlemen. Keep your hands off" summarized local sentiments regarding the Sierra Railway as expressed by the Sonora *Union Democrat*.

Bullock's plans to lay the rails he had almost sold, on his newly acquired right-of-way remained firm and the West Coast Construction Company arrived at Oakdale on March 2, 1897, to commence grading. This company, of which T. S. Bullock was president, and which he had organized in New Jersey to build the Sierra railroad, was to receive Sierra Railway stocks and bonds in payment for completed work. In March, after a long, wet winter, the wagon road from Oakdale into the foothill country was mud, with no end to it, and scarcely any bottom either. Freighting wagons, if not stuck in the mud, could be swamped at creekbed crossings, which were bone dry in summer, but now were gushing torrents forcing drivers to cut the harness and abandon wagons until the water fell. The same inclement conditions were met by the railroad construction company which, before April, had three hundred head of horses, many Fresno scrapers, and four hundred men working ten hours a day, seven days a week on grading, rock work, cut and fill. The roadbed was soon on its way out through grain ranches in the deceivingly rolling hills east of Oakdale. Teamsters on plodding freight wagons headed for the mountains with high loads covered with canvas lashed to the side bars, watched and cursed this competitive monster that was also creeping upward to threaten their livelihood and change their world.

CHAPTER TWO

Sprawling on the south bank of the Stanislaus River at 155 feet elevation, the town of Oakdale was surrounded by grain fields and rolling chameleon-like hills that were green in the spring, orange with California poppies through the summer and dry brown in fall and winter. Several mountain wagon roads converging at this railroad point between the valley and the hills made it a bustling freighting town when the Sierra Railway started building. Teamsters held the rein on strings of mules and horses while they waited at the Southern Pacific tracks to load up with necessities for the mines and mountain towns. Stages drew up before the White House and other hotels and boarding houses. Private conveyances crowded the hitching racks along Railroad and Yosemite Streets while business was done at Haslacker and Kahn's bank, the printing offices of Oakdale's *Leader* and *Graphic* weekly newspapers, Dr. Thompson's sanitarium and half a dozen stores. Here, too, were the opera house and the firehouse from whose bell tower also rang a nine o'clock curfew. But the biggest and busiest places were blacksmith and harness shops, livery stables, saloons, chop houses and an immense red barn where teamsters stabled their horses. A long boardwalk ran past the feed yard to hundreds of homes for teamsters' families on this east side of town, while on the less populous west side of town the homes of hay and barley farmers overlooked oak-studded ranches spreading to both sides of the Stanislaus River. Farmers, doctors, bankers and lawyers all prospered on the teaming business, and yet, there was no public sentiment expressed against the prospect of competing rails.

: 13 :

The January 6, 1897 issue of the Oakdale *Graphic* stated:

"W. C. Potts, assisted by J. W. Brown, F. E. Quail, and J. W. McCrearry, is surveying a railroad starting from the S.P. depot at Oakdale and running to Sonora. The direction will be through Tullock's ranch and Dry Creek Valley to Al Gatzman's ranch and on up Dry Creek."

The Sierra Railway Company's early records have been lost by fire but later records list W. C. Potts as the railroad's superintendent, a position he held for several years. He may, however, have been employed at this time, when Mr. E. Albert was the Sierra's superintendent, in an engineering capacity with the surveyors listed above. Mr. Arnold of Oakdale was in fact the Sierra's right-of-way man, who, as a native, was familiar with land owners in all this area. The rights-of-way he secured, whether sold or granted free to the Sierra railroad, averaged fifty feet in width although they ran as wide as one hundred feet in some instances. The roadbed, starting on wide, sweeping curves out through rolling hills, was graded at less than one per cent, requiring a minimum of engineering work.

During these first miles of construction, railroad graders, known as Cowell's gang, returned each night to Oakdale where they mingled with wagon freighting outfits ready to start a fight at the drop of a railroader's hat. Most of these graders, brought from Stockton by subcontractor Cyrus Moreing, were rough, tough men but no match for burly blacksmiths and teamsters working for such freighters as W. T. Hales of Oakdale or Wesley Haslem of Knights Ferry. In spite of broken noses and property damage, work continued with amazing speed and the graders were moved from Oakdale as soon as the first ten railroad miles were laid with ties.

By this time Bullock's used rails from Arizona had arrived at the Oakdale freight yard. These 40 pound rails had been shipped from Prescott, Arizona, to Redondo Beach, California, thence by water to Stockton and finally by Southern Pacific rails to Oakdale. As soon as enough of this track was laid the Sierra's *No. 1* locomotive, an old recordless 4-4-0, was put to work on them, hauling more rail and work supplies for the growing line. In May, the Sierra railroad purchased its *No. 2* locomotive, an 0-6-0 built for the Montana Union Pacific in 1889. This eight year old rod engine started service on the Sierra's tracks on a diet of four-foot logs but later survived for twenty years with coal stoking and then oil. With these two engines and eleven miles of track, the Sierra Railway Company was in business.

At milepost 6, Occidental (later Arnold) Station was set up with a freight shed for loading baled and sacked grain grown by local ranchers. Beyond this station the right-of-way ran into grazing land where summer's crop of wild oats, though sparse and boulder-strewn, would be saved for nutritious winter feed. As railroad grading continued into spring, carpets of wild flowers almost hid the rocky outcropping which had to be leveled along the right-of-way. In this day of lone men building up the West, even rough graders stepped gingerly among these blooms whose familiar names recalled childhood homes: baby blue eyes, butter-and-eggs, popcorn, lady slippers, fairy bells, paint brush and cream-cups. Bordering these far-flung carpets of wildflowers were miles and miles of boulders loosely stacked on property lines into three and five foot high cattle walls by Chinese "coolie" labor of an earlier day. Here where scattered cattle were now knee-deep in feed but waiting to be driven to mountain pasture or shipped to market, chutes were built beside the tracks. Milepost 11 then became Paulsell Station and the grading camp again moved up ahead.

With a railroad on his ranch, Mr. Al Gatzman invited railroad contractors and construction bosses to his oak-shaded home to celebrate the end of driving cattle to market with the resulting loss of weight on arrival. He, like many other ranchers antici-pating convenient transportation from ranch to town, had offered a right-of-way free to the railroad, and in return was given a life-time pass over the line for his family, but not his cattle! Five freight cars, of which three were cattle cars, were put into service for prompt shipping of these men's spring-fat stock to market, and the following shipping rates were published in the Oakdale papers:

"Two dollars and fifty cents a ton for hay, grain, and lumber; twenty dollars a carload for horses, and cattle, and class rates at four dollars a tonnage shipments, or twenty to twenty-five cents per hundred weight. Signed B. T. Booze, Sierra General Freight Agent."

Five miles further eastward the Sierra's third station was announced as Warnerville, sixteen miles from Oakdale. Although the roadbed still progressed in sweeping curves around rolling hills, the grades were now increased from one to two per cent in preparation for the mountainous country directly ahead, and several bridges were built across dry ravines that became torrents in the winter months. Advance bridge crews had been at work for some time at the Rock River Bridge, which was to be a hundred foot high trestle with spans, girders, all but the rails themselves, built of wood. Just beyond Rock River Bridge was Cooperstown at milepost 20 which, though hardly a town, was the cattle center of Stanislaus County and the first established nameplace contacted by the railroad since leaving Oakdale.

Tracks were laid into Cooperstown in June, 1897, at which time the Sierra Railway printed its first timetable for passenger service as follows: *"Westbound:* — Leave Cooperstown 12:30 p.m. Arrive Oakdale, 1:30 p.m. *Eastbound:* — Leave San Francisco, 9:00 a.m. Leave Oakdale, 2:30 p.m. Arrive Cooperstown, 3:34 p.m." Also, the Sierra's *No. 3* engine came proudly onto the line under its own power from Stockton, where it had been held since coming that far with the rails from the Prescott and Arizona Central Railroad, for which it was built in 1891. This little 4-6-0 Rogers locomotive started its over thirty years of hard and useful work on the Sierra Railway by pulling the first scheduled passenger train, one coach and a mail and baggage car leased from the Southern Pacific, into Cooperstown. Its arrival was to cause the largest assembly of people ever to gather around the old store, saloon and stage depot that had marked this lonely site through fifty years of wagon freighting. Most vehicles by now took the better Sonora or Big Oak Flat roads, leaving this one to become ever rougher and more narrowed by the thorny chaparral that grew everywhere. These dry hills were also spread with wildflowers in the spring but by June their ephemeral life was spent and the drab browns and greens of dry grass, rocks and brush provided camouflage for more rattlesnakes than was usual in these snake-infested foothills. Hundreds of rattlers had already been killed along the roadbed by nervous graders whose rock throwing technique was scoffed at by old timers who "pronged them down" with a stick, by cowboys who considered a snake an easy shot, and by teamsters who could decapitate the varmints with one crack of a bull whip.

The depot site was owned by W. F. Cooper, who also ran the store and saloon. He was said to have stabbed his wife the previous fall in dismal foreboding of winter when his place would be by-passed, if possible, by wagon freighters afraid of bogging down in his clay. Cooper's neighbors to the south and east were ranchers E. H. Smith and John Grohl, but large sections of this country were controlled by cattle interests living elsewhere. Among these were such well-known names as William H. Rushing of the Rushing Land and Cattle Company, Butternut and Miller Cattle Company (Miller and Lux) and Montgomery Horse Ranchers. From Cooperstown into Chinese Camp the right-of-way continued through cattle land which made stock the railroad's biggest freight item to date (1897).

The first two long and two short locomotive whistles at the Cooperstown road crossing were heard by a dozen stage drivers and freighters who had been forced by steam's faster service and cheaper rates to load and unload here, instead of at Oakdale as before. When the smoking little *No. 3* snorted to a stop, passengers carrying knapsacks and valises were transferred to stages by the new stationmaster while whooping cowboys, cursing teamsters and the usual drunks made bedlam among those gathered to welcome this little mixed train. However, when a pretty young woman in divided skirts, crisp blouse and a smooth pompadour rode through the bystanders, there was near silence while she coaxed her skittish horse close enough to the engine cab to shake hands with engineer George Wright, and then whirl away, followed by renewed whoops and whistles.

1897 was called the period of "dreadful depression" in the railroad world. *Poor's Manual* for that year, without looking at the Sierra's busy twenty miles of track, showed no mileage added to the existing 108,000 miles of railroad in the United States and no appreciable increase in their combined $5,373,187,289.00 of capital. But due to these figures of "monstrous wealth," owned by "cruel railroad combines," agitators urged teamsters, liverymen and cattlemen to organize into political pressure groups with representation at the state capitol to stop the creeping Sierra Railway before it left them jobless. Posters were displayed on local roads, depicting the rear of an "Iron Horse" spewing incendiary cinders onto range, grain and timberland. But rugged teamsters and cattlemen preferred independence to organization and the Sierra's steel tracks continued to stretch upwards into the hills, although not without financial difficulty.

At a meeting of Sierra Railway stockholders in San Francisco, Mr. Jesse Lilienthal, attorney for the Sierra Railway Company, recorded two property and chattel mortgages as security for an ultimate $3,720,000 worth of bonds to be secured by the company and sold to raise funds for the prosecution of work. The bonds were printed and largely disposed of, but including both mortgages, the Sierra Railway Company was now bonded for about $30,000 a mile. This investment by private capital during a "dreadful depression in the railroad world," showed courage and determination and also increased the railroad's need to reach the mining country and some of its "pay dirt" as soon as possible.

The above mentioned stockholders' meeting also sanctioned purchase of three 4-4-0 Baldwin locomotives to be bought from the Northern Pacific Railroad, and an 0-6-0 Schenectady to solve the switching problem. Of these Baldwins, the Sierra's *No. 6* engine became their regular passenger train power unit with Engineer George Wright a permanent fixture in the cab. Inspired by Prince Poniatowski and promotional friends at this time, the railroad was presented with a plush, new passenger coach. The elegance of its crystal lamps and the upholstery on its thirty-two seats, accommodating sixty-four persons, makes it likely that the equally elegant and lavish prince may have had a hand in naming it the "Stanislaus," which was not only the name of the county in which the Sierra's rails started, but also the name of his first-born son. This coach was brought into service when a special Southern Pacific train arrived at Oakdale from Stockton with one hundred and four delegates to the Grand Parlor of Native Daughters aboard. An unprecedented crowd, of whom thirty were additional delegates, waited at the Oakdale depot while the two delegate cars were linked onto the "Stanislaus." The three filled cars, headed by the Sierra's *No. 6* covered with American flags, then "whirled away" toward Sonora, where the Grand Parlor was in session. At Cooperstown the delegates were met by carriages in which to complete the trip.

In the mountainous canyon above Cooperstown, construction crews were hard at work. A few miles out of that station, the right-of-way crossed the line into Tuolumne County and started up Dry Creek Canyon for three and a half miles on grades up to three per cent. The necessary water tank at the foot of this grade was named Canyon Tank, which also became the familiar name of the grade above it. Canyon Tank grade has since been lowered, but is still one of the steepest on the Sierra's mainline. During construction, the old *No. 1* work engine, pulling any kind of a load, would fill up with water at Canyon Tank while the fireman stuffed her with wood to build up a full head of steam before starting up the grade. By the time the construction crews were met, the whole canyon was black with smoke. When tracks finally were laid to the top of the grade, another water tank was erected there, and a shoofly put in for spotting cars or a second engine when double-headers would be needed to handle a full consist of freight up the grade.

This point, at milepost 25, was named Rosasco Station, being situated on land owned by extensive cattle rancher S. G. Rosasco, one of several Tuolumne County pioneers of that name.

Leaving Rosasco, the right-of-way leveled out onto a broad flat to which the construction camp was moved from Cooperstown. At the upper end of this flat was Cloudman, which was also a long-standing stage and freighting center on the Sonora road near its intersection by the old Big Oak Flat road. Cloudman was of dwindling importance as a stage stop but of coming importance to the railroad which put in a short spur there for the loading of cattle. This land was owned by rancher James B. Curtin, whose son, John, later became state senator, but who meanwhile, in 1908, sanctioned the installation of the first Tuolumne County telephone toll station in his ranch home there. The vast Curtin range land included plentiful water on this and other foothill and mountain holdings from which the railroad expected to ship better than twenty carloads of cattle a year.

As the railroad turned sharply and continued due north up Dry Creek Canyon for five crooked miles, the construction schedule was so delayed that the Sierra set up a station at milepost 29, halfway up the grade, and made the following announcement to the public:

"We take pleasure in informing you that, effective August 5, a new permanent station called Don Pedro will be opened for both freight and passenger business with an agent in charge. Don Pedro is located one mile south of the old Crimea House. Teamsters are now charging for freight from Cooperstown to Quartz Mountain, Stent, Jamestown, Sonora, etc. $5.00 per ton. The charge from Don Pedro, after the first of August, will be, to Sonora, $3.50 per ton. To Quartz Mountain, Stent, Jamestown, — $3.00 per ton. Freight routed via Cooperstown for mountain points will be carried by this line to Don Pedro and there delivered to teams. Passenger stages and freight teams will meet our trains at Don Pedro for various mountain points as follows: Chinese Camp, Stent, Jamestown, Quartz Mountain, Sonora, Shaws Flat, Springfield, Columbia, Jeffersonville, Soulsbyville, Cherokee, Summerville, Confidence, Jacksonville, Groveland, Big Oak Flat, Tuttletown, Yosemite Valley and bypoints."

B. T. Booze, F. and P. Agent

This roll call of the most historic name places in the California southern mines meant that the Sierra Railway was approaching its goal, although the steep and rough wagon road from the Crimea House into Don Pedro Station did not make it an easy place for flesh-and-blood animals, pulling freight wagons and stages, to meet their master, the Iron Horse. The Crimea House was a deserted early-day staging stop on the Big Oak Flat road, but from Crimea to Don Pedro and back to that road was a hard five mile detour. With a living at stake, stage drivers and teamsters made it, if not always on schedule; and before the grade up Dry Creek was completed, passenger timecards came tersely to read: "Don Pedro. Arrive at 4:40 p.m. — thence by stages."

CHAPTER THREE

SIERRA RAILWAY

Even though, as yet, Sierra trains went nowhere so to speak, patronage of the line exceeded expectations and with California's most flourishing gold mines just ahead, the future of the line appeared very good. One reason, however, for this extensive patronage was that local wagon roads were rutted and deep in summer dust. The people of Tuolumne and Stanislaus Counties, in fact, had proposed maintaining the main roads from the valley to the mines at county expense. It is ironic that movements such as this were in time destined to bring about paved highways, fast auto trucking and the death of many short-line railroads, since California's railroads built and maintained the first good wagon roads from local towns or industries to their stations. The Sierra Railway did its first such work on the wagon road between Knights Ferry and Cooperstown.

Knights Ferry might have become a ghost of the thriving town it had been in placer mining days if the Sperry interests had not located there. The hilly old townsite on the north bank of the Stanislaus River with wheat fields and cattle land spreading westward of it was dominated in 1897 by its flour mills and grain sheds, although considerable business was also done in dairy products and butchering in a sizable slaughterhouse on the river. Fifty years earlier the ferry across the river had been supplanted by a long covered bridge which still carried all the traffic between Knights Ferry and towns on the south side of the river. A two-story stage depot with accompanying saloon and store, located at the junction of this bridge and the Sonora road, was still a popular oasis for thirsty men and animals traveling to and from the mines. Railroad graders and scrapers therefore were put to work on a miserable cross-country trail from the Sonora road to Cooperstown so freight wagons loaded with flour, meat and dairy products would come to the railroad station there instead of turning westward to Oakdale.

Meanwhile, law suits and labor trouble along the railroad right-of-way had increased with the altitude. Ranchers on large tracts of land expected their stock to roam at will and objected to having their land divided by fences. Yet the value of loose cattle soared from the going price of twenty-four dollars a head, to fifty, as soon as hit by a locomotive cowcatcher, which was then no mere decoration. Also, the higher hills were plastered with mining claims of dubious value until disturbed by a shovel or Fresno scraper grading the way for rails. And construction camps, ever magnets for liquor vendors, prostitutes and card sharks, were now invaded by gun-carrying gamblers wagering gold dust and nuggets on anything from poker to pistol-targets and women. Night after night such professionals took the whole savings of graders and tracklayers earning a dollar and a half a day. Losers became disgruntled workers in shorthanded crews, and those hopelessly indebted simply drifted from camp.

Under the best of conditions, grading would have been slow in the canyon above Don Pedro where every rock and shovelful of dirt was moved by hand. Trestles and half trestles were built to make room for tracks. Sweating construction crews labored for two long months in this brush-filled canyon, brittle and dry with late fall heat. This completed piece of track would be less steep but more crooked than the Canyon Tank grade where locomotives had already twice lost traction in spite of sanded rails. Train crews expected worse trouble there come frosty winter time. In the first instance a double-header, hauling six loaded freight cars up to Don Pedro, had been stalled by heavy hail following a most unusual thunderstorm; and in the second case, slippage had resulted from a scourge of grasshoppers whose crushed bodies on the 3% canyon rails made them slick as grease.

In those days operating crews were a self-reliant lot, especially on the Sierra railroad with no dispatcher along the line as yet, nor even anyone with a key. Train crews therefore knew that safe, scheduled runs were strictly up to them.

With tracks at last laid to the top of Dry Creek Canyon, the railroad had reached 1184 feet of elevation, nearly five hundred

The Rawhide Mine at the time it was owned by Captain Nevills. Smelter at left, mill building between the two smokestacks on the side of the hill. Headframe of shaft may be seen at right of smokestack among the center group of buildings.

Hoisting works of Rawhide Mine with teams and wagons hauling mine timbers from the high country. Note huge pile of cordwood behind the boiler room.

Group of mine visitors. Candle drippings on clothes indicate these people had already been underground.

Miners about to go on shift at Rawhide Mine. This picture was made some years later than the above as the hat lamps are all oil.

FOUR PICTURES: DONALD SEGERSTROM

The Harvard Mine and mill just outside Jamestown was one of the major gold mining operations when the Sierra Railway was built. It was closed down in 1917. In 1939 new companies started to open it up but were not in production when forced to close down due to World War II. The large orange headframe seen from the Sierra Railroad just before entering Jamestown was erected at that time and serves to locate the mine.

Small Tuolumne County gold mining operation in the days of steam. This surface plant is typical of hundreds on the Mother Lode.

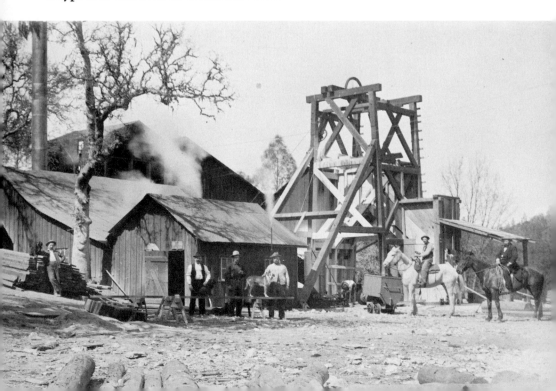

Mill of the Carson Hill Gold Mining Company on the Stanislaus River. Sierra Railway trestle was to the right of highway bridge in foreground.

Prudhomme Hill Mine at Carter's. Sacks in foreground contain concentrate accumulating until a carload lot is available for rail shipment to the smelter.

Visitors arriving at underground station on the main shaft of the App Mine at Quartz. Man holding candle was William Morehead, mine manager, and boy at his right is his son, William, Jr. Picture taken about 1897.

App mine and mill. This was the largest gold producer of Tuolumne County. Although the surface plant was not as impressive as some of the others, continuous production from 1856 until 1920 made up for the much larger surface works that soon exhausted many of the other mines. A depth of 1340 feet was reached which was not deep for the Mother Lode. This mine, along with the adjacent Dutch, was connected by a home-made railway with the Sierra a mile away.

Confidence Mine and mill near Carter's. This mine, like the Prudhomme Hill, was on what is known as the East Belt, a vein paralleling the Mother Lode several miles to the east of it.

SONORA MUSEUM

Part of Soulsbyville in 1875. The mine had three shafts. The mill is located in center of picture, with one of the shafts at group of buildings center right.

One of the shafts of the Soulsby Mine; a lumber drying yard now covers the spot. The masonry foundations of the hoisting machinery may still be seen from the highway between Twain Harte and Tuolumne. The Soulsby Mines, like those of Carter's, were on the East Belt and consisted of veins that were much smaller than those of the Mother Lode. These veins often ran in erratic patterns and where two veins crossed, some phenomenal enrichments could take place. The ore was extremely high grade at these points.

DONALD SEGERSTROM

Mill and surface plant of the Carson Hill Gold Mines on the Stanislaus River. The picture must have been taken in the Spring as the water almost covers the highway bridge.

Chinese Station. Building in center is the storage building belonging to the Eagle-Shawmut Gold Mining Company. Oil facility is by track at left of picture.

Mill of the Eagle-Shawmut Gold Mining Co. This mill had 100 stamps and was one of the largest mills in Tuolumne County. Trestle and track at right are tramway leading to the mine, which was entered from the tunnel higher up on the hill.

View of Columbia in 1878. What resembles beehives in the center of this picture are water-washed marble boulders. Originally covered with dirt, $55,000,000 worth of gold was washed from around these boulders in the early days of placer mining.

Utica Mine and mill at Angels Camp. Hoisting works at left, stamp mill at right. This was one of the major Mother Lode mines but was closed in the early '20s due to labor difficulties and was never reopened. Although it was right in the center of town all that can be seen today is the waste dump shown in the center of the picture.

Guerin & Nevills stage from Milton to Jamestown and Sonora. This was the main public transportation before the coming of the Sierra Railway. Guerin & Nevills were also agents for Wells Fargo & Co.

T. J. Moran team on toll road near Murphys in 1902. A double load of mine timber such as this would be used in not over two days at such mines as the Rawhide and the Harvard.

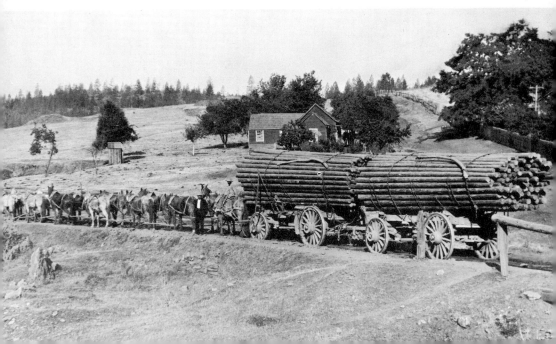

Patterson grade on Sonora Pass road in very early days.

T. J. Moran team on Murphys toll road in 1902. This timber on wagons was destined for Lightner Mine.

of which had been climbed in the last seven miles. At milepost 35 on a placer-graveled flat, a station was set up almost two miles north of Chinese Camp, or the first gold mining town to be contacted by the Sierra's rails. This ended Don Pedro as a stage and teaming junction, for Chinese Camp was a stage and wagon freighting town of fifty years standing with half a dozen roads converging there with the Big Oak Flat road. With the exception of those now paralleled by the railroad, these roads were at a peak of activity, due to the volume of passenger and freight hauling to mining towns and tourist objectives across the Tuolumne River. Above all, to Yosemite Valley which was as yet approachable only by way of its North and South Rims. Chinese Camp was called the North Gateway to Yosemite, although some eighty steep and twisting miles of the Big Oak Flat road lay between them. In summertime the Great Sierra Stage Company carried twenty passengers a day in open stages on the Yosemite Run, either via Milton to Copperopolis and O'Byrnes Ferry bridge, or via Oakdale and Knights Ferry Junction to Chinese Camp. Hence to Jacksonville and a 12 foot wide toll bridge across the Tuolumne River, and on to Priests, Groveland, Cliff House (where tolls were taken), Crockers, and Crane Flat, before descending the North Rim to Camp Curry on the floor of Yosemite Valley. This breathtaking, spine-jolting three day ride was casually undertaken by thousands of people each year, who also had to be fed and cared for on the way. Therefore, the route was also covered by 8 and 12 horse freight wagons, whose jangling bells were anxiously listened for on unpassably narrow curves by stages and private conveyances. For them such an encounter meant backing on hair-raising ledges to some possible passing place. This traffic added to that between towns on the more populous north side of the Tuolumne River for which Chinese Camp was a crossroads, kept it a busy, teaming town in 1897.

San Francisco and San Joaquin Valley newspapers gave considerable space to the Sierra Railway now that it had reached Chinese Camp and the "Mines." Promotional reports pointed out that there was available, ready-rail access to the Mother Lode country for the first time, by which mines would soon be shipping ore more expeditiously and economically, as well as receiving essential timber and mining equipment faster, at less cost. Also made clear was that the staging time into Yosemite Valley via Chinese Camp was now half that of the alternate Southern Pacific route connecting at Merced with stages via Raymond and Wawona. One account in the Oakdale *Graphic* was overly glowing:

> "With this new rail connection we may breakfast at 8:00 a.m. in Oakdale, and lunch at 12:00 noon in Yosemite Valley. One, the midway station of four hundred miles of level wheat land, the other the most sublime of all the sublimities in the everlasting hills!"

This writer's optimism was contradicted when the railroad's timecard gave arrival time at Chinese Station as 5:05 p.m., but the new rail connection was popular with tourists willing to stay overnight at the historic old Garrett Hotel there.

However true it may be, the history of Chinese Camp always starts with some unnamed Englishmen who had settled there before the Gold Rush, and in 1849 are reputed to have done the unheard-of in that locality, which was to become rich without soiling their own hands. This had been accomplished by importing Chinese coolies to wash their dirt and extract its gold for them. With an ever-increasing Chinese population, the Englishmen's diggings became known as Chinese Camp where during the '50's Chinese and white placer miners washed out ten million dollars worth of nuggets and gold dust. By then, the Chinese population, if not the gold, became of enough consequence for four of the influential Chinese Six Companies to place agents there. At nearby Six Bit Gulch, in 1856, one thousand Sam Yops fought one thousand Yan Wos, reducing the Chinese population by unnumbered fatalities. In the white section of town, small homes and tents had been clustered around false fronted saloons, boarding houses, stores, livery stables, harness and blacksmith shops situated on one or another of the roads from north, east, south and west that converged there.

Now, over forty years later, when the Sierra railroad came to Chinese Station, most of the Chinese had found other diggings or larger Chinatowns and the last tong war resulting in fatalities was twenty years past. Without its placer mining population, Chinese Camp was still a rough and ready little town accustomed to all kinds of violence. Only a year before, in 1896, the Sonora-Oakdale stage had been held up by masked men twice in thirty days. After the first holdup, Mr. Barnett, the stageline owner, rode shotgun on the box beside driver Fred Johnson, but failed in his attempt to forestall a second robbery. Since the Wells Fargo iron box and mail pouches were involved, that company assisted in tracing down the bandits and succeeded in recovering the loot.

Only a few months before the railroad came into Chinese Camp, a more tragic holdup had taken place in Morris' General Store where Wells Fargo had an office. Saul Morris was the Wells Fargo Agent but his brother George was acting alone in the office as his assistant when he gave his life in defense of a sack of six hundred silver dollars delivered to him from the Wells Fargo iron box on the Oakdale to Sonora stage. After shooting George in the face, the robber disappeared with the money into the Chinese section of town, leaving his victim unable to utter a sound, let alone name or describe his assailant before he died. Although Saul and another brother, Paul, owned the only telephone in the county which they had strung to Groveland to facilitate orders to be shipped across the canyon, it had been of little use in this robbery-murder due to grades and distance between towns. Instead, marshalls from Jamestown and Sonora were aroused by a man on horseback, but their combined best efforts failed to locate the criminal. Saul Morris was still working with a Wells Fargo Special Agent to solve this case when the railroad came to Chinese Camp, but clues were vague. Mrs. D. Mann and Mrs. Belle Mooney, living across the street from Morris' General Store, had heard the shots. An unnamed man had borrowed a gun from Mr. Solinsky to give chase. "Doc" Stratton had been called in only to find the victim at the point of death.

The above names were familiar ones in Chinese Camp in 1897. Dr. D. E. Stratton, besides being retained by the Eagle Shawmut Mine, had a busy private practice. His rig might be seen, day or night, standing by houses on lonely roads or hitched near town homes, saloons or street fights. During his long, unselfish life there was only one "Doc" in Chinese Camp. At this time, when he was young, Dr. Stratton was called to treat his first of many railroad employees, who was a track layer with a crushed foot brought by him to the Garrett Hotel for close attention. This 10 room hotel on the main street, while innocent of plumbing, had long retained a reputation for gracious hospitality and clean beds, which were not taken for granted in every mining settlement. The hotel had been operated, until lately, by the titled European, Count C. W. Solinsky, who in his long and colorful career in Chinese Camp was banker, storekeeper and Wells Fargo Agent as well as hotel-keeper. This elderly gentleman had entertained the railroad's promoters and looked forward to greeting the first train to come to his town, but unfortunately died in 1896 a few months before that event came to pass. Mrs. Fox, formerly a resident of the neighboring old placer town of Montezuma, now operated the Garrett Hotel, catering principally to the lucrative flow of Yosemite tourists.

Other buildings reminiscent of more populous days in Chinese Camp were St. Francis Xavier Church and the Masonic Hall, both built in the 1850's and still in use at the upper end of town. Crumbling stone walls were all that was left of a Chinese house of worship built at the same time at the other extreme of town which was Chinatown. Also, on Main and Yosemite streets were Egling's blacksmith shop and Wheelock's saloon which each were one of three similar businesses in town. At the T. McAdams General Store, patient Mrs. McAdams found time to sell peppermint lozenges to children, or spools of thread and fitted corsets to their mothers. Morris' Store, run by two enterprising brothers with fingers in staging, telephone lines, politics and many other ventures, were general merchandisers carrying anything from groceries to mining supplies. Because he liked the teamsters and was afraid of losing their trade, Saul Morris was openly opposed to a railroad coming into Chinese Camp, but his brother Paul said rails were progress, which he favored in any form.

Besides the volume in general freight and passengers in and out of Chinese Station, the Sierra Railroad had a very important customer in the nearby Eagle Shawmut Mine, which was the largest, if not the richest, gold mine operating in Tuolumne County. This quartz mine had produced over eight million dollars in gold, and had a forty stamp mill to which the owners contemplated adding sixty stamps more. This expansion would require a large tonnage of equipment, including lumber for new workers' homes as well as the usual supplies for such a mine and its two hundred employees. Chiefly due to this mine and contact with smaller mines in the area, the Sierra Railway Company now issued a new listing for freight rates, adding ores, concentrates and sulphurets at $3.00 per ton.

Although Chinese Station was so far removed from town, over two hundred persons crossed the intervening flat afoot, by rig, buckboard or horseback to line up with stages and freight wagons beside the track and watch the first steam train arrive at their horse-powered town. As the locomotive came in sight, Engineer Wright tied down the whistle cord, causing hitched and unhitched horses to rear, snorting and backing, which added to the good-humored excitement. One horse, however, hitched to a lady's surrey on the far side of the tracks, bolted across a field just as the train steamed up on the intervening track. Several chivalrous males raced in front of the locomotive to catch the runaway, but changed their minds when they met a big red bull that had been diverted from quiet grazing to a fighting stance by the noisy iron monster. As the engine came to a hissing stop, one bullfighter armed with a red bandana and a pistol distracted the bellowing bull while another reached the surrey and drove it back to safety.

Among passengers descending from the train was a highly amused Prince Poniatowski and his party who were met by private conveyance and proceeded to Jamestown. Other passengers bound for nearby towns boarded waiting stages. Those going to Yosemite Valley and intending to pass the night in Chinese Camp were invited to join townspeople, who had brought hard and soft drinks and a hearty picnic out to the depot to share with the train crew.

The day this first passenger train drew into Chinese Station, construction crews were working two miles out of town on the right-of-way to Jamestown. That intended rail terminus, like so many foothill towns, was snuggled in a low spot difficult or costly of approach by rails. But in any case, the Sierra Railway Company would need room there for yards, shops, a roundhouse, water tanks and fuel storage. About fifty acres, large and level enough for all these necessities, had therefore been acquired from one of Jamestown's biggest landowners, G. A. Leland. Here, a mile above Woods Creek where historic Jamestown sprawled, the railroad company established general offices on the second floor of a brand new depot with a curiously Oriental upturned roof line and painted Chinese yellow. About forty yards from it the largest hotel ever to be built in Tuolumne County, the Nevills Hotel, was under construction. As this edifice grew, its three stories were topped by large, rounded turrets, the roof line of which also curled upward in pseudo-Oriental fashion, matching that of the completed depot. This architectural similarity made the hotel appear to be railroad property although it was not. There was, however, an important link between the two buildings — Mr. Bullock.

In his varied capacity as promoter and financier, Bullock had made many business affiliations with important industries and people in Tuolumne County. Backed by the Crocker interests, he had recently promoted the West Side Flume and Lumber Company and owned 570 shares of stock when that company started operations in Tuolumne City (old Summersville). Plans for a similar promotion, the Standard Lumber Company with offices in Sonora, were also under way. Bullock had also become a partner with one of the most influential mining men in the county when he and "Captain" W. A. Nevills financed this elaborate structure named the Nevills Hotel. And, anticipating the town's growth as a rail terminus, these two men, with local partners, had formed a Jamestown Improvement Company to promote one hundred and twenty acres of oak and pine-studded hillside as a residential area near the depot. This development, surveyed into streets and city-size lots, was known as the Pereira Addition, named after Mr. John Pereira, an early settler who originally claimed this, as well as a great deal of other Jamestown land and water rights.

The San Francisco *Call*, December 19, 1897, gave the following report which was reprinted in local papers:

> "Jamestown, the rail terminus, has undergone a magical change. It will be converted into a modern town with avenues and streets properly laid out, water, electric and sewer systems, the plans for which are now under consideration. A large hotel of sixty rooms is being erected, and the bank reorganized to do big business, as the bullion produced in the vicinity of Jamestown amounts to over $300,000.00 a month."

Almost a year previously, this same newspaper had reported that Prince Poniatowski and his associates had bought the Columbia Marble Works, six miles from Jamestown, "where the stone was inexhaustible and would become more profitable when it could be shipped to the cities of California by rail." With fingers in so many pies in this area, the promoters of the Sierra Railway obviously hoped to share in the profits of real estate, lumber, mines and allied businesses as these activities progressed with the coming of a railroad. In this light, the Nevills Hotel was designed to be a local attraction giving a country club appearance to the Pereira Addition beside it. It was also to become the meeting place of prominent local people on business or pleasure, as well as a stopover for mine owners residing outside Tuolumne County, and a temptation to tourists not anxious to "rough it" on jaunts to the Big Trees or Yosemite Valley, both within a day's trip from the hotel by stage.*

The Nevills Hotel foundations and ground floor columns of local green streaked quartz were set on a marble floored porch brought from Prince Poniatowski's marble works. Plans called for wide upper balconies and bedrooms in paneled Ponderosa pine from local mills which, on the hotel front, would overlook the sweep of Table Mountain, with its jutting Pulpit Rock and sixty-foot Peppermint Falls. The rear balconies and dining room were to overlook a garden already laid out with palm trees, rose beds, marble walks and statuary. The large lobby with its marble fire-place was to be elegantly furnished with leather and fine paint-ings. Opening from the marble porch as well as from the lobby, the saloon was to shine with crystal chandeliers, wide mirrors and an imported mahogany bar. The dining room beyond the lobby was to be fitted with mirrored sideboards, white linen and silver. The space between hotel and depot was cemented for a passenger and luggage platform, protected with iron posts and heavy chains from the stage and wagon space behind it. The Sierra rails, with double tracks, were to be laid and abutted just beyond the front of the hotel, so that trains would pull in and back out directly before this imposing length of buildings.

The Jamestown area was the beginning of the mountain and pine region, although the trees of that type growing there were long needled bullpines which attained little more height than the native evergreen oaks. However, the hillsides were thickly "treed" if not forested in the western sense, and full of California red-berry bushes which grew to tree dimensions. On shady Woods

---

*These stages were preceded by a horseback rider blowing a trumpet on blind curves. Therefore the time was better than that possible by private conveyance.

Creek under Table Mountain, an unnamed prospector found the first gold nugget to bring notoriety to Tuolumne County. The resulting settlement that had mushroomed on the site in placer mining days had since dwindled in size but not in importance, for Jamestown, when the Sierra Railway Company chose it as a terminus, was the pivot point of encircling quartz mines. Five hundred stamps in a ten mile radius of the town had produced over two million dollars of gold in that year.

Just westward over Table Mountain was Rawhide Valley with its famous Rawhide Mine, managed by the colorful "Captain" Nevills, who drove his surrey and spanking team of matched horses from his home in the valley over to Jamestown almost every day, to watch the progress of the hotel bearing his name. Pretty little Rawhide Valley resounded day and night with the Rawhide's big stamp mill and chlorination works, as well as to the lesser operations of the nearby Alabama and Omega mines, also under Nevills' managership.

On the southern outskirts of Jamestown were the Ophir and Crystalline mines, whose concentrated wealth, lying one hundred fifty to five hundred feet below the surface and worked by tunnels and stoping upward in the different pay shoots, assayed from $2.00 to $50.00 a ton for ore, and $400 to $500 a ton for sulphurets. Close to the Crystalline Mine, the Cloudman Mine straddled a glaring white outcrop almost on the wagon road into Jamestown. This mine under later owners produced a steady stream of gold until shut down by World War II.

Southeastward of Jamestown was Quartz Mountain, located exactly on the Mother Lode vein. About eight hundred people lived there due to the activities of the Dutch, App and Santa Isabel mines. One mile away was Stent, the "Poverty Hill" of Bret Hart's stories of an earlier day, now boasting a thousand in population and, besides the usual saloons, stores and hotels, the finest opera hall in the county. Stent was home town for one of the most famous of all Mother Lode mines, the Jumper. This mine, owned by capitalists in Glasgow, Scotland, and employing ninety men, was said to produce more free gold than any other mine in the world. The precious metal was often chiseled off shafts in sheets, and so much unique specimen gold was brought to the surface that it was retained from the reduction works and piled "waist-high-to-a-man" in one of the mine's stone storerooms. These and a dozen lesser mines, such as the Hum Bug, pulling its gold out from under Table Mountain, contributed to Jamestown's reputation as the Queen of the Mines.

On both sides of Jamestown's main street were two and three storied stone and wood buildings, the latter with "gingerbread" balconies above doctors', dentists' and newspaper offices. At one end of town was the Jamestown (later, Willow) Hotel. Near the other was the Commercial Hotel, and between were the National Hotel, the Odd Fellows Hall, the marshall's headquarters, offices, stores, livery stables, saloons and an assay office. On either side of the long street, shaded by cottonwood trees, were dozens of saloons flanked by watering troughs and hitching racks. On hot summer afternoons, cottonwood seeds wafted down like gentle snow onto gamblers and drifters dozing in barroom chairs, tilted against saloon fronts, until the evening's excitement began. Between Main Street and Woods Creek, with room enough for men's horses to be hitched inconspicuously, was the Mother Lode's biggest red light district, known as "Back-of-Town."

Sprinkled among Main Street businesses, and on hill slopes east of them, were the homes of Jamestown's five hundred substantial citizens. Many homes whose doors, stained glass windows, tubs and kerosene light fixtures had been shipped around the Horn in early days, were now almost hidden behind magnolia, lilac and rose-scented gardens where they would survive the fires and good and bad years that followed the coming of the railroad. Further southward was Jamestown's graveyard, resting place of good and bad, babies and murderers, with a marker for George Chamberlain, immortalized as Bret Harte's "Tennessee Partner," and one for "Ah Me," knifed in 1852. Also steeply above the main road under spreading oaks was the little red schoolhouse, with splintering benches, a potbellied stove and "two-holer" outhouses. Almost out of town were the modest homes of rancher-miner John App and one of Captain Donner's daughters, who had come this far after surviving her father's ill-fated crossing of the Sierra Nevada summit.

At the opposite end of town was the Pereira Pavilion, where nice people danced and drank pink lemonade until eleven-thirty on Saturday nights. On Sunday mornings, stiffly hatted and booted, they answered the church bells of their choice which rang out about the time folks on the other side of Main Street were going to bed. For Jamestown in 1897 was known as the "rip-snortinest blankety-blank, most altogether roughest town in the mines" where brawlers fought and whooped it up in the glare of saloons and in the shadows of cottonwood trees while good people slept peacefully in shuttered homes set in fragrant gardens.

CHAPTER FOUR

SIERRA RAILWAY

On November 8, 1897, the Sierra's first passenger train into Jamestown came puffing up Woods Creek. Passing in sight of the App and Isabel mines, the Six Spot waved a long plume of smoke, and whistled cheerfully while rounding the last bend to her new home. Approaching the depot, Engineer Wright cut his speed and slowly pulled baggage car, passenger coaches and an observation car past the assembled shouting, hat-waving crowd. The engine's sharp exhaust of steam made horses rear, women scream and men cheer. Conductor Long, in blue uniform and cap, helped hilarious passengers from the coaches to the cemented platform while townspeople swarmed through the train from both sides. After speeches were delivered, Prince Poniatowski drove the "golden spike," but the celebration had only begun. A mile-long queue of men, women and children followed the Jamestown and Oakdale bands down to old Jamestown's flag-bedecked and whisky-redolent Main Street, where miners, cowpunchers, teamsters, blacksmiths and businessmen were prepared to shoot and drink and dance and fight, because Jamestown was a railroad town with Iron Horse wranglers joined in their ranks.

Contests began in mucking and double-jack drilling with a goal of twenty-two inches in ten minutes; roping, gold panning and marksmanship with .45 revolvers at 200 feet. For two days the saloons stayed jam-packed with drunks, semi-drunks and sober-eyed poker players, whose stakes, as likely as not, were pokes of gold dust, or nuggets hijacked from the tunnels of local mines. Only a few men lingered up on the hill of New Town to finger the side rods, control valves and boiler of a locomotive, and become acquainted with its smoke and smell and hiss and pant. Obliging firemen kept up enough steam to repeatedly sound the two long and two short whistles that were to become the familiar cry of the Iron Horse. These were the men, young and not so young, whose enthusiasm for a railroad's equipment, operations, rails and roadbed would lead them to become employees of Jamestown's newest industry, and in some cases to give their whole lives to it.

The Nevills Hotel and nearby surveyed lots symbolized the high hopes of Bullock and Nevills for Jamestown as a swanky rail terminus. But the Sierra Railway itself was operated under rigorous rules of economy while maintaining daily freight and passenger schedules. There were now seven locomotives on the line, including two switch engines. Some fifteen flat cars and two box cars, as well as two "crummies," bore the Sierra's lettering. Passenger coaches, on loan like the one owned by the line, were fitted with wood or coal stoves, iced drinking water tanks, swinging lamps, brass spittoons and lavatories with open tank toilets. The baggage and mail car was presided over by a Wells Fargo Agent and a company baggage and mail clerk, who sorted ordinary mail and tossed off newspapers and packages to ranchers and miners at designated places along the line. Brakemen, firemen and engineers of judgment and self-reliance operated this communicationless road with secondhand engines on secondhand rails pulling heavy loads over grades, curves and bridges. First-rate mechanics and well-fitted shops kept the rolling stock rolling while bridge and road maintenance crews gave them security in motion. These men cooperated for their own lives and livelihood as well as for the economy and efficiency of the railroad.

The Sierra's freight agent contracted for fast and dependable shipment of every conceivable thing from carload lots and corpses to daily bakery products because freight was the railroad's primary objective. Yet the cream of the county's freight was still left to horse power. Freight wagons, bringing marble, lime and lumber to the Jamestown terminus over steep and tortuous grades, were almost as costly to shippers, also paying for transfer time, as was the case when their products were hauled by teams all the way to the valley. The same was true of wagonloads of ore and sulphurets delivered from mines to the nearest rail point, spur or loading platform along the line. Also, if these deliveries bogged down en route to rails, railroad shipping schedules were delayed.

To improve this latter situation at least, the Sierra put its grading crews at work on another wagon road — that between Chinese Camp and Coulterville.

But the heaviest wagon freighting to rails was done from the mines northward and eastward of Jamestown and from the saw-mills above Sonora. To get closer to these two big sources of freight, the Sierra Railway now decided to extend itself in both directions.

There were difficulties in the way of each extension, however. Sonora, five miles eastward, still jealously guarding its teaming and stage businesses, seethed with objections to the railroad's coming. The Oakdale *Graphic* said:

"The Sonora *Banner* doesn't know whether the coming of the Sierra Railway to that country is going to help the people. We think it will be the best thing that ever struck Sonora."

And to quote the San Francisco *Call:*

"The proposed Sierra lines will pass Angels and probably Sonora. At the latter point there are some differences over right-of-way and should these not be arranged the line will be around the town, as rights-of-way for the remaining portions of the road are virtually secure."

Another determined antagonist to the Sierra extending its line to and beyond Sonora, was "Captain" Nevills, who threatened to sue the railroad if it did so, since, according to him, there was an agreement between Bullock and himself that Jamestown would remain the railroad terminus for five years, allowing this much time for a return on money invested in the Nevills Hotel and Jamestown Improvement Company's real estate venture. Nevills favored the railroad's northward extension, however, expecting it to pass his Rawhide Valley mines as well as other mines whose managers, with good transportation, might build homes in James-town's new addition near a cosmopolitan hotel such as he intended the Nevills to be. But Mr. Nevills' desires were of little conse-quence at this moment when California's ex-congressman, James A. Louttit, proposed a railroad to be named the Stockton and Tuolumne Railroad, to run from Stockton to Summersville via Milton, Copperopolis, Columbia and Sonora. This railroad, popu-larly called "The Woman's Railroad," was being actively promoted at Stockton by Mrs. Annie Kline Rikert, who asserted that she would have offices in Sonora within the year. Bullock's answer to this competitive proposal was to engage Charles Erickson and Company, railroad contractors of San Luis Obispo, California, to start grading immediately on the secured right-of-way out of Jamestown toward Sonora, regardless of Sonora's or Nevills' objections.

There had been considerable notoriety ten years previously when the millionaires A. F. "Hog" Davis and James G. Fair of the South Pacific Railroad built expensive trestles over salt marshes from the south end of San Francisco Bay to the city of Alameda only to be refused a franchise into the city limits. Roustabout gangs from the Central Pacific, already serving Alameda, and South Pacific graders had slugged it out while the line was laid through. Tuolumne County residents now expected something of that nature to occur between railroad gangs and teamsters if the Sierra extended its mainline to and beyond Sonora. But to the railroad such a possibility was unimportant compared to the fact that the Standard Lumber Company and the West Side Flume and Lumber Company were both east of Sonora, and both lumber companies, with Crocker money involved, had been promised transportation by the Sierra Railway.

At this point, a startling announcement by Bullock was printed in the San Francisco *Examiner.*

"February 11, 1898. Work commenced today on surveys for three electric powered feeders for the Sierra road to radiate from Jamestown to Sonora, Jacksonville and Angels Camp. Power for the proposed lines will come from the Blue Lakes Electric Plant on the Mokelumne River over a pole line now about completed."

The next day a Sonora paper said:

"T. S. Bullock was interviewed here in regard to his proposed electric railroad from Jamestown to Sonora and other points. He said when rights-of-way were secured, construction would commence immediately and be rushed to completion. He said it was desired to enter Sonora from the north, or south, at the proper elevation and pass directly through the city to Columbia. If favorable action is taken by the authorities at Washington in regard to California marble entering into the construction of the San Francisco post office building, Bullock said, the line would be rushed through to the quarries where five hundred men will be employed. All Bullock asks is depot grounds and rights-of-way through the city. Although many never overlook an opportunity to revile the Sierra railroad, we believe Bullock's wishes will be favorably considered by the Trustees. His proposition is honest in every respect and should act as combination olive branch and pipe of peace."

This friendly attitude, however, was not shared by everyone. As the news got around that Prince Poniatowski, president of the Sierra Railway Company, was also promoter and largest shareholder of the Blue Lakes Power Company and Columbia Marble Works, the idea of electric power on a steam powered railroad seemed more plausible, but many Sonora people still thought the projected electric road amounted to little more than a handle by which to get a franchise through the town, and that once the franchise was obtained it would be used for a steam line which no one would tolerate. While Bullock's petition for a right-of-way over Sonora's Washington Street was under advisement, the voice of the opposition was expressed as follows:

". . . the audacity of the Sierra in having the monumental brass to present such a petition takes away the breath. When it was only a case of skinning, as at Jamestown, and a false boom, it was enough, but when aqua fortis is sprinkled on the raw and rubbed in, we object. The little prince from Russia and his satellites care nothing about Tuolumne, but having gotten so much for the asking would take the rest as vested right. Missionaries who came to enlighten the savages usually offered glass beads or firewater in exchange for favors but we are thought such easy game that even these concessions are unnecessary."

It was understood at this time that Blue Lakes electric power would pass through and supply Stockton on its way to provide San Francisco with electricity. This scheme, the Stockton *Mail* said:

". . . was worked up by C.E.C. of which Poniatowski is a leading spirit and who also proposes to supply rapid electric transit in the mining areas. This syndicate has the cash. It built the Sierra Railway, the cost of which is whispered to have been $375,000. The bonds, amounting to $600,000, were recently bought up by Henry Crocker for the Southern Pacific. If the Sierra railroad is back of this scheme, it must originate from sound commercial reasons."

As a matter of fact, Mr. Henry Crocker did invest in the Sierra Railway at this time to promote his timber interests above Sonora. Prince Poniatowski, on the other hand, was expecting his marble to be used in the construction of the new San Francisco post office building. If Poniatowski's marble was accepted by Federal authorities, he obviously could afford to bring his electric power from Calaveras County to the Columbia marble works and also power a spur track from there through Sonora to the Sierra Railway. While awaiting decisions on these matters by Federal Agents and Sonora trustees, Bullock, who was not one to have all his eggs in one basket, gave his attention to an alternate steam railroad approach to his partner's marble works. This approach was possible as an offshoot of the Sierra's originally planned branch to be built to Angels Camp.

The rights-of-way for the first miles of the proposed Angels Branch from Jamestown to the north had been secured without difficulty. The line started, of necessity, by crossing Table Mountain to Rawhide Valley and Tuttletown. Once tracks were laid to that side of the mountain, they would be within six almost level miles of the marble source. Therefore, a petition was entered at Sacramento for a railroad projection into Columbia, and Erickson's graders and equipment now lying idle on the Sonora route were put to work on the secured right-of-way over Table Mountain.

By this time, the "Woman's Railroad" had secured rights-of-way out of Stockton as high into the foothills as Copperopolis and was actively continuing to sell stock by popular subscription at $100 a share. Its proposed route was still via Columbia to Sonora and Summerville, where Bullock was not only also determined to go, but to get there first.

In the following two months while Washington, D. C., and Sonora were making up their minds, construction workers hacked their way through trees and brush up the side of Table Mountain to a comparatively low place in that mountain's straight back. At that point, graders with powder and shovels began work on a cut wide enough for a train to pass through. Before this cut was finished, the construction company quit the job, having put more time and money on these first two miles than it had anticipated spending on the full mileage to Tuttletown. Also, having looked over the whole route to Angels Camp, the construction engineer

330

Stand of West Side timber about to be cut. Fallers can be seen at work on largest tree in foreground.

Dolbeer donkey on West Side logging operation. This engine was invented by a Eureka lumber operator and quickly supplanted the ox teams that used to haul logs from where they were cut to the railhead. Most steam donkeys were located on hillsides and other points away from immediate water supply. These donkeys with special packs were used to haul water for the ever-thirsty boilers.

311

Logging chute. Logs were pulled over this by a cable from the Dolbeer donkey.

Building railroad trestle on West Side about 1909.

Clavey River bridge on West Side. Mr. Ellis laid this 325 ft. long bridge out in the yards at Tuolumne during the winter shutdown and erected it in the woods at the start of the Spring season. It was 65 ft. high and had a curvature of 30%.

TWO PICTURES: ARTHUR RONTEN

Entire tree upon train at West Side Camp 34. Man in black hat in foreground is Super-intendent Hanlon of West Side Lumber Company.

Another trestle in the course of construction. Note steam donkey on hillside being used for lifting the bents into position.

TWO PICTURES: EUGENE M. PRINCE

West Side No. 8 with train of logs on bridge across the NorthFork of Tuolumne River.

Small power shovel being used in construction of the West Side railroad.

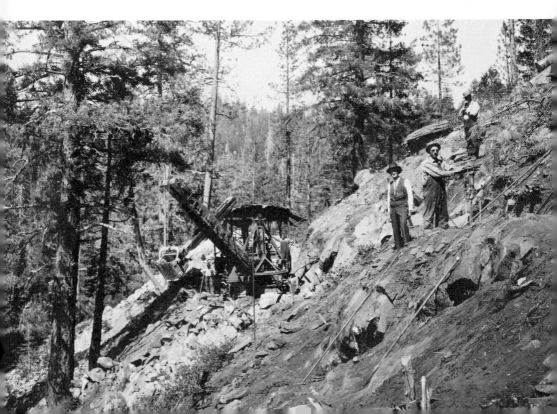

EUGENE M. PRINCE

West Side No. 7 emerging from deep cut between North Fork of Tuolumne River and Camp 8.

Typical type of construction and terrain on West Side lumber railroad.

ARTHUR RONTEN

View of West Side mill taken from dock by engine house. Logs are dumped from cars into the pond where they can be stored for use as the mill demands.

Douglas Fir logs being hauled into mill. Endless chain runs in slot in foreground which pulls logs out of pond.

Logs on deck of mill waiting to be taken to the saw. Partially cut log can be seen on saw carriage at right.

Log being cut. The log is on what is called the carriage, and is moved back and forth at high speed by steam pistons. Man at left is sawyer who controls the action of the carriage and loge turner. Setter rides the carriage and advances the log at each cut in response to hand signals from the sawyer.

Lumber stacked in drying yard at West Side mill. This lumber was stacked from an "A" frame with tongs pulled by a horse, just like hay in a loft.

Clear sugar pine plank 3"x35"x16 ft. This was premium grade lumber and used mainly for drain boards before the advent of more modern materials.

Four narrow gauge Heislers standing outside engine house, West Side. Logs in pond in foreground must have been dumped off flatcars on track at edge.

The continuation of picture on page opposite, showing two of the Shays. Date of these pictures is unknown, but the classic automobile at extreme right should give some indication. A modern day photo would show little change.

SIERRA RAILROAD

Log pond and engine house of Pickering Lumber Company. Sierra main line passes behind log train.

Dry storage of logs at Pickering mill. Logs were piled here so that the mill could operate long after snows had shut down logging in the higher country.

Closeup of log piles. Steam crane in distance is loading logs for the short trip to the pond.

TWO PICTURES: SIERRA RAILROAD

Drying yard at Pickering Lumber Company.

Overall view of Pickering Lumber Company operation. Sierra main line makes big curve at left. Mill is at extreme right.

now took a dim view of the possibility of crossing the Stanislaus Canyon which, he said, was too steep for tracks, let alone equipment, and too wide for bridging.

After hearing this verdict, Bullock, carrying papers of engineering figures about which he knew little, and of his railroad's bonded indebtedness about which he knew much, took the train to San Francisco where he met with friends Poniatowski and Will Crocker. After hearing his engineering dilemma, it was suggested that he contact a young civil engineer named W. H. Newell, who recently had come to Henry Crocker, a Southern Pacific executive, with a letter of introduction from the Mexican Central Railroad. Bullock had heard of Newell's railroad location work in mountainous Mexico and had seen his engineering of the Tampico Jettees when he, Bullock, was in Mexico promoting the sale of his own railroad there. He therefore took the train back to Stockton where Newell was locating a short line called the Stockton Terminal and Eastern Railroad. Bullock presented his problem as a well-paying engineering challenge, and had little difficulty in obtaining Newell's promise to look the situation over as soon as possible.

Before Bullock's return to Jamestown the Sierra Railway had its first fatal accident. The victim, Conductor William G. Bailey, was a cousin of Bullock's who had recently been brought out from New Jersey. A special freight train had left Jamestown at six o'clock on a Sunday morning headed for Cooperstown, with Engineer Wright, Fireman Messenger, Brakeman E. W. Miller and Bailey all riding in the cab. Pulling into Chinese Station at about twelve miles an hour, the engine derailed at a switch and ran on the ties for almost forty feet before sinking to soft roadbed and toppling over into the ditch. Bailey, who had been sitting on the fireman's bench, was thrown through the lookout window and crushed to death as the boiler rolled over on him. Wright shut off the steam from the cylinders and went over with the engine as did Messenger, but neither was hurt. The brakeman was climbing over the tender when the engine hit the dirt and he jumped to safety. Sierra switch stands had no lock on them and could be thrown open by anyone with malicious intent, but Wright was positive the switch was open to the mainline fifty feet before he reached it. In spite of his insistence that spreading rails had caused the accident, padlocks were installed on all switch stands along the line after this accident.

That March, when Bullock brought two bankers to the Nevills Hotel for inspection and appraisal, the hotel was electrically lighted top to bottom. It was an imposing sight which the Oakdale *Leader* commented on as follows:

"Jimtown is noisy. Whistles blow night and day, cowbells ring, the milk man shouts 'Milk' loud enough to be heard on the north branch of the South Fork of the Tuolumne and, a lot of roosters think it's broad daylight because the Hotel Nevills is a blaze of electric lights. Old Jimtown has its crooked main street with magnificent stores, dingy Chinese washhouses, old stone buildings, new brick buildings, alleys and byways. But who would think Jimtown would wake up and put on fresh airs, fresh paint and a pile of style? Jimtown on the hill! Clean, wooded, the uplifting outline of Table Mountain and the Nevills Hotel. Every convenience in every room, hot and cold water, bath, electric lights, — and the cuisine! Manager J. H. Van Horn looks after all guests, if need be for such in those surroundings!"

While the questions of power, rights-of-way, depot sites and marble-versus-granite in the post office building dragged on, the railroad maintained busy routine service. Passenger trains "whirled" up and down between the valley and the foothills on such crowded schedules that an experiment was tried using an extra Pullman train. Beginning May 15th, chiefly for the accommodation of tourist travel to Yosemite Valley, two sleepers were put on a night train, leaving San Francisco at 4:30 p.m. and arriving at the Nevills Hotel at 1:00 a.m. This train left Jamestown at 6:00 p.m., arriving at San Francisco at 12:15 p.m. Tickets were immediately in demand but the service was hardly begun before it lagged for an obvious reason. People who could afford a Yosemite trip and indulge in Pullman accommodations would not swelter from 1:00 a.m. to 6:00 a.m. in the hotbox which a sleeper (without fans or air-conditioning) could become when the temperature stood at 100°. Especially so when one of the best hotels in the state was only a few feet away. As soon as day coaches were added to this train for passengers with hotel reservations, the Pullman Company lost out almost altogether. The temptation to sidetrack the sleepers a half mile out of town was resisted and, with insufficient patronage, the Pullman service was discontinued as of July 1st.

With the terminus still at Jamestown, the Great Sierra Stage Company, renamed the Nevills and Guerin Stages, accommodated tourists on the Jamestown to Yosemite run. This speedy service left the Hotel Nevills at 6:00 a.m., arriving at Priests Station for lunch, and at Crockers Resort for the night. Service from that point to the floor of the Valley ran morning and evening. With the Morris brothers as agents in Chinese Camp, stages also met the daytime passenger trains at that point and covered the same route. Priests and Crockers resorts had been show places of years' standing on the Big Oak Flat road, and the latter near the Tuolumne and Mariposa Big Trees offered such rustic yet homelike charm that many Yosemite-bound tourists got no further.

That summer Newell came to Jamestown to inspect the Sierra's engineering projects. En route by train, he had a four hour look at the line's crookedest piece of track while a derailed freight held up passenger service near Don Pedro Station. The day after his arrival in Jamestown, he and Bullock drove by horse and buggy along the Mother Lode mines to the Stanislaus Canyon, and crossed the river on Percy Wood's hand-operated ferry. After stopping in the canyon for note taking and discussion as to the possibility of a rail crossing in this disputed area, they continued to Angels Camp. A few days later a similar trip was made afoot and horseback past Sonora to Tuolumne City.

On his way back to Stockton, Newell left the train at Chinese Station and rode horseback to Cooperstown where he again took the train. After these trips he agreed to engineer the Sierra's main-line extension to Tuolumne and the Angels Branch. Also, he recommended realignment of the present roadbed with a seven mile detour westward of Don Pedro Station. In the fall of 1897, Newell joined the Sierra Railway Company as its Engineer in Charge of Locations and Surveys with two draftsmen assisting him in the Jamestown office and a crew of surveyors in the field.

The first annual meeting of the Sierra Railway Company was held in San Francisco on July 16, 1898. Directors A. Poniatowski, S. D. Freshman, Samuel Susaman, Hall McAllister and Frank Pierce were re-elected, and Henry J. Crocker also elected to the directorate. Officers of the company were: A. Poniatowski, president; H. J. Crocker, vice-president; J. M. Bonner, secretary; S. D. Freshman, treasurer; C. N. Hamblin, auditor (replacing P. M.

Peck); T. S. Bullock, general manager and W. H. Newell, chief engineer. The extended construction program was sanctioned and the purchase of more rolling stock authorized.

The "Woman's Railroad" had become a highly controversial subject in Tuolumne County. While some people believed the line would come in to Columbia and Sonora bringing better service than that offered by the Sierra, others called the line a purely promotional scheme. An engineer's drawing of a 500 foot high railroad bridge designed to span the Stanislaus River canyon below Melones had been published in local papers. Erickson Company graders, hired away from Sierra construction work, had thirty-five teams and plows on the line's right-of-way out of Stockton, and Mrs. Rikert had made her appearance in Sonora. "The Sierra Railway is a good road," she said, "but does not fill the bill. They charge twenty dollars a ton to get ore out, so ore has to assay twenty dollars a ton to pay to take it off the dump. We could haul this ore out for nine dollars a ton."

To counter this remark, Bullock, quoting Engineer Newell, said the road proposed by this lady was impossible to build due to the route chosen, and therefore they were foisting worthless stock upon a credulous public. Whereupon Bullock was requoted as having called Mrs. Rikert "a high-toned thief and mesmerizer of large-figured checks." But the friendly *Mother Lode Magnet* of Jamestown said:

"When the Sierra Railway was first mooted, the conservative element wondered if it would be built or would pay. It was built and has proven a benefactor to our community, lessening freight charges and bringing us in touch with the outside world. The cost of construction of the electric roads they propose for the use of the people of three counties will foot up to a large sum. The bridging of the Stanislaus River, alone, will require an enormous expenditure of money. Why should we encourage a competitor?"

Three things then happened to bring the whole situation to a head. The Sonora trustees refused to grant a franchise for a right-of-way through the city for the Sierra Railway. A dispatch from Washington, D. C., said Federal investigators had found that granite was more accessible than marble and better in every way as structural material for the San Francisco post office building.

Thus, with no right-of-way through Sonora, and no marble contract, Bullock and Poniatowski decided not to supplement the power generated at the Columbia Marble Works. Though this ended talk of electrically powered extensions to the Sierra Railway, the extensions themselves remained a very live issue.

At this time, also, the "Woman's Railroad" began to topple. Erickson's graders put an attachment on that line's property for unpaid wages and were immediately rehired by the Sierra Railway to proceed with track laying toward Sonora. Mrs. Rikert then blamed Sierra officials and the war (Spanish-American) for her failure.

"This is all twaddle," a local reporter said. "Mrs. R's road fell in the consommé simply because laboring men must be paid. Our own opinion of the Sierra road is not an exalted one but they did put their road through and in many respects it has been a blessing. Their service may not be the best but it beats the pack trail all hollow."

That August, with daytime heat at 104 degrees, some financiers spent a week at the Nevills Hotel reviewing their investments in local mines, lumber and railroads. W. H. Crocker, H. J. Crocker, C. F. Gardner and H. McIntyre were there with Bullock to discuss promotional plans for the West Side Flume and Lumber Company, including eight miles of narrow-gauged logging road already located by Newell and now under construction from the millsite in Tuolumne into their timberland. Although Poniatowski was also interested in this lumber, he brought Count Le Hon, a European authority on marble, to this meeting to promote the sale of his Columbia marble.

After inspection trips made during the day's exhausting heat, these gentlemen relaxed in the spacious Nevills Hotel. Bartender John Murphy, recently of the Palace Hotel in San Francisco, served drinks from his well-stocked bar. In the cool dining room, uniformed waitresses served local and imported delicacies prepared by a French chef with Chinese assistants. After dinner, rattan rockers on the upper balcony encouraged the peaceful contemplation of old Jamestown and majestic Table Mountain with twinkling lanterns marking mines where men were still tunneling for gold. By the end of the week, several conclusions reached by these financiers were made public in San Francisco and New York.

Le Hon's finding that Columbia marble, while not as colorful, was more durable than the finest from Italy, led to investment by Eastern capital in Poniatowski's marble. Poniatowski's statement that mining had by no means reached its maximum development was backed up by several options taken on local mines. The owners of the West Side timberland decided to open their logging road to tourist travel as soon as it reached Hetch Hetchy Valley and Bullock, holding the key to all this promotion, promised rail service to Tuolumne by Christmas and the branch line to Tuttletown ready for ore and marble hauling before then. In fact, during their meeting these financiers had watched Sierra tracks branch from the main line below the hotel and continue northeastward through the hills to Kentucky Flat before crossing the Fahey place, on the right-of-way to the southern suburbs of Sonora.

When the Sierra railroad negotiated to buy a depot site between N. L. Knudsene's lumberyard and the county hospital, outside Sonora's limits, county supervisors said the site was reserved for a future county high school. This angle was disputed by townspeople who wanted the railroad and felt that a depot site had better be found before the line by-passed them and grass grew on their unused streets! The issue raged, unsolved, while the Sierra's new passenger and freight agent, S. H. Smith, composed articles for the West's leading publications advertising mining and agricultural resources in its vicinity. To further increase local good will and prosperity, the railroad installed a 22,000 gallon tank in upper Jamestown to be used by the Tuolumne County Water Company for fire protection. A better wagon road was built from Jamestown to Stent and the Jumper Mine. Free telegraphic service previously offered on Sundays, when passenger trains did not run, was supplanted by a special train which ran seven days a week between Sonora and Stockton, carrying a combination passenger-baggage car painted bright yellow, which arrived in Stockton at 11:15 a.m. and left there at 1:20 p.m. With this service in effect, the railroad sponsored the first Tuolumne County reunion ever held in the home county, which prior to rails would have been impossible, involving a jolting daylong trip up and back by wagon road. The railroad's interests also built and inaugurated a new Jamestown bank. When the California Miner's Association entertained the American Institute of Mining Engineers, the railroad offered delegates a special car at half fare in order to induce them to come to Tuolumne County. And when the Collector of Internal Revenue imposed a one-cent war tax on each bill of lading in freight shipments, the Sierra absorbed the tax. Wells Fargo, on the other hand, was sued by shippers, as that company, quite understandably, insisted the tax should be paid by shipper or consignee.

A report from Sacramento on July 20, 1898, said:

"The entire session of the State Board of Equalization today was occupied in listening to the appeals of representatives of the Carson and Colorado Railroad Company and the Sierra Railway Company of California to reduce the assessed valuations of the corporations' properties.

"T. S. Bullock, General Manager of Sierra, and S. D. Woods of Stockton, its attorney, told the board they believed $2,500 a mile would be fair valuation upon which to base an assessment. The road has operated since November last, and cost in the neighborhood of $207,000. Mr. Woods said its prospects were good and he thought the board should be lenient in its first assessment. In reply to this remark, Chairman Morhouse said: 'Don't you know it takes a nervy man to set here and vote for a reduction of a railroad assessment!' "

It must, in fact, have taken more nerve than was available, since in August the Sierra Railway was assessed by the State Board of Equalization at $4,000 per mile, or on $162,400 for 40.61 miles. In spite of the resulting high tax on a company whose financial statement in 1898 showed a meager $16,368.16 surplus earnings after operating expenses and fixed charges, the little Sierra proceeded with expenditures befitting its determination to grow. A three stall roundhouse and enlarged machine shops were completed in Jamestown. A Thomas Flyer touring car was put on track wheels in the Jamestown shop for use as Bullock's "private car," and a Model K Winton was converted to a six wheel car for W. H. Newell's use and for twice monthly trips made over the line by Mr. Harry Guilds, paymaster. The Rogers locomotive *No. 3* was laid up for extensive repairs, but the two 4-4-0 freight engines met daily schedules which included sidetracking while passenger trains high-balled through. Grazing livestock no longer raced, manes and horns flying, away from engines whose steam whistles and squealing wheels told ranchers and miners the time of day.

Eighteen men, under Sierra direction, were now cutting Columbia marble slabs for use in the construction of a depot on the finally acquired site at the south end of Sonora. Sonora, however, after objecting to rails, now also put its foot down on traction engines with hard tires and ten-ton blocks of marble cutting up Washington Street on the way from Columbia to the depot site. Furthermore, Bullock's bill introduced into the Senate to allow a branch line from Tuttletown to the Columbia marble works had been filled. This was frustrating to railroad officials determined to haul this freight item, wherever consigned and particularly now, to Sonora. Newell therefore put half of the construction men still working between Jamestown and Sonora onto the Angels Branch to hasten its completion as far as Tuttletown. A short spur track was to reach from there to Jeffersonville so marble, wagon freighted from Columbia, could be loaded onto flat cars spotted on the spur for ultimate rail shipment over Table Mountain to Jamestown and then Sonora.

Table Mountain is an ancient lava flow forty miles long with a flat top averaging over half a mile in width. Its sides, where it intersects the Mother Lode, are perpendicular walls of solid basalt five to eight hundred feet high. The existing railroad cut, through the lowest pass of this basalt table, was 40 feet deep and 15 feet wide. Although the bottom of the cut, at 1,710 feet elevation, was only some 300 feet above Jamestown on the one side and Tuttletown on the other, the climb to it was so short and steep it was called a hurdle. To reduce these grades, widen the cut and reduce curvature to 29 degrees, still the heaviest on the Sierra railroad, took a gang of men a month working with powder, hand shovels and a steam-pistoned drilling machine on a tripod (quite an innovation). The work was finished and tracks were laid to Tuttletown and the marble spur before the mainline reached Sonora. When the *No. 3* engine proved inadequate to pull the first marble loads up to the cut, the Sierra's old *No. 4* engine was put on the job though it squeaked through the cut, scraping dirt fore and aft.

Some idea of local conditions while Sonorans debated whether or not to have a railroad, may be had by the following excerpts from newsprint at the county seat:

May, 1898: "B. T. Booze, Gen. Pass. Agent, Jamestown, announced stage connections with the rails at Jamestown to and from sixteen Tuolumne County towns including a daily stage, Sonora to Jamestown, to connect with all trains, and a handsome three seater buggy, daily, for private use."

June 24, '98: "Word comes to us that there can be no viler or more offensive den than the so-called dance hall in Jamestown."

"Thirty Sonorans attended the social hop at Hotel Nevills."

"There are two mails a day for Sonora. One on 1:00 a.m. and one on 5:00 p.m. trains. (Jamestown to Sonora by stage.) A year before this we were lucky to get any mail at all, yet the old mossbacks are against improvements."

Aug. 19, '98: "Preparations are being made to extend the railroad to this city. Grading machinery is here. The company desires to establish the depot on county property and the county to make a present of the site. Otherwise depot will be located two miles out of town. Let it go there. The company better awake to the fact they will have to pay for the land they use. The county is not making presents of real estate. The Sierra Railway has not let the milk of human kindness run away with it — the same rule should prevail with the people."

"Sierra's road will ultimately cross the mountains and connect with a transcontinental line in Nevada. If all current rumors concerning railroads are founded on facts, the iron tracks through Sonora Pass will be so thick that space there will be at a premium."

"Brake beams dropped down on a special freight car ahead of three coaches on the evening passenger train, while rounding a curve between Don Pedro's and Chinese Station. Impossible to move coaches past ripped-up track so passengers finished the trip crowded into a box car. Mails and passengers arrived an hour late."

Sept. 2, '98: "Grading on Sierra Railway, Jamestown to Sonora, calculated to be completed in three months. Be the depot where it may, Sonora will go right along as before."

Sept., '98: "We pray the first act by the Iron Horse in this city will be to run over and mash the life out of a beastly cow that nightly roams the south end of town with a ding-dong bell around her neck."

Oct. 8, '98: "General W. H. L. Barnes of San Francisco spoke to Republicans in Sonora. He termed the Sierra line 'the most inexpensive road.' He forgot that the Sierra built the best road they could with the money they had and that the Southern Pacific wouldn't have a road at all if they had to pay their debts."

"When the Sierra extension now under construction is complete, that line will penetrate further into the Sierra Nevada Mountains than any other road in the State, with the exception of the main line of the Central Pacific."

Dec. 3, '98: "Newell's survey party is at work on main line cutoff."

"Senator C. N. Felton and W. C. Ralston at Nevills Hotel on return from Melones Mine where a 100 stamp mill will be erected."

"Twenty-five stock cars brought to Jamestown for shipment of Miller and Lux cattle."

"Proposed Sonora depot will be 20 x 40 feet and two stories high. Lower story to be of marble brought from the Columbia quarry by team to Jeffersonville, and thence rail via Table Mountain and Jamestown."

"Business men of Sonora pledge $1,000 towards Sierra's payment of depot site at south end of town."

Dec. 23, '98: "The firm of Cy Moreing and Son of Stockton engaged by Newell to grade the new piece of road from Rosasco to Chinese. A number of high trestles and sharp curves will be avoided."

"Injunction taken out restraining the Sierra Railway from passing through private property at the south end of Sonora."

Jan. 2, 1899: "Sierra officials say it is the best paying short piece of road in the state."

"Prince Poniatowski lost a princely sum at the races."

Jan. 11, 1899: "Regular Sunday contingent of visitors to the point south of town where grading is going on were treated to a sight not on the construction program. When a large horse and cart backed too far, animal and vehicle somersaulted forty feet to the bottom of the grade. Small damage resulted."

"Sierra freight shed, 40 x 104 feet, at Sonora is complete. A 'Y' and spur track with sidings will be put in the yard this week."

Feb., '99: "Crew of surveyors under engineer Newell of the Sierra Co. busy on proposed extension of rails to Summerville [Tuolumne City]. Rights-of-way secured. New depot and huge sawmill and hotel will be stationed in the immediate neighborhood of Summerville."

"Sierra passenger depot at Sonora will not be built until track completed and graders have reached city limits. Marble for depot will be hauled in over Sierra tracks."

Feb. 10, '99: "Meeting of Sierra Railway stockholders in San Francisco. All present officers re-elected."

"County gold output for 1898, $4,000,000."

Jumper Mine working full handed and forty stamps dropping. Thirty stamps operating at Rawhide. 183 men employed at Eagle Shawmut."

Feb. 20, '99: "Excursion Sonora to Stockton planned. First passenger train (no excursion) will leave Sonora, Feb. 25, at 7:10 a.m. — to arrive San Francisco, 4:15 p.m. Returning arrives Sonora 5:23 p.m."

"Railroad ball planned Saturday evening at Turn Verein Hall. Reception for railroad officials at Hotel Victoria."

Such bits of newsprint indicate Sonora's acceptance of rails to their community, if not to their town. In fact, after watching the last pieces of forty pound steel rail laid, jubilant Sonora men and women rode flatcars on the construction train returning to Jamestown. As many as could rode stages back, and the rest walked, but these were the first passengers on the Sierra's extension to Sonora. The roadbed had been laid on 2% and 3% grades through some large cuts and fills. A spur had been added at Fassler Station half a mile below Sonora to accommodate the Lime and Plaster Co. From there the tracks curved around the hill and were in sight of Sonora's freight sheds. When the depot was built there, it was to be painted yellow above the marble siding and have a gabled roof curling upwards at the corners to match the Jamestown depot and Hotel Nevills.

Although Sonora had been settled and named by Mexicans and South Americans around a hundred years before, its fifty year-old past as the "Metropolis of the Southern Mines," was most proudly recalled. The polyglot of Americans and Europeans who invaded Sonora during the Gold Rush brought a mixture of languages, professions, cultures and crudities, which, combined with the fortunes made in local lump gold, gave the settlement a truly metropolitan flavor in the 1850's. Fabulous pocket mines then made Sonora the county seat and kept it rich and busy for over fifteen years. The Big Bonanza Mine, straddling Main Street, was one of the richest pocket mines in the state while operating on Sonora's rutted and sidewalkless Washington Street, where merchants, doctors, bankers, craftsmen and stablemen were in business for the miners. Rich, poor, lawful and lawless Sonorans of that populous day dueled and shouted on the court house steps or in saloons, while music was played in the plaza, in bagnios and for operas in Turn Verein Hall.

But now, in 1898, the Big Bonanza had been "temporarily" shut down for over thirty years. The specialty shops, bagnios, señores, señoritas and bonanza kings were gone. Most of the reduced (3,000) population still wore guns and miner's boots, however, and owned at least one gold specimen or other souvenir of a "strike," a hanging, shooting or mob trial of the good old pocket mining days. Ninety per cent of the local newsprint dealt with hopeful strikes, claims, veins and new life in old mines; while elsewhere in the U.S.A. people looked forward to electricity, telephones, gramophones, luxury steamships and railroads in the Twentieth Century — just around the corner.

But Sonora was still the county seat and still the largest town in all the encircling counties where men with political and financial aspirations in Tuolumne County were settled. Their tall Victorian homes financially supported by businesses unrelated to the mines, spelled a different future for Sonora. This mixture of the new among the old was obvious looking down Washington Street from the north end of town where the old race track was across the road from Macomber's new bottling works producing fine cider from one of the county's oldest crops, apples. Senator James B. Curtin, of the pioneer Curtin cattle ranch below Jamestown, now lived at this end of town in his elegant home, complete with ballroom on the third floor. At the head of Washington Street was the historic Episcopalian church and parsonage house, occupied by young and progressive Deaconess Elizabeth Dorsey. On down Washington Street was the newer "Gem" saloon and cafe owned by pioneer miner T. F. McGovern, collector of its fabulous display of gold specimens. Long-time County Supervisor Tom Hender and very young County Sheriff R. L. Price lived in nearby hillside homes as did newcomer C. H. Segerstrom, Sr., who was expanding from the abstract and title business into real estate and banking. On the town plaza run-down Turn Verein Hall was overshadowed by the new county courthouse under construction. Around this central area were the printing offices of four weekly newspapers ranging from fifty to one year in standing. Sprinkled on down this main street were the Tuolumne County and Citizens banks, with Wells Fargo express offices around the corner.

At the junction of Washington Street and Sonora Road, were the City and Victoria hotels, where four and five stages a day stopped before wheeling off to stables farther down the street. Senator Shine's stable in Sonora was then said to be the largest in the state, while stableman D. E. Guerin was noted for his classy single drivers, double teams and four-in-hands. On the eastern hillside was the Sonora grammar school in which five teachers taught two hundred and fifty pupils.

Above Washington Street to the east was the imposing home with glass tropical conservatory of Dr. E. T. Gould, owner of the Sierra Hospital. Southward on Washington Street was the old Europa Hotel, solidly stone-built and long popular with residents of Italian descent. Further southward was Maltman's Reduction Works, having its ups and downs in tune with the quartz mines on which it depended. And the Sonora Foundry, one of whose owners, J. B. Damas, invented miners' improvements such as the air cushion rock drill and the rotary hoist.

As businesses and homes dwindled away on the southern outskirts of town, Washington Street became a crisscross of wagon trails divided by a cow corral. Standing off to one side was the new county hospital, its tall porches laced in wooden "gingerbread," and on the other side, a lumberyard. Between and beyond were the Sierra's freight shed and switchyards with adjoining land enough to accommodate the Hales and Symons warehouse and freight business in another year and, still later, the Standard Lumber Company's huge sash and door planing mill. By then these big industries would crowd and dwarf the depot, to make the area busier and noisier than any in town. But meanwhile, F. T. Duhring, Sonora's Wells Fargo Agent, and R. Briggs, Sierra's station agent, held lonesome sway at this Sonora "outpost."

On February 26, 1899, the above-mentioned and many other equally noteworthy Sonora citizens united in sudden enthusiasm to greet the first train to their community in a manner befitting

the "best town in the West." Folks from all the surrounding countryside came afoot, on horseback and in carriages to the south end
of Sonora. Before noon, two thousand spectators crowded on, or
near, the freight depot where picnic baskets were spread and
booths set up for the sale of tamales, cider, beer and whisky. Members of the reception committee wearing badges on long dress
coats were prepared to deliver speeches before delegations from
Stockton, Oakdale and San Francisco. When the "T-O-O-O,
T-O-O-O — toot-toot" sounded at the road crossing, it was said
that a cannon could have been fired up Washington Street without
hitting a living soul while all eyes watched the Sierra's *No. 6* come
around the turn pulling three loaded coaches. As the train snorted
to a stop, the noise of whooping crowd and frightened horses was
climaxed by blasts of giant powder set off on the adjacent hill. If
the train was seven minutes late no one cared now, by five-thirty,
when some saw two trains come in and some saw none. Speeches
by Mayor Burden and attorney Crittenden Hampton praised the
enterprise that had brought a train into Tuolumne County. Bullock and Prince Poniatowski returned the compliments from the
train's rear platform after which railroad dignitaries were escorted
into town by the Columbia Cornet Band.

Folks who wished were allowed to climb aboard for a close
look at a train while others hurried back to town to secure front
row locations at the plaza where fireworks were to be set off.
These folks were somewhat thwarted by rows of patient Indians
already seated there in beaded hat bands, bright silk neck scarves
and brilliant squaw dresses, because a train was nothing in their
lives, but fireworks meant a chance to watch the town and people
become exceedingly well lit up.

That night at a banquet at the Victoria Hotel, S. D. Woods,
Stockton attorney for the Sierra, prophetically said:

"The headlight of a railroad is the headlight of civilization.
Mr. Bullock has built this road without U. S. Government
subsidy and is established with great corporate interests which
will keep it in business for fifty years."

Within a week a local paper reported:

"New fad. Sonorans walk to Jamestown and ride back on
on the cars."

Also this amazing conclusion:

> "We accept it as a vast improvement over staging and teaming, but we do not go into a frenzy of exuberance and shut our eyes to the cold-blooded proposition that the railroad is here to increase its bank account by service given to the people. It is out for the coin."

It must be admitted that the Sierra was not operating a railroad for its health, but it put Tuolumne County on the map and did everything possible to bring in new industries, as well as to bolster established ones. Especially the mines, whose bulk and packaged ores and sulphurets made up 50% of rail freight at this time.

Sulphurets, or local sulphide ores, are iron pyrites in which gold is a considerable constituent. These cube-shaped concentrates assayed from 40 to 900 dollars of gold to the ton. A few local mines claimed to have shipped sulphurets which assayed as high as $5,000 a ton, although sustaining records are not available. Finer sulpherets subjected themselves to cyanide treatment, but chlorination was the usual method used in reduction. Ores from the Jumper Mine, carrying 3% sulphurets, were passed away until 1900 when reduced by a 20 ton cyanide plant built at the Jumper mill. Sulphurets from mines without chlorination or cyanide plants were hauled to reduction works, such as Maltman's of Sonora, or to plants in the San Joaquin Valley and on San Francisco Bay. This freight item was therefore a major reason why the Sierra railroad continued construction work, as fast as possible, to the operating mines of the East Belt and those along the Mother Lode vein toward Angels Camp.

CHAPTER FIVE

Even while the celebration at Sonora was being held, railroad graders were strung out for miles along the right-of-way, already cleared of trees and brush, to Tuolumne City. Curving past the county hospital on a long fill, the grade bridged Sullivans Creek, proceeded to the Junction Mine and then up Buck Horn Hill to the Black Oak Mine and Campbell apple orchards. From this summit the grade descended to Tuolumne City where station and yard sites had been purchased. Engineer Newell, usually afoot, and dressed in Rough Rider style popularized by Teddy Roosevelt checked surveys and construction specifications at sites like Sullivans Creek, where the highest bridge so far along the line was being built on a 20 degree curve. From there he might ride his motor track car to the almost finished six mile cutoff below Chinese Camp where he had a survey party camped in a field west of the Crimea House.

South of Jamestown the new route by-passed Don Pedro Station, running from Rosasco to Keystone, a previously busy staging crossroads, where an old blacksmith shop was now being removed to make way for tracks. The right-of-way then turned northeast through the Red Hills, the McCormick cattle lands and Mountain Pass, to an intersection with the present line, thence by an improved grade on to Chinese Station. This new route, though longer, would eliminate seventeen bridges and reduce grades and curvatures in the previous seven miles of dangerous roadway to minimize accidents, maintenance and operating expenses.

As Moreing's graders approached Rosasco Station, a familiar figure was greying John Rosasco on his big black stallion who rode out each day to watch the progress. One day he saw the graders cut through a quartz ledge with streaks of gold shining through it and heard Moreing's orders that gold or no gold, work would not be slowed or the ledge disturbed beyond the right-of-way. But the graders spent their few daylight hours before and after work pounding and washing the rock in the cut. Many a pan full of loose rock washed out in the nearby creek by those inexperienced miners produced over fifty cents worth of gold, and among them, the men cleaned up about a hundred dollars. After the graders moved on, a powder monkey encouraged by Rosasco set off a charge of dynamite in the ledge beyond the right-of-way. The barren quartz uncovered was discouraging news to graders who had thought pretty good wages might be made prospecting there when steady jobs became scarce after the grading rush was over.

Graders were employed at an all-time high in Tuolumne County working ten and twelve hours a day, six days a week. As soon as this cutoff was completed, these men would join Erickson's gang on the main line construction into Tuolumne City to speed that work to conclusion, and then start again on the Angels track from Tuttletown to Angels Camp. Surveyors had already staked out the latter right-of-way to the Stanislaus River, and mines along the extended survey were clamoring for rail service such as that already available to the Rawhide group. However, Sierra tracks were now anathema to "Cap" Nevills, who was not only suing the railroad but involved in two other lawsuits.

In the Nevills Hotel's first active months, Nevills had frequently driven over from Rawhide Valley in his fringed surrey, with stylishly dressed guests protected by dusters, goggles and gauntlets. But since bringing a suit against Bullock, co-owner of the hotel, for laying rails beyond that point, Nevills had quit patronizing his elegant enterprise and did his entertaining at the Victoria Hotel in Sonora which he also owned. Though half the size and elegance of the Nevills Hotel, the Victoria was Sonora's best, and here Nevills was undisputed king. He now joined in Sonora's opposition to the railroad. While his suit against Bullock and the Sierra Railroad was in the courts, Nevills was dismissed by the Guild Mining Company after ten years of managing that company's mines. He had promptly brought a counter suit in Superior Court to have himself reinstated. A third suit, labeled as "racy" by the Sonora *Banner* and "the case of an old man making a fool of himself by getting stuck after a woman," may have been the case of a newspaper making the worst of a personal affair, but it did not improve the defendant's temper. The suit against the Sierra Railroad (actually Bullock) was settled when Nevills received half the value of the Nevills Hotel after it was put up for a loan at a Stockton bank. The prosecutor also won his second case in September, 1901, when the Oakdale *Leader* reported:

> "W. A. Nevills was in town with his wife enroute to the Rawhide mines of which he recently regained possession. From Oakdale, Mr. Nevills traveled by private conveyance to view the roads leading to the mines over which he proposes to do his freighting in the future. Mr. Nevills said he would put on three heavy freight teams on October 9th, and increase the number as need demanded, saying he would prefer paying wagon freighters eight dollars to paying the railroad people six dollars a ton. Mr. Nevills is a fighter. The citizens of Jamestown, including the miners, rejoice over his regaining management of these mines."

However, as tempers cooled, the Rawhide, Omega and Alabama mines became paying customers of the Sierra Railway Company. Nevills was, by then, free of law suits and soon afterwards sold his ranches and mines in Tuolumne County, as well as the Victoria Hotel, and quietly retired to a luxurious home in San Francisco. Thus ended the career in Tuolumne County of one of its most colorful figures—both friend and foe of the Sierra Railway.

After the Sierra's mainline came into Sonora, it was predicted that rails would not reach Tuolumne City within a year's time unless work went faster there than it had from Jamestown to Sonora. This prediction proved true. Though only fourteen miles southeast of Sonora, Tuolumne townsite lay in a wide valley at 2563 feet elevation, to be approached by a pass at Buck Horn Hill, four hundred feet above it. This route, located by Newell and maintained through the years, necessitated not only the 145 foot long, 8 bent Sullivans Creek bridge previously mentioned, but the longer, though less high, Black Oak bridge at 2900 feet elevation, and also a 260 foot long, 22 foot high bridge spanning Turn Back Creek close to Tuolumne City. Construction of these bridges with cuts and fills along the continuously curving roadbed was done in icy midwinter at a pace much slower than work in the less rugged lower country in the dry season. Rails were not laid into the new terminus until January of 1900.

Stations along this added main line were: Standard, at the Standard Lumber Company's future millsite just above Sonora; Black Oak, at the successfully operating Black Oak Mine; Campbells (later Ralph's) Station at the highest elevation on the line, and Tuolumne City, center of the East Belt quartz mines and new home of the West Side Flume and Lumber Company.

Tuolumne City was the name given the new lumber town in 1898, and so recognized by the Federal Post Office. But confusion about the town's names was to persist for years. In 1858, the first Lode mine in this belt was located at a little ranch settlement on Turn Back Creek called Summersville. The mining camp of over a thousand population, which then sprung up around this Eureka mine, was named Carters. The community was commonly called by both names before the coming of the lumber industry. By whatever name, it was a pretty place encircled by hills, about three thousand feet high. Looking directly across the valley from the slopes of Buck Horn is the majestic cone of Duckwall Mountain, separated from the town by the precipitous Tuolumne River Canyon. The forested sides of Duckwall Mountain rise almost six thousand feet with the taller snow-clad peaks of Yosemite Park still beyond.

In this direction south and east of Tuolumne City lay a tremendous tract of virgin timberland extending to the Yosemite National Park boundary and crossed by the Clavey and Cherry rivers. Within this area lay a 60,000 acre tract of timber owned by the West Side Flume and Lumber Company. The word "Flume" suggests that logs were originally intended to be flumed out, but this impractical intention was supplanted by a narrow gauge logging road. The ten square mile tract was estimated to contain a billion feet of merchantable timber but actually cut out more than twice that much in its productive years. In 1898, having purchased its town and plant site adjacent to old Carters, the lumber company began construction of a double-band sawmill designed to cut 18,000 feet per hour. This amounted to about 45,000,000 feet per year of lumber, the handsome freight potential for which the Sierra Railway had come to Tuolumne City.

Near the millsite the lumber company built offices, a large store and a warehouse to which the Sierra's tracks were laid and beside which their depot was built. The narrow gauge tracks of the logging road, named the Hetch Hetchy and Yosemite Valley Railroad, curved around Carters toward the Tuolumne River canyon and Duckwall Mountain. Beyond the millpond and tracks was the town square with residential streets running from those of old Carters into the southerly hill slopes.

When the Sierra's first train was due to arrive there, the last load of logs for the winter had been hauled into town by the logging road and piled beside the millpond. The West Side Flume and Lumber Company's first operations in the woods were closed by snow, and the lumber jacks, 300 strong, moved into town bringing Tuolumne City's population to a total of 382.

The adjoining town of Carters had over 500 residents, of whom about 300 were mining men. Like all mining towns, Carters had more than its share of saloons, gambling rooms, dance halls and "bad" houses. The Summerville hotel, recently built in Carters, offered rooms at fifty cents to a dollar a night with meals at twenty-five cents and up. The old Baker's Hotel charged up to two dollars for a room but advertised that it intended to give free carriage service from the coming passenger trains to its doors. These typical Mother Lode hostelries provided seldom-occupied parlors for ladies, and a pool room and saloon, both well occupied and familiarly redolent of stale cigar butts, whisky and tobacco-spattered spittoons. Upstairs bedrooms provided wash stands, pots, slop jars and double beds with open springs, the latter allowing minimum concealment for lice and fleas. Such furnishings, including insects, were common to all California mining hostelries in those days when fleas flourished all over the state. The San Francisco fire in 1906 left that city less notoriously flea-ridden and at the same time inland areas somehow experienced the same happy fate, perhaps due to those assiduously-used deterrents, Buhack Powder and Kerosene.

To mining residents in Carters the East Belt was the coming, biggest gold-producing section in all the Mother Lode. Miners worked in the Buchanan Mine, between the North Fork and Tuolumne River. In the Providence and Draper mines, pounding proceeded full blast beyond the town, as in the Columbus, Carlotta, Dead Horse, Grizzley, New Albany and half a dozen other nearby mines. The Pine Nut Mine on Turn Back Creek had a carload of sulphurets already waiting at the railroad depot and the Black Hawk Mine had mule-teamed five tons of plumbago ore from the mine site (later Twain Harte) to the terminus for rail shipment to Stockton, and thence by water to London, England. This unique shipment netted the mine about five hundred dollars after shipping costs. Large ore shipments were expected from all the above-mentioned mines as well as the Confidence and Soulsby mines, each in its own little settlement, but close neighbors to Tuolumne City. This was also very handsome freight potential for the Sierra Railway.

The Soulsby Mine, richest on the East Belt, having produced $6,500,000 by 1900, was operated by Cornish coal miners imported for the work in 1858. Four hundred and ninety-nine of these Cornishmen had sailed from England to San Francisco and ridden freight wagons from there to the Soulsby Mine. As they were joined by wives and sweethearts, these men built the town of Soulsbyville, which remained strictly Cornish for many years. Although by 1900 a few outsiders lived in town, the miners themselves were a closed society of churchgoing Cornishmen who nevertheless were said to be systematically hijacking gold from the mine and hoarding it against the day when the gold-bearing veins would run out and their source of livelihood cease.

Between Soulsbyville and Carters was a reservation of Mi Wuk Indians. In 1900 Chief Fuller was a young, locally respected giant with about a hundred tribesmen. For many years he was a familiar local figure whose uncommonly accurate predictions of the weather for each forthcoming year often appeared in print and were taken more seriously than the highly technical weatherman's. In 1900, Chief Fuller and his tribesmen spent their spare time and money in Carters.

The almost simultaneous opening of a sawmill and arrival of a railroad to the "Summerville-Carters-Tuolumne City" area, was bound to mean a Big Time to this eighty per cent male community, all united in welcoming rails but divided in bloodthirsty hostility between mine and lumber factions. On February 1, 1900, when the Sierra's first passenger train, loaded with delegates and jubilant local riders, came sliding down Buck Horn Hill, the crowd awaiting it had already squared off in two enemy camps. Red smoke flared from the huge conical burner at the West Side's $350,000 mill whose screech of saws was music to new residents and abhorrence to old. The train came in sight as she rumbled across Turn Back Creek with Engineer Wright holding his whistle cord down. At the depot the flag and hat waving crowd closed in on the train and passengers with whooping hospitality, and the celebration began. Veterans of the Mexican and Civil wars, hook and ladder units from old and new towns, the drum corps of five lodges, a few school children and many Indians marched past the depot in a two mile-long parade. Speeches by lumberman J. T. Adams and financier-promoters Henry Crocker and Thomas Bullock told of the prosperity to come with railroad payrolls added to those of the "woods" and the mines. "America" and "Yankee Doodle," played by competing bands, were punctuated by cannon fire. The parade then straggled back to Carters in a cold drizzle where fists flew in free-for-all fights as the scheduled celebration proceeded. Anger and liquor-strengthened men swore by blasphemous oaths to beat their opponents in log-chopping, triple jacking, bucking, drilling and target shooting. After sawyers in two men teams cut three feet of fir in two minutes, jealous miners instigated a tug of war on a mine cable which ended in a draw due to bleeding hands. At dusk, legally sober Indians went home and the saloons resounded all night with brawling fights, which were to continue for years, between the citizens of old Carters and new Tuolumne City.

With its fifty-eight miles of main-line track now complete, the line was operating at its busiest peak in combined freight and passenger service. Freight trains, double-headed on the grades, brought boxcars from railroads all over the United States into Tuolumne County. Grain, coal, crude oil, dynamite, mining and lumbering machinery were imported as well as the bulk of each mining town's needs. Returning to Oakdale with lumber at $2.50 a ton, lime and ores at $3.00 a ton, cattle at $20.00 a carload and mixed incidental freight, the rails' capacity business was expected to last indefinitely. The quartz mines, while dwindling in number, were larger and deeper than ever before. Tuolumne County was still the leader of California mining sections with 345 patented mines, 545 quartz claims located and recorded and 1,086 stamps working. These and every other nearby industry were customers of the railroad in some degree, with lumber now vying with the mines for first place.

The Sierra's *No. 1,* or down train, left Tuolumne City every morning at 6:18 a.m., arriving at Sonora at 7:00 a.m. and Oakdale at 9:50 a.m. On this train was the through combination coach which was taken directly to Stockton over S.P. tracks, where passengers for San Francisco and way points transferred to S.P. main line trains. The returning *No. 2* or up train left Oakdale at 2:35 p.m. and was back in Tuolumne for the night at 6:15 p.m. Fare per passenger, Oakdale to Jamestown, was a dollar and a half; to Sonora, a dollar seventy-five; and to Tuolumne, two dollars. Local rates were made for the forty-five and twenty-five minute rides between Tuolumne and Jamestown, respectively, into Sonora to accommodate workmen, businessmen and drummers commuting to the county seat. Traffic on these local trains almost doubled a few years later when the county's first high school was built in Sonora and children came to it by rail even from Calaveras County. In the wintertime, boys and girls from Tuolumne City might climb aboard with snow glistening on caps, boots, and lunch boxes. Gathered around the stove with the snow melting into puddles, they laughed and talked above the clickety-clack of the wheels while cars swayed around turns, or crept across trestles with steam hissing onto icy tracks. When the locomotive whistle announced arrival into Sonora, the youngsters set out in laughing groups to walk the mile and a half to their high school.

After this regular morning down train had pulled out of Jamestown, a "special" was made up there, where buckboards had brought teenage youngsters from the surrounding mines and towns to meet with Jamestown's pupils and other commuters, all headed for Sonora. The demand for this kind of service grew to such an extent in the next five years that the Sierra sometimes ran as many as six local passenger trains daily.

The Sierra's motive power still stood at seven engines, in spite of the fact that the old "One Spot" had been ignominiously disposed of. The two 0-6-0's were used as work and switch engines while the *No. 3* Rogers and two 4-4-0 Baldwins made scheduled freight runs. The *No. 6* was on passenger service. There is no record of a *No. 8* on the line, but a new Heisler Locomotive became the Sierra's *No. 9*. This short, geared engine with 45-degree pistons and cylinders was bought for use as the extension continued beyond Tuttletown.

During the rainy winter of 1899, while construction work had been progressing on tracks to Tuolumne City and on the Chinese cutoff, the Sierra's trains suffered several accidents. Because there had been no fatalities, the Sierra Railway Company was said to have a horseshoe around its shoulders. The up passenger train had been stopped between Jamestown and Sonora by a cave-in of dirt on a big cut and passenger coaches were backed down to Jamestown where passengers transferred to stages. A box car of freight tipped over near Chinese Station due to the wet and muddy roadbed, and a few miles out of Oakdale the baggage car and two coaches on the passenger train turned over. This latter accident was caused by the sixty-five ton Schenectady locomotive (later the Sierra's *No. 5* switch unit) when it was being brought to Jamestown as a dead engine attached to the passenger train. Its weight had spread the old forty-pound rails laid on ties on a rain-soaked roadbed. Among passengers badly shaken up by the tipover was the wife of "Captain" Nevills, which served to increase her husband's antipathy toward the Sierra Railroad. Although big headlines read: "Wife of Millionaire Nevills Seriously Injured," this was not true. But it was not a pleasant experience for her or any of the passengers who were thrown in a pile of seats, stoves, trunks and other coach furnishings. Among others slightly injured in the wreck was Mr. Frank Rockwell, messenger for Wells Fargo, who narrowly escaped a load of buckshot from his gun which went off while he was buried under a pile of trunks in the baggage car. Superintendent Potts, among many uninjured passengers in this accident, had the injured and uninjured transferred to box cars and taken to Sonora for medical attention.

As a result of these accidents, a hundred workmen increased the ballast on the whole line, and in spite of this diversion of manpower, the Chinese cutoff was rushed to completion. Just before the final grading was done on this detour, Bullock took an excursion of 150 local people to a point about two miles below Chinese Station where they climbed a hill giving a safe view of the new grade. At a pistol shot fired by Bullock, Hugh Desmond, the construction foreman, answered by calling out "Fire!" and a five-ton blast of dynamite was set off in the final cut just below. The 9,800 pounds of Judson powder and 250 pounds of dynamite, distributed in thirty holes, raised the mass of earth 500 feet into the air with rock fragments estimated to have been blown 4,000 feet high. The following crash was heard as far away as Jamestown, where people who had not seen the explosion decided they had been close enough. The next day a steam shovel cleared the debris to complete the detour into Chinese Station, and rails on the tracks previously used via Don Pedro station were torn up.

Newell's desk in the Jamestown depot was stacked with profiles, cross sections and specifications for bridges, rails, switches and other material to be used on the continuance of the Angels Branch. Location and contour maps stretched across the drafting boards, were the result of many walking and horseback trips along the Mother Lode quartz vein from Tuttletown to Angels Camp. At the intervening, and supposedly impassable, Stanislaus River canyon, as one local writer put it: "Newell and his transitmen climbed up and down all around the Stanislaus canyon staking out the snakiest railroad ever to be built." The contract for grading this road, as taken by C. Moreing and Son, called for a standard gauge roadbed to include all designated sidetracks and switches. Rails of not less than forty-pound steel were to be laid on 8 foot redwood or oak ties, numbering 3200 to the mile. The contract also included labor, material and supplies for grading, cuts, fills, bridges and culverts. The Sierra Railway agreed to pay the contractor fifteen of its first mortgage bonds, fifteen of its second mortgage bonds and three hundred shares of its capital stock for each completed mile.

Branching from the Sierra's main line in front of the Nevills Hotel in Jamestown, the Angels extension bridged Woods Creek at the north end of town and crossed John Black's dairy ranch before starting up the grade to Table Mountain cut. Sloping steeply down the west side of the mountain, the tracks swept widely around Rawhide Valley and the mines operating there before curving northward to Tuttletown. This much of the line, including the Jeffersonville marble spur, had been in use for months and was accepted as finished, except for minor corrections of ballast and curvature. But there was no hurrying out of

Tuttletown, for Newell's blueprints called for a fifty-foot high, seventeen bent wooden trestle where the line continued northward contacting the ten operating mines located between Tuttletown and the Stanislaus River.

Tuttletown had been a crossroads of mining activity since placer days. It was then the center of a cluster of mining settlements so close that pioneers from Jackass Hill, Mormon Gulch and a half dozen other places on the west side of Table Mountain walked into Tuttletown to shop. Mark Twain and Bret Harte were among those people collecting notes for tales such as "The Twins of Table Mountain" and "Outcasts of Poker Flat." At that time two main roads crossed at Tuttletown. One running in a generally north-south direction between Angels Camp and the Big Oak Flat road via Robinson's Ferry, and the other running in a generally east-west direction between Stockton or Milton and Columbia via Reynolds Ferry.

There were also intermediate roads coming into Tuttletown, making it a populous and busy place in '49'er days. But at the time of the railroad's coming, the community was reduced to permanent scattered residents numbering between three and four hundred people. By then it was the center of big and little quartz mines and the home of miners regularly employed in them. Swerer's stone-built store where Bret Harte had clerked was still in business there. Beside it were two saloons and the old-time Cremer house, also of that day. Other big mines situated near Tuttletown, besides the Rawhide Valley group, were the Rappahanock, Isabella and Tarantula mines. The renowned Patterson Mine on the north edge of town had been a rewarding one to its early owners in the 1870's and '80's even though three Wells Fargo shipments of five thousand dollars worth of bullion and three hundred ounces of gold dust from the mine had been stolen by notorious Black Bart during that activity. Closed down in 1891, this mine with its 500 foot shaft full of accumulated water was to be reopened and a twenty-stamp mill added because of anticipated rail shipping service.

But at this moment of readiness to proceed with the railroad, Bullock made the announcement that instead of going ahead, the Angels Branch would end at Tuttletown because exorbitant prices were being asked for rights-of-way over mining properties. Especially, he said, in the vicinity of the Melones mines on the Stanislaus River, where Mr. W. C. Ralston not only made rights-of-ways prohibitive, but insisted on decreased freight rates to his operations. After a month of this standstill in railroad work, the Sierra Railway's half finished bridge across the Stanislaus River was put up for sale and Tuolumne and Calaveras counties asked to bid on it. It was pointed out that the concrete piers and wooden supports for this bridge, erected under Newell's supervision, could be the base for a suitable bridge built for horse-drawn vehicles at this point between the two counties where such a bridge was so sorely needed.

Perhaps this offer of sale by Bullock was a bluff. Perhaps Ralston's demands were a ruse to get railroad freight rates reduced from $8.00 per ton for miscellaneous shipments from Oakdale to his mines, although this seems unlikely since Ralston admitted paying $12.00 per ton for his present wagon freighted shipments over the same route. At any rate, the bridge was not sold but work was held up for almost a year before the necessary rights-of-way were arbitrated over this precious mining property.

In March of 1901, when activity began again on the Angels Branch, the largest steam plow ever seen in this foothill country arrived by Sierra tracks to Tuttletown where it was put to use on grading. Two hundred graders and bridge workers encamped there in tents were advised, at the risk of losing their jobs, to avoid brawling with miners and teamsters. This order was due, in part, to a grader who had been knifed and treated at the Cremer House there the previous Christmas Eve, and who had later stabbed two miners because he was not sure which one had been his assailant.

As the Tuttletown trestle neared completion, pick and shovel crews with powder monkeys, Fresno scrapers and the big steam plow were pushing the roadbed northward toward Jackass Hill. There, in placer days, Mark Twain, among hundreds of others, had prospected, but quit his backbreaking work only to learn that his successor took $20,000 out of his abandoned diggings! Millionaire J. Ogden Mills took his first fortune out of one of the pocket mines which honeycombed Jackass Hill. In 1900, several deep quartz mines were established. Two of the largest were the Atlas Mine with a shaft 120 feet deep which was now being sunk to 600 feet in hopes of more gold, and the long-lived Norwegian Mine. Between these mines Newell had set up a survey camp in tents on a comparatively level pastoral point above the river. His right-of-way on the other side of the river was now being brushed out and the roadbed on this side had been graded this far. From here the railroad was to take off by double switchback on its descent down the Stanislaus River canyon.

For years the Stanislaus River had been wagon-crossed at Robinson's Ferry by rafts attached to guide cables. In placer mining days, Robinson's (later Woods) Ferry had been the thriving community called "Slum Gullion" by Bret Harte. In the late '50's, richly producing quartz mines such as the Calaveras, Columbia and Melones were working in this canyon. Melones, largest of these mines, in its earliest activity, had been worked by fifty hand mortars and arrastras to produce fortunes in virgin gold from its surface veins. In the late '60's it was taken over by legal shenanigans and lay idle for fifteen years with an unclear title. In the '80's most of the nearby mines had petered out and the population of Robinson's Ferry had dropped to a handful of white and Chinese gold panners working over the tailings with remarkably good returns. However, when the Melones Mine finally came into lawful hands, it was converted to deep mining operations at almost prohibitive cost, due to its location at 750 foot elevation in the bottom of a canyon without adequate transportation or power.

Prince Poniatowski had promoted the sale of the Melones and adjoining properties to W. C. Ralston in the name of the Melones Consolidated Gold Mining Company in 1900 with W. J. Loring as superintendent. The Stanislaus Electric Power Company had contracted to provide power for the 120 stamp mill now being built by bringing water from a higher river source through sixteen miles of wooden flume, and dropping it into a power plant site beside the stamp mill. For years miners had been chipping at the Melones mine tunnel which now ran back straight as a die for 4,000 feet under Carson Hill, tapping the old tunnels of the South Carolina Mine running in from Coyote Creek and two other mines located above on Carson Flat. One miner working in the Melones at this time described how those who wanted to go to church on Sundays had to climb up 800 feet of ladders from this tunnel to reach the wagon road to Angels Camp and then walk eight miles to town. Now, by means of this long tunnel, practically all the ore from the Carson Hill diggings and glory hole was to be dropped down shafts and raises to electric trains in the tunnel and pulled out to the new mill on the banks of the Stanislaus.

This huge project had turned Robinson's Ferry into a hive of industry. Besides the mining office, bunk houses for 125 new workmen had been built there, and dozens of saloon men trying to lease ground were being resisted by Mrs. Woods and the Melones Company who wanted no liquor sold in camp. A recreation room for reading and billiards was to be built instead.

The survey camp on Jackass Hill in Tuolumne County overlooked the river canyon with the Melones Mine at the bottom and the opposite Calaveras County crest directly above it. Indian Gulch sloped up that north side of the canyon toward the mines on top of Carson Hill which had produced the most notorious fortunes made in Calaveras County from 1850 to 1880, and where several deep mines were still lucratively operating. To run a railroad across the deep Stanislaus canyon between these two fabulous hills of mining activity and, at the crossing level, to contact the Melones Mine, was a tough engineering proposition. The decision to do so by switchbacks on either side of the canyon with grades on which a train could safely scale the cliffs, was called preposterous and scoffed at as an utter impossibility by many contemporary railroad engineers. But, with Bullock's confidence and the Sierra Railway Director's sanction Newell was now preparing to prove that it could be done. His drafting table was set up in a tent under over-hanging kerosene lamps, for night work, while the survey crew slept in other tents and were provided with breakfast, dinner, and box lunches, at the nearby McArdle ranch. Here, in sight of each step of construction, the camp would remain until a train had been run from one side of the controversial canyon to the other.

On the Tuolumne side of the canyon the roadbed was to descend by a double switchback called the McArdle Switch, starting, as it did, on that ranch property. Dropping down Soldier's Gulch and crossing Joe William's cow corral on the edge of the steep ravine, the switchbacks, tangents and curves wound downward to the level of the almost completed railroad trestle across the river, a seven hundred foot drop in four miles of track with grades up to 4.15 per cent and 27 to 28 degree curves. Climbing from the river on the Calaveras County side, only one switchback was to be used, although a longer one, to be called the Pendola Switch. Eight miles of track with grades equaling the previous ones were required to reach that crest, 660 feet above the river. The finished roadbed on these grades and curves was to be suitable for locomotives pulling heavy freight loads as well as passenger trains.

The Moreing grading firm kept two hundred men working on the Angels Branch, but it was twelve months before trestles, bridges and switchbacks completed the twenty-one mile long Angels Branch. These miles, almost funicular in effect because more perpendicular than horizontal, required painstaking cooperation by construction and survey crews.

After exceptionally heavy winter rains, the steam shovel had to re-clear six hundred feet of roadbed at the Bond Mine site near the McArdle ranch before tracks were laid, ballasted and ready for freight service. Two carloads of freight for the Melones Mine were hauled to the McArdle ranch in February, 1902, to be unloaded there and wagon-freighted to Robinson's Ferry. A short spur was added here to accommodate a boxcar in which meals were cooked and served. The "track layers," as distinguished from "muckers," on the railroad's direct payroll, returned to Jamestown when the price of these meals was raised from 20 to 25 cents each. Meals here, as at all camps along the line, consisted of ham, "hen fruit," spuds, beans, biscuits and coffee for breakfast. Noon and evening meals included steaks, mulligan stews, vegetables, spuds, cakes, pies and gallons of coffee. Vinegar and raisin (or fly) pie was a favorite dessert. Serving platters and pie pans filled with these foods were placed on the table in reach of everyone, beside stacks of bread, pounds of butter, cans of Eagle Brand cream and coffee mugs, to be replenished as desired. But since seventy-five cents for three "squares" was almost half of a man's daily pay, wages were increased fifteen cents a day, and work happily resumed.

Grading on switchbacks from the spur to the bridge had to be done by blasting powder and hand shovels before the cumber-

some steam shovel could be used there. The same procedure followed on the Calaveras County side of the canyon except that
the steam shovel could not be used at all until hauled across the
bridge. All hands at this time were therefore concentrated on
these approaches to the now completed bridge. This single track
wood and steel-trussed bridge, with concrete abutments at each
end and eight approach bents, was a little over 300 feet in length,
and some fifty feet in height at mid-river. As soon as bridge and
roadbed to Melones Station, or Robinson's Ferry, were complete
with rails, a test locomotive crossing would be made prior to hauling the steam shovel and other equipment over it.

An unrecorded locomotive engineer on the Sierra's *No. 9*
complacently made this first run across the Stanislaus River
bridge, but when he looked from the river crossing up to the top
of the opposite cliff, which would be his next test run, he turned
to the fireman in his cab and shook his head dubiously, saying,
"Gee Whiz." Whereupon, that high crest on the Pendola Switch
became officially known as Gee Whiz Point.

The grading camp at last was moved to Calaveras County as
work continued on the muddy, rocky roadbed up Indian Gulch.
This much construction had been accomplished with remarkably
few casualties considering that many of the workers were un-
accustomed to rugged, mountainous country. One man had been
needlessly crushed to death under a falling boulder. One had his
leg amputated at the knee when some powder he was thawing
out exploded prematurely. Another was blown into the air by a
misfire hole in a cut. One young fellow, after lassoing a tree limb,
had climbed a tall pine to signal across the canyon but was so
furiously attacked by a squirrel that he let go and fell 150 feet,
breaking a leg. Encounters with rattlesnakes were common, but,
fortunately, the only two victims of bites were saved by quick
lancing of the wounds. Snakes, in fact, resulted in less loss of
work hours than the poison oak growing all along the line.

There were happier incidents. The nuggets found, especially
after rains along the right-of-way, caused flurries of hunting and
picking at rock with little bearing on the roadbed. The rule was
"finders keepers," but prospecting had to be curbed after work
stopped for a whole morning when a nugget the size of the finder's
thumb was uncovered. One morning a grader with a heavy

hammer had been finishing off a cut in quartz formation when the piece he struck off from the ledge revealed a streak of sparkling gold. Without comment, he hacked off as much ore as he could stagger away with and proceeded to leave the cut as well as the job. Seeing him go, and taking a close look at the ledge, each man in the work gang took a turn at the gold-bearing rock until it was demolished. Their combined recovery proved out at about three hundred dollars, or enough to keep every grader's hopes up in each cut along Jackass Hill. Though no more gold was recovered there, hopes remained high for the other side of the gold-strewn Stanislaus canyon.

Leaving Melones Station, tracks were to run almost all the way up Indian Gulch before switching back and climbing on a 3.68 grade up to Gee Whiz Point. Switches on both sides of the canyon were designed to take a three car and caboose freight train and were graded to that length, although it was expected that the average consist, with heavy loads such as ores and mine timbers, would be two cars and a caboose on these canyon cliffs. The *No. 9* Heisler locomotive performed well but needed help, so the Sierra bought its second geared engine *No. 10*, selected especially for this run. It was a Shay (Lima) which Newell preferred for use over those grades and curves. The intricate parts of this little two-truck engine with vertical pistons and cylinders were a challenge to mechanics in the Jamestown shops, but it performed so well there that two more Shays were ordered to complete the needed power units on the finished Angels Branch. Although the Sierra's *No. 4* Baldwin could and did make this branch run, the curves put rod engines at such an angle that sand could not flow to the rails for traction on wet or frosty tracks. Blasting and grading on the Pendola Switch was slowed by rains, and the added dangers involved in wet blasting and equipment on slippery rocks made it impossible to predict when Gee Whiz Point would be reached, let alone the long, twisting grade beyond it where the roadbed was to curve around the mountain as it climbed to the town of Carson Hill. *The Mountain Echo*, newspaper of Angels Camp, reported:

"The road will be zig-zag from the river to the top of the hill requiring four miles of grading at a certain point to gain one mile of distance on an air-line. It is given out that the road will be completed for train service by next June."

Mr. and Mrs. T. S. Bullock with son Jack on lap of Mrs. S. H. Smith, wife of Sierra's general passenger agent. Velocipede was made of bicycle tubing with wire spoke wheels and was very light. These vehicles were fairly common around the turn of the century.

Prince André Poniatowski was one of the co-promoters of the Sierra Railway as well as many lumbering and electric power interests. He was the first president of the railroad.

PACIFIC GAS & ELECTRIC CO.

W. H. Crocker of San Francisco provided the financial backing and served as vice president of the Sierra Railway.

CALIFORNIA HISTORICAL SOC.

Thomas S. Bullock conceived the idea of building the Sierra and served as its General Manager.

W. H. Newell, long-time Chief Engineer of the Sierra. At the time this picture was taken he was chief of location of the Mexican Central Railroad, a position he held just prior to coming to Tuolumne County.

SIERRA RAILROAD

Looking north from G Street onto West Railroad Avenue in Oakdale about 1920.

Cooperstown about 1900.

MRS. E. ZIMMERMAN

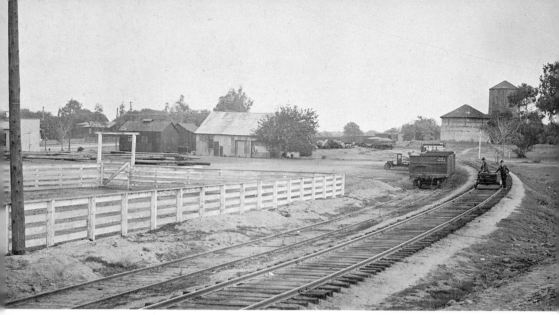

Entering Sierra yards at the outskirts of Oakdale. It is here that interchange is made with the Southern Pacific and Santa Fe.

Cooperstown in 1923. Station is hidden in the trees; the Wye is located at the right.

Paulsell. Warehouse at left, section gang house at right.

Cooperstown station in the early days.

SIERRA RAILROAD

Hetch Hetchy Junction. Sierra main line is at left, while the Hetch Hetchy turns off at right. New roadbed was used as far as Jacksonville, where the old grade of the Yosemite Short Line was used.

Chinese station.

MRS. E. ZIMMERMAN

Fashionable Winton No. 6.

Celebration of arrival of first train at Chinese. Track is not yet in shape for heavy use.

Sierra motorcar No. 7 being used as paymaster car for Standard Lumber Company Railroad.

Arrival of first train at Chinese. This engine bears No. 2 and is a Heisler. It is not on any list of known Sierra engines, but there were many strange engines on the line in early days and not all proved suitable for retention.

Excursion goes across Woods Creek trestle in celebration of the finishing of the Don Pedro cutoff realignment.

Portion of the old Don Pedro line.

SIERRA RAILROAD

Engine No. 3 split a switch, with this result. Engineer Newell stands on engine, while son Paul faces camera. Paul Newell is currently a director of the Sierra Railroad.

Early inspection party. Ball fringe curtain on window at left would indicate a private car. Man third from right is Prince Poniatowski.

West bound passenger at Lime Spur about 1910.

First passenger train arriving at Jamestown. Passenger station and general offices had not yet been built.

This motorcar with the fringe on top was one of several owned by the Sierra.

One of the several special cars built for the once-popular excursion business.

Inspection party at Jamestown. Man in center of observation platform is Prince Ponia-towski. The car is on the Sonora track and, judging by its condition, it did not extend very much further at the time this picture was taken.

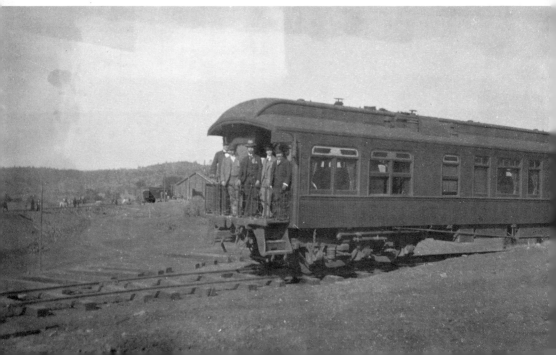

Interior of general offices at Jamestown about 1905. Man by stovepipe in rear is General Manager C. W. Hamblin. The paymaster, Harry Guild, sports an elegant moustache.

View of Sierra Railway shops and yards. Roundhouse at extreme left, car shops center, yards right. Steam shovel used in building Angels Branch in front of roundhouse.

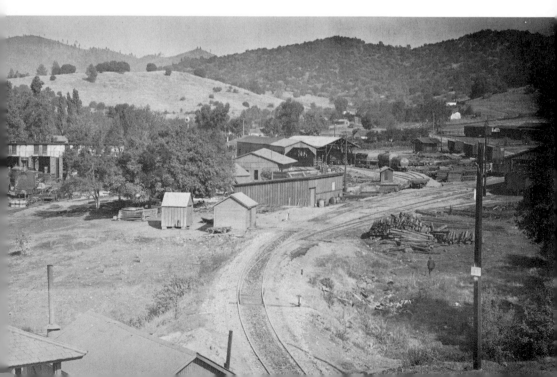

Jamestown, California about 1902. Nevills Hotel and Sierra yards in right background.

Eastbound train from Oakdale stands in front of Nevills Hotel while passengers, mail and baggage are exchanged with Angels passenger train.

Nevills Hotel. Annex at right was mostly used by Sierra Railway employees.

Nevills Bar was known far and wide for its ability to take care of weary travelers.

Menu

SUNDAY, JANUARY 1, 1899.

✶

SOUP

Chicken a la Rein   Cousomme Clear

———

Steamed Little Neck Clams a la Bordelais   Celery
Ripe California Olives   Shrimp Salad en Mayonaise

FISH

Fillet of Halibut Beurrenoir   Pomes de Terre a la Duchess

———

ENTREES

Ox Tongue aux Champigons
Val au Vent of Oysters   Baked Apple Dumpling. Rum Sauce

ROAST

Prime Rib of Beef au Jus
Young Turkey. Oyster Dressing. Cranberry Sauce

VEGETABLES

Steamed Potatoes   Mashed Potatoes
Sugar Corn   Stewed Tomatoes   French Peas

PASTRY

White Mountain Cake   Lady Fingers   Jelly Cake
New England Plum Pudding. Brandy Sauce
Lemon Cream Pie   Roman Punch   Pumpkin Pie
Swiss Cheese   American Cheese   Nuts and Raisins   Assorted Fruit
Tea   Coffee

⋅⋅─⋗◄▮►◄⋅⋅

MEAL HOURS.

BREAKFAST	LUNCHEON	DINNER
6.30 to 9.30 A. M.	11.00 A. M. to 1.30 P. M.	5.00 to 7.30 P. M

Menu of the Nevills Dining Room was the best on the Mother Lode and quite acceptable anywhere.

Wine List

CLARETS.

	P:s.	Q:s.
Hotel Nevills...	$ .15	$ .25
Inglenook, B. I...	.25	.50
Cresta Blanca Souvenir	.50	1.00
St. Julien (DE LUZE & FILS)..	.75	1.50

CHAMPAGNES.

Cresta Blanca.........	1.00	
Paul Masson.........	1.00	
G. H. Mumm & Co	2 50	4.50
Pommery Greno	2.50	4.50

MALT LIQUORS.

Guinness' Stout (Stone)	.30	
Tennant's Ale (Stone)...	.30	
Wieland's Beer,		
(Patent Stoppers, ...	.15	.25
Schlitz Beer (Export) ...	.25	.50
A. B. C. Bohemian Beer		
(Export)................	.25	.50

RIESLINGS.

	P:s.	Q:s.
Hotel Nevills......... ...	$ .15	$ .25
Mont Rouge	.25	.50
Gutedel (I. de Turk).....		.75

SAUTERNES.

Cresta Blanca Souvenir	.50	1.00
Haut Sauterne (Berts) ..	1.00	2.00

MINERAL WATERS, ETC.

Bartlett Springs Water..		.25
Apollinaris	.25	.50
Veronica Water		.75
Belfast Ginger Ale.......	.25	
Sonora " "	.15	
Macomber Cider...........	.25	.50

WHISKIES, BRANDIES, ETC.

	Qts.			Qts.
Jesse Moore's "C "........	$1.50		Burke's Garnkirk (Scotch) ...$2.00	
Jesse Moore's A. A.	2.00		Dewars Extra Special	
Taylor's O. F. C.	2.00		Scotch Liqueur.......	3.00
Keystone Monogram	2.50		Sazarac Brandy	2.50
R. G. & Co., Special Reserve	3.50		J. F. Martel.	2.50
G. & W., Canadian Rye	2.00		Boord & Son, Old Tom Gin...	1.50
			A. V. H. Gin	2.50

FRENCH CORDIALS AND LIQUORS, per glass, 25 cts.

CORKAGE.

Still Wines 25   **Champagnes** 50

The wine list was probably used more than the menu, and the prices shown are quite a factor.

CALIFORNIA HISTORICAL SOCIETY

Nevills Hotel in its heyday. Sierra general offices and passenger station are at extreme right.

This is all that was left of the Nevills Hotel the morning after the fire. It was never rebuilt. The foundations may still be seen a few feet east of the general offices.

The first general offices of the Sierra did not last as long as the Nevills Hotel. This picture, taken at 7:35 a.m. on May 1, 1913 shows what happened. All the important records of the company were destroyed in this fire.

SIERRA
RAILWAY COMPANY

OF CALIFORNIA

———●———

PCE. A. PONIATOWSKI, PRES.   H. J. CROCKER, VICE-PRES.
SAN FRANCISCO, CAL.   SAN FRANCISCO, CAL.

T. S. BULLOCK, GEN. MGR.   W. C. POTTS, SUPT.
JAMESTOWN, CAL.   JAMESTOWN, CAL.

S. D. FRESHMAN, TREAS. JAMESTOWN, CAL.

B. T. BOOZE, GEN. PASS. AND FRT. AGT., JAMESTOWN, CAL.

R. M. PECK, AUDITOR, JAMESTOWN, CAL.

General Offices, Jamestown, Cal.   Pacific Standard Time

No. 3 Daily	No. 1 Daily ex. Sunday	Mls.	MAY 1, 1898	Mls.	No. 2 Daily ex. Sunday	No. 4 Daily
4:30 PM	8:30 AM		Lv..San Franc'o..Ar		7:15 PM	12:15 PM
10:30 PM	2:35 PM	0	....Oakdale (1)....	41	1:30 PM	10·20 PM
10:44 PM	2:49 PM	6	Occidental	35	1:18 PM	10:08 PM
10:58 PM	3:03 PM	11	......Paulsell......	30	1:05 PM	9:55 PM
11:16 PM	3:21 PM	18	..Warnerville....	23	12:47 PM	9:37 PM
11;25 PM	3:30 PM	20	..Cooperstown (2)..	21	12:40 PM	9:30 PM
12:19 AM	4:24 PM	29	.....Don Pedro	12	11:55 AM	8:45 PM
12:40 AM	4:45 PM	35	... Chinese (3)....	6	11:30 AM	8:20 PM
1:00 AM	5:10 PM	41	Ar.James'own (4).Lv		11:10 AM	8:00 PM

Nos. 1 and 2 regular Mail and Express Trains.
Nos. 3 and 4 have Pullman Sleepers attached.

Connections.—(1) With Southern Pacific Company. (2) Stages for La Grange, Haywards and Sellecks. (3) Stages for Chinese Camp, Montezuma, Jacksonville, Big Oak Flat, Groveland, Coulterville and famous Yosemite Valley. (4) Stages for Quartz Mountain, Stent. Rawhide, Sonora, Tuttletown, Springfield, Columbia, Jeffersonville, Soulsbyville, Cherokee, Summerville, Carters, Arastraville, Sugar Pine, Confidence, Angels Camp, Altaville, Murphys and Calaveras Big Trees.

Freight wagons being loaded at Jamestown depot for re-shipment to the mines and to Sonora and points beyond not yet reached by the railroad.

Willow Bar in Jamestown, a frequent watering place for Sierra travelers.

One of the Sierra's immaculately kept little motor cars.

Picture of Engine No. 20 taken at Baldwin Locomotive Works on its completion.

Freight wagons hauling goods from Sierra depot through main street of Jamestown.

Loading supplies at Sierra's Jamestown depot. This was the end-of-rail for a time and interchange with wagons was an important business.

SIERRA RAILWAY CO.

First Popular Excursion of the Season

MAY 15, 1904

—FROM—

OAKDALE

—TO—

SONORA

Account of Baseball Game

Sonora vs. Oakdale.

Special train leaves Oakdale at 8 a. m.
Returning leaves Sonora at 8 p. m.

Fare for Round Trip, : : : $1.00

Music going and coming by the Oakdale Band.
Take your best girl and come along.

S. H. SMITH, Gen. Pass. Agent.

Passenger train loading at Sonora depot.

Railroad is on other side of fence. Automobile stands on one of the better roads in the Mother Lode region.

EUGENE M. PRINCE

20

Sonora in 1900. Tower of Victoria Hotel may be seen down the street.

Tuolumne County reunion reception in Sonora June 16, 1899. County hospital stands in back of train.

TWO PICTURES: DONALD SEGERSTROM

Victoria Hotel. This building has been rebuilt and is currently the well known Sonora Inn.

View of main street, Sonora. Offices of the *Banner* are next to the theatre at left.

Columbia's finest turn out for Sonora's railroad celebration.

Sonora station upon completion. Wainscoting on first floor is marble from Columbia's quarries.

Sonora. Standard Lumber Company's planing mill and door factory at left. Roof of Sierra freight station can be seen in front of passenger depot. County hospital at extreme right.

An active day at train time.

Standard Lumber Company at Standard City. Picture taken from Sierra station.

Sierra Railway station at Standard City.

Standard Lumber Company's mill and plant, 1923.

Ralph Station showing fruit packing plant. Track in foreground was Sierra's. That in front of building is Standard Lumber Company's line into timber country.

SIERRA RAILROAD

Sierra passenger and freight station at Tuolumne.

Turn Back Inn, Tuolumne's finest hotel, stood where the Veterans' Memorial now stands. The hotel was destroyed by fire.

DONALD SEGERSTROM

Page from the Oakdale Graphic.

Sierra Railway Company

OF CALIFORNIA.

❧ ❧ ❧

TRAINS LEAVE AND ARE DUE TO ARRIVE AT

OAKDALE.

LEAVE	From Feb. 18, 1906.	ARRIVE
2:40 p m	Angels, Tuolumne Sonora, Jamestown Chinese & Cooperstown	10:18 a m

For Freight and Ticket Rates, or other information, apply to Station Agent, or address

S. H. SMITH,
Gen. Pass. & Freight Agt.
Jamestown, Cal.

SANTA FE

New Time Card.

NORTH BOUND.

Leave	........Oakdale.........	10:35 a. m.
"	.... Riverbank	10:50 "
Arrive	.... Stockton	11:20 "
"	.......Richmond.....	1:35 p. m.
"	.... Berkeley	2:05 "
"	.... Oakland	2:20 "
"	.....San Francisco.	2:30 "

SOUTH BOUND.

Leave	.....San Francisco.....	10:55 a. m.
"	.... Oakland	11:00 "
"	.... Berkeley	11:15 "
"	.......Richmond.......	11:40 "
"	........Stockton	1:50 p. m.
"	.... Riverbank	2:27 "
Arrive	........Oakdale.........	2:40 "

NORTH BOUND.

Leave	.........Oakdale.........	3:10 p. m.
Arrive	.... Stockton	4:30 "
"	... ..San Francisco.....	10:55 "

SOUTH BOUND.

Leave	.....San Francisco.....	7:30 a. m.
"	.... Oakland	7:30 "
"	.... Berkeley	7:35 "
"	.......Richmond....	8:18 "
"	.... Stockton	10:55 "
Arrive	...... Riverbank	11:34 "
"	.......Oakdale........	12:00 m

Close connections with Sierra Railway trains without change of cars between Tuolumne and San Francisco. Also close connections at Riverbank for Merced, Fresno, Visalia, Tulare, Bakersfield and all points East and South.

Paints. See F. A. Sawyer.

Southern Pacific Time Table.

Changes in Time Card, commencing Wednesday, May 3d.

PASSENGER TRAINS.

No. 151.

Leaves Merced................	...8:10 A. M.
Arrives at Oakdale..............	10:20 A. M.
Leaves Oakdale.................	10:30 A. M.
Arrive at Stockton......	11:40 A. M

No. 152.

Leaves Stockton	1:10 P. M.
Arrives at Oakdale................	2:30 P. M.
Leaves Oakdale...	2:35 P. M.
Arrives at Merced................	4:10 P. M.

FREIGHT TRAINS.

Southern Pacific mixed train, freight and passenger, No. 306, leaves Stockton at 7:45 a. m., leaves Oakdale about 10:20 a. m., arrives Montpelier 11:15 p. m. Leaves Montpellier 11:55 a. m.; leaves Oakdale 1:30 p. m.; arrives in Stockton at 4:00 p. m.

5000 Telegraphers NEEDED

Annually to fill the new positions created by Railroad and Telegraph Companies. We want YOUNG MEN and LADIES of good habits to

Learn Telegraphy

AND R. R. ACCOUNTING

We furnish 75 per cent of the Operators and Station Agents in America. Our six schools are the largest exclusive Telegraph Schools in the world. Established 20 years and endorsed by all leading Railway Officials.

We execute a $250 Bond to every student to furnish him or her a position paying from $40 to $60 a month in States east of the Rocky Mountains, or from $75 to $100 a month in States west of the Rockies, immediately upon graduation.

Students can enter at any time. No vacations. For full particulars regarding any of our Schools write direct to our executive office at Cincinnati, O. Catalogue free.

The Morse School of Telegraphy

Cincinnati, O.	Buffalo, N. Y.
Atlanta, Ga.	LaCrosse, Wis.
Texarkana, Tex.	San Francisco, Ca

Job work...*Neatly done* *at the* Graphic

Sierra shop crew about 1904. Man at top left is Gus Swanson.

This ungainly vehicle was acquired from the Hetch Hetchy to try out as a possible way of handling LCL freight. It did not prove successful and was later changed back into a truck with rubber tires.

The Sierra's Shay No. 12.

Engine No. 7 was bought from the Northern Pacific and was later resold.

Construction engine used on Relief Dam. This engine was brought part way by rail and then had to be hauled by wagons as far as roads would permit. It was then dragged by mule team to the location of the construction project.

Building Relief Dam. Picture shows the great difficulty of getting the materials to the job.

Heisler No. 9 with Combine No. 5 attached. This was probably the Angels passenger train.

The No. 36 was the last and largest new steam locomotive to be made for the Sierra. It is currently kept for possible standby use at the Jamestown roundhouse.

DONALD DUKE

West of Chinese. This grade almost always required two engines or doubling the hill with one.

Nine-car passenger train headed by two locomotives.

SIERRA RAILROAD

February 1949 saw an exceptionally heavy snowfall for the Sierra. With its greatest elevation being a little less than 3000 ft., one or two light falls of a few inches annually are about par.

Sonora-bound train works hard up the grade by Lime Spur in a light snowstorm.

Same train as above, crossing trestle east of Sonora.

SIERRA RAILROAD

Don Pedro dam under construction. A branch was built from the Sierra especially for this project.

Model of No. 38 as furnished by Pacific Fast Mail of Edmonds, Washington.

JOHN ALLEN

The Sierra is known for its steam, but like other railroads it had to exist, and in 1955 these two Diesels were purchased from Baldwin. They are now the line's principal source of motive power.

The Sierra bought No. 38 from the Weyerhauser Timber Company in 1952 in an effort to stay with steam. The engine proved very effective, but its availability and cost of operation could not compare with a Diesel.

STANLEY A. SNOOK

1951 excursion train blasting up one of the steep grades in the line, near Ralph.

Two engines with the daily freight head up the steep westbound grade out of Chinese.

JIM BAKER

The Sierra had her share of wrecks, but this is not one of them. Here is a paper dummy being blown up for the movie Duel in the Sun.

Semi-rotary snow plow on Hetch-Hetchy railroad being operated by Sierra. Elevations of over 5000 ft. were found on the Hetch Hetchy line and called for much more complicated treatment.

Hetch Hetchy railcar No. 19 crossing Jacksonville bridge a few years before abandonment.

But two months later, the *Mother Lode Magnet* of Jamestown printed:

"About thirty-five laborers employed on the Angels extension were let out last week with two miles of grade complete on the Calaveras side and Contractor Moreing expecting to spend the next four to five weeks on one and one half miles of heavy rock work, if weather permits."

Weather did not permit and not even Carson Hill was reached by June, 1902, or the date when the whole branch road was supposed to have been open for service. But there were more complications than grades and granite in the Stanislaus canyon that winter. The Stanislaus Electric Power Company's water flume, sixteen miles long and six by ten feet in size was in the process of being strung along the precipitous walls of the Stanislaus canyon. The work gang on the flume project was about equal in numbers and weight to that of the railroad gangs, but their divergent loyalties resulted in vicious rivalry between the two. As the flume and ditch approached Melones, the two gangs were working almost side by side. The whole canyon then resounded to catcalls, practical jokes, fist fights and knifings. A climax was reached the evening the flume workers, en masse, invaded the "Jerries" camp and the resulting free-for-all, helped along with weapons like railroad ties and flume boards, caused such wreckage and broken bones that work on both projects was suspended for two days.

The hard winter dragged on without other work cessation, and one day in April the *No. 9* and *No. 10* engines together backed two flat cars, carrying the steam shovel, up Indian Gulch and then switched to head steeply up to Gee Whiz Point. After the shovel was unloaded, the train reversed its first procedure as it backed down the steep descent. This trip spelled victory for Newell, the location engineer whose doubted ability to cross the Stanislaus canyon at this point by rail was now an accomplished fact. And for the locomotive engineers also, who had easily controlled the sturdy gears and compact mechanism of their power units on the grades of the crossing. With only those winding miles to the top of Carson Hill left to build, the railroad estimated that freight would be picked up and delivered at that point by July.

The town of Carson Hill (then called Irvine) was far from bustling. Its rich and raucous heyday had lasted for thirty years but in the last ten years it had dwindled to a routine little settlement of ranchers and miners working in unpredictable quartz mines. However, each foot of ground and each building was reminiscent of some gold-inspired history. One such building, reeking of golden romance, was the old Rooney House where magnate James G. Fair met and courted his bride of a pioneer Carson Hill family. The old Irvine home had been built by pioneer William Irvine who had once owned most of the town.

The story of Carson Hill gold claims in the '50's is one of the most exciting and confusing in all of California's intricate stories of early mining. This conical hill, fabulously laced with gold veins that crossed and crisscrossed each other was a jungle of mining claims. Surface gold there had made millionaires overnight, after which many claims were abandoned, only to be reopened to make new fortunes, or new paupers. Nowhere were claims more disputed and contested with more complicated "on-the-spot" sales and "sheriff's" sales of mining properties than at gold-laden Carson Hill.

This confusion persisted through the 1880's when deep quartz mining prevailed. The largest and richest mines then working were the Morgan Mine, the Reserve Mine and the Carson Hill Mine. In those flush early days, the Morgan had produced the famous "Calaveras Nugget," weighing 195 pounds, worth $43,500. This mine's surface gold had been reaped by Mr. William Irvine, who, with his son, Louis, had closed it down too soon. The mine was later bought and reworked for a two million dollar profit by Mr. James G. Fair and now twenty years later, again lay idle with Mr. Fair's daughter in legal custody. The exchange of title to this mine was described as a "deal" in which Irvine double-crossed Fair and was, himself, recrossed by that financier.

The Reserve Mine was on the property of pioneer Emile K. Stevenot, early-day mining engineer, who through the years had worked, sold and regained possession of his mine. The Reserve Mine close to the Morgan Mine started the huge glory hole which dominated the southern view from the townsite in 1902. It had been enlarged to its present enormous size by subterranean workings from the Morgan Mine.

After giving up its golden surface wealth, the Carson Hill Mine had been closed, sold, resold, reacquired and manipulated in ways disputed to this day by factions of divergent loyalties. Its ore vein went so deep that it also was worked later some 700 feet below the surface at the level of the Melones Mine tunnel. In fact, as the railroad drew near, a plan was afoot to reopen all the Carson Hill mines in a big way: a plan that was to lead to still another legal entanglement between Melones and Carson Hill mines.

The few remaining stores, saloons, homes and barns of Carson Hill's fifty residents in 1902 were scattered along the old stage road which circled the whole mountain on its way up past the mine to the town before continuing on to Angels Camp. Old mine dumps were everywhere — in back yards, beside the little school house, near the church and even on Boot Hill. Most of the population were miners surreptitiously high-grading closed mines on the hill and working at the enlarged Melones operation four miles down in the canyon. The Carson Hill saloon was doing a flourishing business as its patronage was augmented by miners living in the bunk houses at Robinson's Ferry where saloons were denied. Prospectors lodged at the Rooney House still scoured the hills in search of new surface gold. Speculators drifted in and out of town gathering specimens of gold quartz and information on properties with lapsed taxes, hazy titles or forgotten liens. All of these people, as well as the few who chose to live there with or without the mines, welcomed the railroad as a useful asset and one likely to put their dwindled community back on the map. Perhaps even to bring new life to abandoned mines, which, of course, was the hope of the railroad itself.

The senior Mr. Stevenot of Carson Hill offered the railroad a considerable right-of-way through his property in return for a lifetime pass and a private flag stop. His elder son, Fred Stevenot, was destined, some fifty years later, to become the owner of all these mines, including the Melones group.

The first train into Carson Hill must have been a relief, if not an impressive event, for everyone. After long association with construction problems and men, the whole town came to doors or windows when they heard it pound up the canyon and rumble across the trestle before it steamed into sight. By then, each miner and resident felt that he, or she, had had a personal hand in the arrival of this train. The most lasting impression of Carson Hill at this time for at least one person there, however, was not of a train. Ten-year-old Paul Newell with his father in Carson Hill remembers the awesome glory hole, out of bounds for young fry, and of hurrying, not only to be on time when Schoolmaster March called his fourteen pupils to order, but also to get past one house in town where an austere old man was always sitting in a rocker on the front porch with a shotgun across his knees. Perhaps this long-remembered old man, reported to be a descendant of the Irvine family was guarding against crooks who had threatened to take over his family's early-day claims. It was conceivable that he might even come to grips with the ghost of some claim-jumping contemporary, for Carson Hill was a ghost town and a place where claims had been, and still were, taken over in the name of the dead, as well as the living.

CHAPTER SIX

In the 1850's Angels Camp had grown fast in a small draw where the Mother Lode had been exposed by Angels Creek and its tributaries. Fortunes in loose gold and nuggets picked and panned and sluiced from crevices and creeks in this area helped finance some of the earliest established quartz mines in California. The trail that connected their shafts, all within a mile of each other in this draw, later became the Main Street of Angels Camp, solidly flanked on both sides by saloons, livery stables, hotels, assay offices and all the other activities that made this the "Roaring Camp" of Mark Twain's day. In the next twenty-five years first one side of town would burn down and then the other, but overnight they were rebuilt around the life of these mines.

Throughout these years Angels Camp was the largest town in Calaveras County. Its population, once over 5,000, dropped to 500 and climbed to over 2,500 during the quartz mining era, but was again dropping with the use of more modern mining methods at the turn of the century. Poor, hazardous roads from the San Joaquin Valley into this gold-famous county were still the life lines of supplies and communications, as they were into all Sierra Nevada foothill counties not contacted by rails.

Mark Twain and Bret Harte tales of Angels Camp in its boom years are a cherished part of its past glory which, in fact, led someone to describe Angels Camp seventy-five years later as "the town where Mark discovered a jumping frog." The gambling spirit that pervaded such tales was a common trait among these people. It was the spirit which had brought them West, the spirit by which they lived and the spirit which still prevailed in Angels Camp in 1902. Wells Fargo shipments of gold bullion out and coin of the realm into the county might be less since the busy days of Black Bart and Joaquin Murietta, and the odds on spectacular new gold "strikes" reduced, but the right to stake money, courage and even lives on any gamble was still each man's prized prerogative. Quartz miners were "risk" miners working long hours underground without safety insurance or security of any kind, let alone that as yet unheard-of "Social Security." Mine owners and business men were equally gamblers since gains or losses in the mines spelled success or failure for all. And so, though law and order prevailed in Angels Camp in 1902, so did gambling — at work and at play. Faro and red dog dealers did a good business. Poker games were always in session in a dozen saloons. Angels Camp, like Sonora, had its race track where folks gathered after church on Sunday afternoons, taking children who might have worked hard through the week so they could bet their pennies on a nag. Behind the swinging doors of any saloon someone was always holding the stakes on who would be wearing Gertie's garter for a sleeve band next week or whether Joe Dokes' mule would climb Hard Scrabble Street. The local press complained of no newsworthy events in those days before the railroad came to Angels.

In 1902, travelers coming from Tuolumne County to Angels Camp crossed the Stanislaus River by Wood's Ferry, and drove in sight of the new railroad tracks through Carson Hill to a junction with the Murphys road just above the railroad's Angels Camp depot site about a mile out of town. The road from there to Main Street was lined with lumber and feed yards, livery stables and mine dumps, while Main itself was solidly flanked by business houses and mine offices crowded between operating mines. At the southern end of town were the Angels and Commercial hotels where miners and drummers waited for stages that wheeled up on regular schedules uninterrupted any longer by highway men. On a level area eastward of Main, along wooded Angels Creek, were the congested red light district and Chinatown.

The Angelus Mine shaft and mill property stood prominently to the west, and a few yards east of mid-Main Street was the famous Utica Mine which had been operated by Loring before he took over the Melones Mining Company. At one time Utica gold was often so pure it was not even put through the mill. The fabulous mine was still operating in 1902, using power from the Murphys area, which had been generated in town since 1899 and which also supplied some businesses with electric lights.

Behind the Calaveras Hotel on one of the short streets between Main and Bush was Dollings Hall, popular setting for dances and theaters in Angels Camp. The residential areas of town rose steeply behind it on the upper side of Bush Street and Democrat Hill, even though a pipe three feet in diameter, like a huge snake, was being laid along Bush preparatory to reworking the dumps and tailings of mines above it. Cottages and gardens sat primly in a high row along the sidewalk four and five feet above the seasonally dusty and muddy traffic on Bush. Other homes clinging further up the slopes of Democrat Hill were accessible by trails and steep roads such as Hard Scrabble Street, which was log and stone cleated all the way up to ease the climb for horses. For forty years milk wagons and water carts scrabbled up this street to reach families who, lacking plumbing in the modern sense, trod perilous paths to back-houses perched behind bushes and trellises. At the foot of this hill, washrooms and privies emptied into a gully between Main and Bush which was purged each winter by water gushing down the gully to Angels Creek.

There was no high school in town or county in 1902, but many young folks were emerging as doctors, lawyers and merchant chiefs through higher education obtained elsewhere. Three weekly newspapers — the *Angels Record, Calaveras Prospect,* and the *Mountain Echo* — were then printed in Angels Camp.

At the north end of Main Street where the road from San Andreas, the county seat, dipped into town, were the grammar school, the Catholic church and graveyard, besides the thumping Stickle Mine and Mill. This big mine had recently been sold by Captain Nevills of Rawhide to the Utica Mining Company, which had also bought the nearby Lightner Mine. The twenty-stamp mill and hoisting machinery of the latter were run by electricity brought from Poniatowski's Blue Lakes power plant. Among other mines then operating in the vicinity of Angels Camp were the Zeiley, Angelus, Coleman, Gold Cliff and Thorpe, the latter then under option to Prince Poniatowski. It was largely to reach these mines and their freight potential that the Sierra Railway Company had gone to the enormous expense of building its Angels Branch.

The eight miles of road between Angels Camp and San Andreas was then a busy thoroughfare traveled by wagons, stages, private conveyances and horseback riders on the way to other central Mother Lode mines, if not heading all the way down to the San Joaquin Valley.

Between these towns but closer to Angels Camp, was Altaville, the site of a few new houses, a blacksmith shop and the Demarest and Fullen Foundry. This iron works was now operated by young D. C. Demarest whose knowledge of metals led him to become a Federal authority on the metallurgy of ores some sixty years later. As a young man in 1898 he installed the first Pelton wheel to operate in Angels Camp. It was small, but effectively ran the press of the *Mountain Echo* newspaper. This was the forerunner of the Peltons that within a few months powered the hoists and mills of many mines. Now, in 1902, besides making and repairing mining machinery, Demarest had made the moving parts for a turntable designed by Newell for use at the Sierra's Angels Camp depot. The finished parts, wagon freighted through Angels Camp to the depot at the far end of town, would soon be followed by other loads of machinery from Altaville for shipment to mines along the Sierra.

Such traffic, besides stages and private vehicles from other Calaveras County towns, was, in fact, to cause a lively congestion of men and beasts on Angels Camp's Main Street when the trains began to run. Looking forward to that day, stores and saloons were stocking up, new businesses were opening and mining operations were reviving. There was talk of building a stone bridge across Angels Creek at the foot of Main Street, also of regrinding the tailings of all the mines and bringing electricity and telephones into every business in that new rail terminus.

The little Sierra depot and turntable were quite a ways from Main Street, but it was a conveniently level site from which to turn future tracks toward Murphys and then the Big Trees area where tremendous logging activity was going on. Logs and lumber were hauled to Angels and the sawmills in the vicinity of Murphys. Teamsters such as those working for T. J. Moran cracked whips over twelve and fourteen head of mules and horses pulling huge logs and mine timbers from above Murphys to Angels Camp over a toll road costing $1.30 per trip. Some of these logs and lumber was hauled on down to the San Joaquin Valley over those dangerously narrow roads. At this time the *Mountain Echo* said:

". . . millions upon millions of feet of the finest spruce, sugar pine and cedar timber in the Big Tree area are uncut because it cannot be brought to tidewater profitably without the aid of a railroad. Fortunately, this will soon change with the advent of the Sierra Railroad. Also, the valuable iron mine above Murphys, belonging to Mr. Jas. L. Sperry, formerly of the Big Trees, will be opening up."

Besides lumber and ores to haul from the Murphys area, 6,000 head of cattle were being driven out of these mountains to local slaughterhouses or down to winter feed on foothill ranches. All of these totaled a very large freight potential for a railroad, yet this extension by the Sierra Railway Company eastward towards Murphys was never built. Perhaps the mammoth logs from towering Sequoia and sugar pines were too long and heavy for the twisting Angels Branch. Local mills and teamsters evidently refused to cooperate with rails. Possibly the Sierra directors were relieved of their early promise to bring rails to the Sperry holdings because they knew the iron mine would not materialize and the glorious Big Trees soon would be sold to the state to be saved for posterity. For whatever unknown reason, Angels Camp remained the lifetime terminus of this branch line.

The Sierra's new *No. 10* Shay locomotive and the old *No. 9* Heisler were as yet the chief power units on the Angels Branch. A short little passenger coach and a combination passenger mail car specially designed to fit these curves had been built by Holman and Company of San Francisco, and were numbered 6 and 5, respectively, to make up the Angels Branch daily combination passenger train, which was to remain in service for over twenty years.

It was estimated that over three thousand people from San Andreas, Mokelumne Hill, Copperopolis, Murphys, Fourth Crossing, West Point and many other Calaveras County towns came to Angels Camp on September 10, 1902, to see the first scheduled railroad train in their county. Only five minutes late, the bunting-draped *No. 10* roared, smoking and whistling, into the depot ahead of the two short coaches loaded with railroad "brass" and special guests from as far west as San Francisco. After fireworks and speeches at the depot a reception was held at Dollings Hall, where Master of Ceremonies Lewis Tullock, elegantly dressed in a long Prince Albert coat, gave the principal speech. With dramatic eloquence, he alluded to the railroad contingent as "Empire Builders" and to locomotives as "the artillery of commerce."

This official train was fine, everyone said, but Angels Camp people and businesses asked the Sierra Railway Company to arrange a special excursion from Oakdale and way points into Angels Camp. An agreement was made and this excursion left Oakdale ten days later on Saturday, September 20th, scheduled to return Monday morning, September 22nd.

At the special rate of $2.00 per person for the round trip seats were so oversold that the problem of accommodating the excursionists was acute since the long, standard-sized coaches used on the main line could not negotiate the sharp curves of the Angels Branch. Flat cars were converted to open excursion cars at the Jamestown shops and the train made up there in two sections. Each consisted of three excursion cars and one small coach headed by a geared engine. Excitement and pandemonium prevailed, aided by liquor, basket lunches, ladies in leg o' mutton sleeves and ostrich plumed hats, men in frock coats and in Levis. The trains stopped frequently for mountain drinking water, which was not only therapeutic but an excuse for the boys "to help the girls" on and off those high-stepped flat cars.

At the awe-inspiring Stanislaus canyon, passengers craned their necks to see down the autumn-shaded slopes where poison oak was at its reddest and wild grape twined bright yellow and red leaves up the trunks of pine and oaks. Crossing the river, gay blades threw caps and lunch boxes overboard into the water, then whistled and sang, "Halleluiah, here we come," as the trains chugged up Pendola Switch.

The excursionists were met at the Angels depot by the Sixth Regiment Band of Stockton, and in town by the Utica Band of Angels. On the bunting and flag draped Main Street, carnival attractions were offered by the Chutes Company, imported for the occasion from the renowned "Chutes at the Beach" in San Francisco. That afternoon "Professor" Vosner made a balloon ascension, taking a parachute jump from a height of about 2,000 feet, and landing heroically near the Ghost Mine. Local stages drove guests out to see nearby mining operations. Dancing continued day and night at Dollings Hall until repeated steam whistles warned that the returning excursion trains were made up and ready to depart for Jamestown, Tuolumne, Oakdale and Stockton.

After the above celebration the Calaveras *Prospect* said:

"The railroad will bring new men and ideas into our midst, and arouse us to the fact that we have been asleep while the world has moved along and left us. We should start by becoming better acquainted with our neighbors who, though only across the canyon, have had the benefit of rails longer than we — but who shall not surpass us now."

With these words as their war cry, the local citizenry promptly arranged for a return excursion trip from Angels Camp to Tuolumne City. On Sunday, the 4th of October, at 7:00 a.m., two trains left Angels Station with 445 passengers on board accompanied by the Angels Brass Band, which played at every station until arrival at 10:30 a.m. at Tuolumne. Although such a crowd had not been anticipated, an inter-county drilling contest and baseball game between the Carters' and the Angels' teams were attended by some 600 people. Returning excursion cars carried hilarious victors of both big events safely back to Angels Camp over "the most popular road in the country!"

Daily passenger service on the Angels run had been inaugurated with a $1.50 fare for the hour and forty-five minute ride. Regular trains left Angels Camp every morning at 6:45, arriving at Jamestown at 8:30 a.m. Leaving Jamestown each afternoon at 4:40, the train returned to Angels Camp by 6:35. When this schedule was announced, a new timetable for the main line was also published showing the running time between mountain towns and Oakdale to have been shortened by nearly an hour. This was possible since trains now ran as straight passenger and express trains, instead of as mixed trains as previously, obviating freight stops. Freight trains making regular trips over the main line and Angels Branch were augmented by specials carrying emergency freight or perishables such as dairy products. Rates between Oakdale and Angels Station were $4.50 per ton for carload lots and $6.50 for less than carload lots. As soon as these rail rates were made public, the freight teamsters of Milton set wagon freight between that town and Angels Camp at $5.00 a ton. "It is generally conceded," said the Angels *Record*, "that freight cannot be handled by teamsters at a $5.00 rate, but as the offer was made, it looks as if the shippers have the best of it any way it goes." The *Record* was correct. Wagon freighting from Milton to Angels was discontinued two months later, as was the Southern Pacific branch line, Stockton to Milton, which had fed the freighters. This left Angels Camp almost entirely dependent on the Sierra line for transportation.

Although a rod engine could make the Angels run without taking on water, geared engines had to stop each trip at the water tank installed on the Melones side of the Stanislaus River bridge. But the little Shays pulled heavier loads of ores, mine timbers and oil cars, than the later used rod engines ever did. When the large new *No. 12* Shay chugged up the Pendola grade with a full consist, the whole town of Melones quivered and dust rattled through the timbers in the mine tunnels below.

The Angels Branch passenger stations located at Omega, Tuttletown, Melones, Carson Hill and Angels Camp, brought the Sierra's full line of stations to eighteen. Passengers over the Angels Branch in the summertime made the trip by daylight, and often leaned out open windows to look at scenery or wave to friends at farms, mines and road crossings, if they did not mind an occasional cinder in the eye. In the winter, however, the trip to Angels was made by dusk with windows closed and wood stacked beside the corner stove. Passengers assisted the conductor in keeping up the fire or adjusting the damper, and tried to read by the big swinging oil lamp glowing cozily overhead.

Although the Sierra's train crews understood that service over the Angels Branch had to be handled with more than ordinary caution, it was still the era of the "flying" switch. The brakeman, flapping his elbows as a signal to the engineer, would let a car go off, coasting, into a switch or sidetrack. Then racing afoot to catch up with the car, the brakeman would climb the ladder and again sprint along the top to grab and wind up the brake wheel. In those days before automatic brakes, brakemen and all the crew were "risk" operators living dangerously and liking it that way. The Sierra's spurs and sidings, too often on grades, were therefore a tempting testing ground for risky practices. Also, a thrilling sight for bystanders who never seemed to tire of watching the execution of a "flying" switch.

However, competent service over the Angels Branch became routine as mining activity was spurred on by rail transportation. Freights ran day and night passing the twinkling carbide lights of small mining operations and the strings of electric lights and flaring furnaces at big mines and mills. The Rawhide chlorination plant had been overhauled in 1902 to treat eight tons of concentrates daily. The Patterson Mine's mill, working twenty-four hours a day, was a beacon light at the Tuttletown trestle. The Bell Mine was shipping two or three carloads a day of sulphurets and the Atlas Mine, on Jackass Hill, had received many carloads of mine timbers and machinery to sink its main shaft from 120 to 600 feet. The Norwegian Mine was in its third cycle of peak production; below it was the tremendous activity at Melones. As the Melones Mining Company came into full operation treating the ores of six mines under one hundred and twenty stamps and a chlorination plant, with power provided by the completed flume, electrically run mine cars pulled a continuous stream of ore from the longest tunnel in the Mother Lode country. For fifteen years, to the tune of a twenty million dollar production, the Angels Branch was the life line of transportation, mail and supplies for this activity at the bottom of the Stanislaus canyon.

While the Angels Branch was being built and put into routine operation, things had been happening along the Sierra's main line. The four year old railroad had become a well-established transportation system between the valley and the mountains. Local newspapers printed at Oakdale, Jamestown, Sonora and Tuolumne, carried train schedules and daily items that opened with: "Among out-going passengers on today's train were..." People dressed up and went to depots to meet friends or just to watch other people and the panting engine with its shuttling rods and hissing steam. The trains were not only being used, but broke the monotony, in these comparatively unexciting times, for local descendants of Forty Niners!

In 1900, a short commotion had been caused by a last breath fight against the railroad by Hales and Symons, who wagon freighted merchandise to and from rail points all over Tuolumne County after most other big freighting outfits had bowed out of business. It seemed to have become customary for freighters to buy a piece of land, with its ranch house, barn, spring and fig tree, on which to settle down to cattle raising. But not W. J. Hales, or T. F. Symons. When Hales closed out his big freighting business in Oakdale in 1897, he had stated that his headquarters, henceforth, would be at the other end of the Sierra Railway, and that was where he intended to keep it. But when he insisted upon hauling hay and grain from Jamestown to Sonora, and on bringing loads of sulphurets from mines in the Tuolumne area down to Jamestown for further shipment to reduction works in the valley, the Sierra Railway Company objected to this parallel hauling. The quarrel culminated in the railroad giving Hales sixty days in which to remove his warehouse from railroad property in Jamestown. In return battle, Hales joined with Symons to get contracts from many Sonora merchants for hauling their freight to and from Oakdale at cheaper than railroad rates. Bullock then announced that he would "give these wagon freighters a run for their money." Expecting railroad rates to drop competitively after this threat, and since wagon freighting was slower in any case, most of the merchants canceled their teaming contracts. This dispute, "Horse vs. Steam," was finally settled amicably when Hales and Symons moved into larger quarters built beside the Sonora depot, and accepted exclusive contracts for all hauling to and from Sierra trains at that point.

Jamestown lost this freighting business in 1901, but W. C. Minaer continued to run his regular ad, "Call on me for a livery to the mines," for most of the quartz mines were still working profitably and, in some cases, spectacularly. The Jumper had yielded $417,300 in 1900 and doubled its output the next year. Among Wells Fargo reports of August 7, 1901, was the following:

"Half a ton of gold was stolen from the Selby Works by robbers who broke into a safe and stole 37 bars of gold valued at $280,-000, the largest theft of gold bullion known in this country. The Selby Smelting and Lead Company at Vallejo Junction on the Southern Pacific tracks is the largest on the Pacific coast and refines most of the gold produced in California. These bars of refined gold from ore from the Jumper Mine in Tuolumne County were brought to the smelter by Sierra and S.P. rails."

Free gold and gold-bearing quartz from the famous Jumper Mine continued to be shipped to this smelter, however, and Jumper Gold Syndicate stock was selling at eleven dollars a share on London and Glasgow stock boards. This mine's productivity plus the yield from hundreds of other mines stamping out gold in Tuolumne County was largely responsible for the San Francisco mint breaking the coinage record in 1901, converting eighty-one million dollars from bullion into coin, making double eagles, eagles, half eagles and standard dollars. New and rich finds had been made in the old Confidence, Draper and Isabel mines, and six new stamp mills were erected in the county. These included a twenty-stamp unit to be added at the Mazeppa Mine as soon as an eighty horsepower boiler, which came by rail to Jamestown, was installed. An eight and a half pound nugget, containing $2,400 worth of gold found on an old gravel claim at Yankee Hill near Sonora, spurred mining operations in several local river beds such as the lower Stanislaus River where an earthen dam was built to hold back water while dredges worked.

While the Angels Branch was being built, the Sierra Railway Company and the West Side Flume and Lumber Company had made a huge combined play for outside capital to invest in Tuolumne County. Both companies backed by Crocker interests were then planning to open their Hetch Hetchy logging road to passenger service by running excursion cars over it in the summer season. Henry Crocker, William Crocker, Prince Poniatowski and T. S. Bullock intended to extend their logging road through to the Hetch Hetchy Valley, which was considered comparable in beauty to Yosemite Valley and close enough to it, they said, for the two to be connected by stage coach service. It was anticipated that such a move would attract a large tourist trade via Tuolumne City and incidentally bring the West Side Flume and Lumber Company's timberland to the attention of financial investors. To promote this plan, two hundred influential guests from San Francisco and other cities were invited to a weekend party on May 25, 1900, with a trip over the completed part of the logging road as the highlight of the occasion. Special Pullman trains brought these guests to the Nevills Hotel at Jamestown where all expenses were paid by the railroad. The next day the Sierra's *No. 3* Rogers pulled eleven open excursion cars to Sonora, and the *No. 7* followed with one car to which seven more filled with local guests were added at Sonora. As these two units were taken to Tuolumne City, Bullock pointed out progressive opportunities and sights of scenic interest to one group while Newell did the same for the other. At Tuolumne, the West Side Flume and Lumber Company's sawmill blasted greetings to the visitors who saw logs being chuted into the pond, put through the sawmill and stacked in drying piles. In the center of town building lots had been surveyed around a plaza and foundations laid for the spacious Turn Back Inn, the second largest hotel in Tuolumne County. There the special guests boarded two trains of open excursion cars backed, instead of headed, by the lumber company's *No. 1* and *No. 2* Heislers, which proceeded to push them on grades and curves into the forests. In this way the excursionists had an uninterrupted view and minimum risk of smoke and cinders from wood burning engines while being shown some of the most spectacular scenery in the West. Leaving Tuolumne, with Duckwall Mountain silhouetted straight ahead, the trains twisted around the intervening pine-forested canyons catching breath-taking vistas of snow peaks towering distantly above and the North Fork of the Tuolumne River winding far below like a shining silver thread.

On arrival at a logging camp situated in deep forests twelve miles out of Tuolumne City, guests were met by Henry J. Crocker dressed in corduroy outing clothes and mounted on a large black mule. He and Bullock, on crutches due to a sprained ankle, were hosts there during a sumptuous lunch spread on long tables under giant trees while Cruse's Orchestra from Stockton played soft music. After lunch, guests watched woodsmen felling, barking and limbing logs which were then snaked to landings by horses and donkey engines. A relief map of the Clavey and Cherry River canyons, Lake Eleanor and the Hetch Hetchy Valley was displayed showing the proposed route by which the Crocker interests intended to reach those wonders of nature. And with the odor of pines on a cool late afternoon breeze, guests were returned to Tuolumne. There arrangements had been made for dinner and dancing in a decorated hall over the lumber company's store and warehouse. Guests who so chose returned for the night to the Nevills Hotel where another dance was beginning.

During these festivities, local and city reporters had busily gathered names and figures for their next day's papers, which gave a great deal of space to this lavish fiesta. Writers waxed poetic over scenery and food besides quoting large figures of lumber productivity in that area. Articles concluded with the following resolution, drawn up by guests on the special train returning to Stockton and San Francisco, which was signed by all, including some of the most prominent names in California's financial world:

"We, the undersigned guests of the Sierra Railway Company and the West Side Flume and Lumber Company on the grand excursion given on their respective roads on May 25 and 26, 1900, desire to express our pleasure for the entertainment and hospitality of our generous hosts. As a token of the esteem in which we hold the officials of said companies we hereby tender the following resolutions:

Resolved, the exact information conveyed to us by this object lesson, the magnitude of the enterprise, the hospitality extended to us, renews our faith in the undeveloped riches of our mountain districts as one of the many opportunities of employing local capital.

Second,— The courage and enterprise of our hosts in pushing to a successful completion the Sierra Railway and the West Side Flume and Lumber Railroad justified the confidence and hearty support of the citizens of our state.

Third,— We desire to commend the skill, care and success of the engineers in safely handling the entire trains under extremely difficult circumstances.

Fourth,— Success to officers of the Sierra Railway Company: Prince Andre Poniatowski, Pres.; Henry J. Crocker, Vice-Pres.; T. S. Bullock, General Manager; S. D. Freshman, Chief Engineer; W. H. Newell, Maurice Casey, Hall McAllister, W. F. Pierce, Samuel Sussman,— and to officers of the West Side Flume and Lumber Company: Henry Crocker, Pres.; Wellington Gregg, Vice-Pres.; Charles F. Gardner, Secty. and Treas.; W. H. Crocker, T. S. Bullock."

The indomitable Mr. Bullock no doubt had planned to combine passenger service with logging over these narrow gauge rails that twisted and squirmed into such spectacular country approaching Yosemite National Park. To this end he completed his large two story hotel at Tuolumne, which he named the Turn Back Inn.

Lacking the pompous splendor of the Nevills Hotel in Jamestown, this long two story structure in shingled California style was gracious, comfortable and modernly plumbed. A fifteen-foot wide veranda overlooking spacious lawns was cool in summer while a huge log-burning fireplace and leather furniture made an inviting lobby when snow came to Tuolumne in winter. This hotel was opened in January, 1902, at which time Bullock said,

> "Eventually Yosemite travel will all come up through Tuolumne. Frankly, that is why I built this hotel. It would not now pay on the present transient travel to this town but when this narrow gauge is built to Hetch Hetchy, this will be a night and day stopping-off place coming in and out."

The ultimate goal, however, shared by his associates in this venture, H. J. and William Crocker, was to exploit their timberlands. And this end was achieved in January, 1902. At that time, a reporter asked Bullock about the reported sale of the Sierra railroad to the Santa Fe Company.

"You may say," replied Bullock, "that the Sierra is not for sale. I never heard of the report, but it must have originated from the sale of my lumbering interests in the West Side Company to Mr. J. T. Adams."

In 1903, the whole 60,000 acres of West Side timberland were sold to a group of eight lumber men from Michigan and Wisconsin who had cut out their holdings in those states. Since the sale was consummated by J. T. Adams, manager of the lumber company for the Crockers, who temporarily remained in that capacity as well as that of co-owner, there was little change in working personnel and business continued without interruption. Under the direction of the new owners, the West Side Lumber Company thereafter dealt strictly in lumber.

Just before this sale the towns of Carters and Tuolumne had come into publicity on their own through association with Prince Poniatowski. When the San Francisco *Examiner*, in a derogatory report on Poniatowski's promotions, had mentioned Carters as "a little logging camp," localites indignantly rebelled insisting that Carters was a mining town and Tuolumne a "phenomenal" mill town, and that the two combined, with a population of 2,200 people, was no "logging camp." The *Examiner* had also accused Poniatowski of using Congressman Wood's mailing frank for shipping enormous quantities of bulky reports by the Department of Agriculture and the Commissioner of Forestry over the Sierra railroad at the time when mail was weighed to fix federal compensation. These shipments, the paper charged, would mean $30,000 a year to the railroad in its contract for carrying the mails. Unlike the mine and mill towns, the railroad did not rebut these accusations even though an investigation by Federal authorities produced no charges. Poniatowski, however, was said to have taken a leading part in having the *Examiner* cut off the list of papers received, thereafter, at clubs such as the Pacific Union Club of San Francisco. Also, at this time Poniatowski was under fire by H. J. Crocker, who brought suit against him and Bullock for some $64,000 worth of Sierra Railway Company bonds which Crocker said was due him. Shortly after this, Henry J. Crocker was voted out of the Sierra Railway directory and former Congressman Woods, who had been legal advisor to the railroad for some time, was elected in his place.

With William Crocker's money still behind him, Bullock continued to expand in Tuolumne County. He negotiated the purchase of another tract of timberland, almost as vast as the land just sold but running northward into mountains of the upper Stanislaus River watershed. At the same time he bought out Bradford's mountain sawmill and timberlands at Empire City some twenty-five miles above and east of Sonora, as well as his planing mill and sash and door factory in Sonora. Knudsen's mill and lumberyards in south Sonora were taken under lease. These combined properties became the holdings of the Standard Lumber Company which had been incorporated two years before. The entire rough lumber output was to be brought by six-horse teams to the enlarged Sonora planing mills, sash and door factory, and lumberyard for further shipment over Sierra rails.

In 1901, a fire which razed several buildings in Carters was only brought under control by a shift in the wind, for the water supply had failed. Immediately C. H. Carter promoted a community ditch to divert extra water from the North Fork of the Stanislaus River. That same year, and for much the same reason, two other Tuolumne County towns suffered much worse fire damage. Flames consumed half of Chinese Camp, and on a hot, dry day in August almost the whole town of Quartz Mountain burned down. Horse carts were rushed to the latter from Jamestown, Sonora and Stent, but water was inadequate and flames mercilessly destroyed over twenty dwellings and eleven places of business. Quartz was never rebuilt.

Although a great deal of California crude oil had been shipped out of the state since the first 6,000 barrels went by tanker in 1896, the local uses for oil in 1900 were limited. Since 1898, however, when the utility of crude petroleum on public highways was first tested, many California counties were finding that oiled roads developed a tough surface which was easily repaired and improved by each successive treatment. When the Southern Pacific railroad spoke seriously of converting to oil for locomotive fuel because it was safer and should be cheaper, as it had proven to be for forging and welding, the Sierra Railroad also experimented with oil. In 1901, a broken locomotive frame in the Jamestown shop had been straightened and welded in place by an oil burner under air blast at a cost of $18 when coal forging that job would have cost $150. From then on, oil cars were spotted at the Tuolumne and Jamestown shops as they had been previously spotted at mines using steam power, and there was talk of trying that fuel out on a locomotive.

In 1901, the railroad had its second series of accidents. In the first of these a carload of lumber and one of ore jumped the track and rolled all the way down a 200 foot embankment. Another flat car of lumber had jumped the track on a bridge near Cooperstown, tearing up about 300 feet of ties and rails before the train could be stopped. A few days later a freight engine had left two cars at Cooperstown before pulling all it could handle up the Rosasco Canyon, and was backing down for them when the engine's tender left the track on a low bridge. About thirty feet of ties were torn out before the tender went over the bridge and the engine settled down on it. Minutes later, the regular morning passenger train came down the grade but fortunately stopped short of the torn-up bridge. Passengers assisted in moving the wounded freight crew to the ranch home of E. H. Smith while the Cooperstown station agent telegraphed to Jamestown that the train crew had all been killed.

When Bullock, Superintendent Potts and Dr. Condon arrived on the scene by special train, Edward Dolan, brakeman, appeared, in fact, to be dead and Fireman Henry McAdams in a deep coma. Less seriously injured were A. D. Crowe, engineer, and E. W. Miller, conductor. These men were taken on the special to Sonora Hospital where all but Dolan were pronounced out of danger. The passenger train was four hours late when the tracks were cleared for it to go through. As an anti-climax to this accident, a Southern Pacific locomotive, having pulled a special passenger train into Jamestown the same day, collided head-on with the Sierra's *No. 4* engine right in the Jamestown yards. Although no one was hurt, both engines were badly damaged.

These accidents added up to a great deal of expense in road and equipment repairs as well as in damage suits. Dolan sued the Sierra for $25,000, which was finally reduced to $7,000 by the railroad attorneys. Smaller injury suits resulting from these accidents, plus a suit brought for fire damage done by a section crew burning brush along the tracks, added up to another $7,000 loss by the railroad.

In spite of disasters, the financial statement of the Sierra Railway Company in March, 1902, gave quarterly earnings in excess of expenditures as $31,923.15. A small figure now, but at that time it gave the Sierra railroad the reputation of being the best paying short line railroad in the state. In the following two years the whole main line was reballasted and freight and passenger service over it continued uninterrupted. The regular up and down passenger train pulled three coaches and a baggage car. This train was met twice daily at Sonora by stage driver and mail carrier George Trask and at Jamestown by Frank Butterfield, both of whom became familiar to passengers through long years of continuous service. The two daily freight trains on the main line were usually made up at night by switch engines that assembled cars from spur tracks. After the Harvard Gold Mining Company paid $350,000 for the Erin Go Braugh and Cloudman mines on Whisky Hill near Jamestown, their mill was enlarged to treat the combined ores in 1902, and the Sierra built a mile long spur to it. This spur allowed empties to be loaded with sulphurets direct from the mill and shipped from there (until 1914) to reduction works at Selby on San Francisco Bay. The Dutch Mine at Quartz put in a mile long privately built spur track from which the Sierra hauled cars loaded with bulk or sacked sulphurets. Also, every night at least three carloads of lime products were removed from Fassler spur, which served the quarry and plant that later became Pacific Lime and Plaster Company. On one occasion three lime cars were allowed to run away near Jamestown and three miles down the road they derailed, spilling their entire contents to make a scene resembling a snowstorm in July. Such ore shipments, added to carloads of lumber and cattle made up most of the outgoing freight. Tons of mixed cargo were shipped back into the hills for people still catching up with the inventions, novelties and necessities of the "outside" world.

To handle this traffic, the Sierra's equipment was increased and improved. A two-stall roundhouse was built in Tuolumne City and pits laid for a four-stall roundhouse in Jamestown. Of the 35 freight cars in local service, all but ten were on lease from the Southern Pacific Company, but at this time ten more were purchased from other roads and were relettered and numbered accordingly. Their shops were equipped with electric motors for lathes, presses, rattlers and flue-cutting machines. A stiffleg derrick and two-way traveling crane were installed, as well as other shop supplies. The Sierra's *No. 5* Schenectady, had been sold and shipped to Hawaii. *No. 10* Lima was the first of their locomotives to be refurbished with acetylene headlights, and air as well as steam brakes. Slowly all seven main line locomotives were brought up to date, and in 1904 the Sierra's brand new Baldwin 2-8-0 came on the tracks as their prideful *No. 18* locomotive. The Sierra's roster of engines does not include any numbered *13* to *17*, but in this interim several newspapers reported:

"A new locomotive arrived in Oakdale from Schenectady, N.Y., consigned to Sierra Railway Company of California. It is of special design for heavy mountain work and is the only one of its class in the state." Since a heavy new Schenectady locomotive being deadheaded over the line two years earlier had spread the rails and rolled passenger coaches down the bank, it seems obvious that such a locomotive was on the line, if only for a short time.

Six regular Fairbanks Morse, three-cylinder, two-cycle track cars were owned for the use of section crews. Laborers riding on the high seats over the motors of these track cars held onto their hats while whizzing gleefully down grade although they knew what went down on the Sierra tracks must chug upward, slowly, sometimes even having to be pushed. The "Special" track car with four front wheels and two back drivers accommodated four passengers and was used so much that every part of it had been worn out and replaced. Forgetting big business for one time, Henry Crocker and Bullock had ridden this track car out of Tuolumne the day after the excursion party there. On the way to the Nevills Hotel, holding Stetson hats in hand and Bullock's crutches on the back seat, the bareheaded financiers "let her go" down Buck Horn Hill grade with the same breath-taking abandon as track crews reveled in.

The gala atmosphere of the Nevills Hotel had paled since the days when "Captain" Nevills drove over from Rawhide Valley in his fringed surrey with the stylish guests, but in the summer its accommodations were popularly reserved by tourists and socially inclined localites. In fact, with the largest suites reserved for railroad officials, an annex had to be added to the depot end of the hotel for the use of transients and single railroad employees. In the winter of 1903, however, the number of unoccupied rooms in the Nevills Hotel inspired the ever belittling San Francisco *Examiner* to report that "mice and spiders are holding carnival in Jamestown's palatial hotel."

At that time the Pereira Addition, hopefully promoted almost five years before, was as untenanted as the day it was subdivided, although old Jamestown was still thriving on the trade of 800 quartz miners and mill hands working in the vicinity. After Nevills sold his shares in the Jamestown Improvement Company, it had disbanded, and the weed-overgrown subdivision became Bullock's private property. Unsuccessful inventions and projects by men of schemes and dreams are not necessarily unstable or impossibly visionary because they fail. Locations on the eastern seaboard with less natural attractiveness, resources and potentials than Jamestown had become flourishing and fashionable communities in the 1890's due to a railroad, a luxurious hotel or promotional money. If times had turned better instead of worse, Jamestown might conceivably have become the Saratoga of the Mother Lode, and Tuolumne a popular tourist resort. The survival of the Sierra Railroad at this time when money was becoming scarce was exceptional, and consequently the essence of this history.

CHAPTER SEVEN

SIERRA RAILWAY

Many transportation schemes besides Bullock's electric ones were projected in Tuolumne County around the turn of the century, with none carried to fruition. Table Mountain was going to be tunneled, electric trains were going to cross the upper Tuolumne River, and some Oakdale citizens secured miles of rights-of-way for a Modesto-Yosemite Railway that died the year it was born.

When these competitive threats did not mature, the stock and trade in stage lines went up. As a result, a concrete two-way wagon bridge supplanted the old wooden one that used to sway over the Tuolumne River at Jacksonville, and Paul Morris of the Big Oak Flat Toll Road Company did needed work on that road. The Big Oak Flat and Yosemite stages, with Sierra Railway backing, made the trip from Chinese Station to Yosemite Valley in one long day, changing horses five times. After 1400 people were taken over this route in the summer of 1901, an attempt was made to use motive power; the next year six eleven-passenger auto buses with baggage racks on top were ordered at $2,000 each. Morris bet $500 that no automobile carrying twelve persons could make the trip in as good time as the horse drawn stages, and collected his money after a trial run to Crocker in 1903. This trip cost two sets of tires, two sets of brakes, a broken spring and a week's wages for several employees besides gasoline and oil.

Automobiles were beginning to filter in, however, and Tuolumne County got some roads scraped and oiled. The road from Cloudman, where the supervisor lived, to Jamestown was the first to get the treatment. The section of road between Jamestown and Sonora was greatly improved and a concrete bridge built over Woods Creek, which became a popular Sunday afternoon drive for a fellow with a surrey or single seated rig and a best girl to sit beside him.

County supervisors also made an effort to have the old Mono highway over the Sierra Nevada mountains to Bodie repaired, for by now it was considered "almost impassable." Such an admission about a road in Tuolumne County, at that time, meant anyone but a hardened teamster carrying his own repair kit and plenty of axle grease would be tempting Providence to try it. The county surveyor pointed out that the Mono road job would take a long summer and at least fifty steadily employed road workers at two dollars each per day to merely patch washouts and clear the road of boulders. Supervisors then found that there were not fifty such laborers available due to the Sierra railroad's activity.

Immediately after rails were laid into Angels, the engineering crew, replete with transits, levels and drafting table, was packed up and moved to the Sugar Pine Hotel on the Mono road above Sonora, to locate a broad gauge logging railroad which would branch from the Sierra's main line near Campbell's Station and reach into the Standard Lumber Company's mountain timberland. While surveying this branch, Newell was advised by Bullock to bear in mind the railroad's possible future extension northward across granite canyons into Calaveras County and eastward over the Sierra Nevada mountains into the state of Nevada!

Location work began at Campbell's Station and turned up the ridge that divides the Stanislaus and Tuolumne watersheds. The Mono road following up this ridge was crossed by an overpass at the Confidence Mine, after which the right-of-way wound along the west slope of the ridge to Lyon's Dam on the South Fork of the Stanislaus River and proceeded upstream to Rushings Meadows, then across to Spring Gap and Strawberry. Before leaving the ridge, the railroad was to connect by inclined rails with two little narrow gauge logging roads serving the Empire and Cold Springs mills then being operated in the Tuolumne River canyon by the Standard Lumber Company. Of these, the Empire Mill alone was cutting 40,000 feet of sugar and yellow pine lumber daily, which the new branch was to haul down to Sonora.

To the Sierra's civil engineers this project was a challenge of future possibilities in the stimulating mountainous terrain. Here, the air was spiced from that feathery green ground cover disdained by cattle and called Mountain Misery by cattlemen. Bright green deer brush grew among waxy manzanita leaves on brown-red branches. Towering above these man-high scrubs were the majestic ponderosa and sugar pines. Far vistas disclosed hazy blue mountains whose crags and precipices challenged passage to man or beast, let alone steel rails. Yet those were the granite canyons between this ridge and the Calaveras Big Trees, and those were the snowy peaks with the lowest pass at 11,000 feet over which Bullock blithely talked of extending his railroad. But with the location of a comparatively short logging road as their immediate objective, the engineers rode horses or walked with transits on shoulders, along and across this mid-slope section of California's most austere mountains.

The old Sugar Pine Hotel, to which the survey crew returned at night when possible, was still an active and hospitable stage depot managed by the pioneer Carr family. Twelve-horse teams coming from mountain sawmills raised great clouds of dust as they rattled past the hotel with an average of 1,000 feet of lumber to a horse. In the fall, huge herds of cattle surged past the hotel on drives from forest grazing to the foothills. Sometimes bellowing herds were bedded down overnight behind the hotel, and after dinner cattlemen joined teamsters and engineers on the hotel veranda. Two such evenings that fall were spent anxiously looking across the Tuolumne canyon where the sky flamed angry red and the wind was acrid with smoke. By leaps and bounds the forest fire raced from treetop to treetop and burst like bombs when the oozing resinous sap of red hot tree trunks exploded. That devastating scene, which would be black and barren for years to come, substantiated the lumberman's motto of the day: "Let us get the trees before the fires do." Sad though the knowledge that the proud stand of magnificent pines on Mono ridge would soon be chopped into chaos by lumbermen, this death at least was less complete to the forests than fire.

Survey and cross sections for the railroad location were handed over to Bullock in mid-November, 1902, but the projected Sugar Pine Railroad was not incorporated and financed until the spring of 1903. Then, with snows melted and frozen ground thawed out, grading commenced on the right of way and tracks were laid to Newell Station, the line's first, which was at the foot of a steep grade to Mono ridge. Construction work on the Sugar Pine Railroad continued through that year until Bullock diverted plans and funds to the promotion of yet another railroad into timberlands adjacent to Yosemite Park, where competitive rails threatened to go ahead of him.

Suspended work on the Sugar Pine branch left logging transportation from the Standard Lumber Company's mountain mills to horse and mule teams. It was a hard interim of competition with the West Side Lumber Company, whose twenty miles of logging road and concentrated one mill in Tuolumne were turning out 80 to 90 thousand feet of lumber around the clock. Meanwhile, Tuolumne City was self-sufficiently progressing and Carters steadfastly upholding the mining tradition; but neither town offered much attraction for outside industry or tourists. Sierra passenger trains pulled into the end of the line almost empty. The Turn Back Inn had become a temporary residence for a few mine owners and Sierra and West Side officials. To encourage local business, the railroad promoted summer baseball excursions and, in 1902, sponsored their first winter pilgrimage to the place of contest between Fresno and Carters in "the great game of football." Rates to Carters of one dollar for the round trip from local points and three dollars from San Joaquin Valley points made ticket sales exceed expectations, necessitating three excursion trains. Carters hotels provided lunches at twenty-five and fifty cents before the game; the saloons took over after the visiting team won. The open excursion cars pulled out of town in a sleeting rain, causing a sellout of all current copies and back sheets of the *New Era* newspaper for head and seat protection.

Such expeditions benefited business in Carters but did little for Tuolumne. That section of the community was growing in its own atmosphere of screeching saws on fresh cut lumber. The regularly deposited savings of mill and timber employees had warranted a local commercial bank, a modern hospital and two new churches. Through a case of mistaken identity, Tuolumne's new Episcopal church tower housed an old engine bell removed from the Sierra's *No. 2* locomotive when it was dismantled in Jamestown. Supervisor Booker had suggested placing the bell in the vacant belfry of his own Methodist church. Although the railroad happily responded, it was shipped to the Episcopal church and ringing proudly from its tower before the mistake could be rectified.

About this time, Poniatowski's marble works in Columbia was sold to Mr. J. J. Crooks and eastern associates, who also purchased the adjoining Tuolumne County Power and Light Company. This source of power and light might have been bought by Tuolumne County if the local mine situation had not made money so tight in Sonora. On October 14, 1901, the Citizens Bank of Sonora had closed its doors, after which angry depositors met at Turn Verein Hall to elect a committee to audit the bank's accounts. A block of 52,000 shares of thirty-five year old stock in the old Bonanza Mining Company was among mine assets held in the bank's loan portfolio, which was sold at twenty-five cents a share in the drawn out dissolution plan.

In Jamestown the railroad had installed Thompson arc lights in the shops and yards. Cars loaded with giant powder or dynamite for mines were being delivered by special freight trains. Fifty track layers were installing $100,000 worth of 60-pound rail between Cooperstown and Jamestown; and the twenty miles of old 40-pound rails were to be relaid on the Sugar Pine Railroad, after which tracks would at last reach the Standard Lumber Company's mills. Sierra Railway was not affected in 1902 when a conductors' and brakemen's union demanded a 20% increase in wages. But in 1903, when the Brotherhood of Locomotive Engineers threatened to go on strike, some of the Sierra's engineers were members. Since the strike was not called, the railroad was saved from having to carry out Bullock's ultimatum which promised "permanent walking papers" to any employee who walked off the job.

Liveries from Jamestown to the mines were still in demand, especially to the Jumper where a 20 ton cyanide plant was being added at the millsite. To facilitate this travel and their own depot-to-mine wagon freighting, the Sierra had oiled, scraped and re-oiled the road from Jamestown to Stent, Quartz and the Jumper Mine until it was the best in the county.

Oakdale was no longer a "Teamster Town." The only wagon freighting of consequence was hauling grain to Oakdale warehouses and to the Sperry mill, which had moved there from

SIERRA RAILWAY CO.

Grand Harvest Festival

..EXCURSION..

OAKDALE
— TO —
ANGELS

Sunday, Aug. 14

Baseball Game--Angels vs. S. M. & P. Co.

Big Barbecue

FARE, Round Trip, $1.00

Special covered excursion cars—no flats. Through train   Accommodations for all.   Special arrangements for large crowd.

Excursion train leaves Oakdale 8 a. m.
Returning, leaves Angels 7 p. m.

Knights Ferry, making grain the town's largest year around business. Oakdale was a railroad town. Besides being on Southern Pacific and Sierra tracks, the Santa Fe railroad had built their long talked of spur from Riverbank into Oakdale for the transfer of passengers and freight to and from the mountains. The Sierra down-train, leaving Sonora at 8:25 a.m., pulled into Oakdale at 10:00 a.m. with first and second class passengers bound for San Francisco via either S.P. or Santa Fe with arrival around 4:45 p.m. Luxurious private cars from railroads all over the U.S.A. were brought to Oakdale to be coupled onto Sierra trains and later to be sidetracked along the line while V.I.P.'s visited the mines, timberlands or world-famed scenic sights accessible by stage from Sierra stations.

In these years when the Sierra Railway was introducing Tuolumne County to the West, their 35 foot excursion cars with three foot high sides and iron barred tops, over which canvas could be spread against sun or rain, were in constant use the year around. Trips were advertised throughout California in 1903 to 1906 by newspapers, magazines and handbills.

In June, 1904, after regular and special trains had been routinely and uneventfully operating for two years on the Angels Branch, a shocking tragedy occurred. The regular morning passenger train descended the Pendola Switch, and after crossing the river came chugging up the McArdle switchback with the two usual coaches, carrying seventeen passengers including the Valente sisters of Angels Camp, traveling to a funeral in Sonora. Backing up the switch, the train crew was horrified to see a loaded boxcar and flat car, brakes loosened by the vibration of the train engine, slipping toward them out of the El Rico siding near the top of the grade. The engine ground to a stop and the conductor and brakeman ran through the coaches ordering everyone out. Moments later the two loosed cars came crashing into the rear of the train. By then everyone had either jumped off or scrambled into the forward combination coach, except the two Valente sisters who clung to the platform between the coaches, and were fatally crushed when these cars telescoped. After the bodies had been removed and a few minor injuries given first aid at the McArdle ranch house, the engine and little combination coach, loaded with its surviving but saddened passengers, pulled out for Jamestown. Besides a large damage suit paid to the Valente family, a drummer sued the Sierra Railway Company for a sale he did not make because of missing his connection with the San Francisco bound train, which, by the size of the amount won, must have been the most important sale of his life.

The *No. 6* coach was no sooner repaired and normal operations resumed on the Angels Branch than an accident took place on the main line. On a frosty morning in 1904, the *No. 6* locomotive pulling passenger coaches jumped the tracks between Sonora and Sullivan Creek bridge. Although the engine and baggage cars careened over on their sides, no passengers were hurt, and the undamaged coaches were pulled to Tuolumne by another engine. Shortly after this, the little *No. 3* jumped a split switch and tipped over near Chinese Station, coal and water spilling from her tender like the entrails and blood from a wounded animal. But the little Rogers was destined to have more lives than a cat. On that occasion another engine pulled her onto a butterfly rail with the help of a pulley anchored to a deadman, and she rolled onto the main track as good as ever.

In January, 1905, the Angels *Record* reported:

"On Monday morning a big crowd of passengers bound to the City and intermediate points, found when they reached the Sierra station, that the fare had been raised to $4. Objecting to the advance, some came back to town and went down below by way of Milton, two stages and two surreys being loaded with the travelers."

This fare increase may have caused regular passenger traffic on the Angels Branch to fall off but the Sierra railroad made up for it by increasing excursion traffic on that scenic branch in 1905. That summer the line sponsored seven gigantic excursions which made favorable headline advertising in all but one instance. The Sierra also offered what was called "auto service" along the line to private parties, which kept the Winton and Thomas Flyer track cars on the go. The San Francisco *Chronicle* reported:

"The Sierra is probably the first railroad in the United States and certainly the first in the West to put a railroad track automobile in service for the use of its patrons ... on the basis of one full-fare round trip rate between terminal points for each of three possible passengers plus $5 per hour for chauffeur. Time to be computed from departure of auto from roundhouse until return. Minimum charge $15."

The Sierra's scenic Sunday excursions into the mine and Bret Harte country, jointly sponsored by the Southern Pacific and Santa Fe railroads, finally snowballed into a debacle. The first of these excursions, Stockton to Angels Camp at $2 the round trip, took 300 passengers in six closed and open-sided excursion cars, pulled first in two and later four sections. Crowds met the trains at every station and bands kept up lively tunes aboard except at the Stanislaus River crossing where musicians and revelers alike took time out to "oh" and "ah" at the scenery. The following week nearly 500 people from Angels Camp and other mountain towns took a round trip excursion to Stockton using ten S.P. coaches for the valley part of the trip. These happy travelers left the depot in Stockton at 6:00 a.m. and were home by midnight. The next Sunday the Santa Fe took four loaded coaches from Stockton to Jamestown where passengers transferred to the Sierra's open cars fitted with four lengthwise rows of seats to double their usual capacity. On Sunday, October 8th, $4 round trip tickets were sold to 1500 people of the bay cities for an expedition to Sonora and Carters. Both Santa Fe and Sierra were swamped. Due to completely inadequate accommodations, the eighteen coaches supposed to reach Sonora at noon did not arrive even at Oakdale until 2:00 p.m. The fourth section of this excursion arrived in Sonora at 11:35 p.m. with disgusted camera fans, frightened women, hungry children and angry men. As one reporter commented:

"The four or five hundred people in the Ferry Building Sunday morning who, as the gate closed on them with money in hands shouted 'We want to go to Sonora!' — were born under lucky stars."

For the rest of that year, excursions were limited to one or two hundred passengers taken to Angels, for instance, when the Valley Brew baseball team of Stockton went there to play the local nine; or Stockton to Sonora when Sonora played the Farmington team. On the occasion of this latter game a Stockton reporter wrote an item which was intended to disparage but apparently only whetted readers' appetites for rail excursions:

"The excursion ran from Stockton to Jamestown, and there split up. One hundred tourists took the scenic railway to Angels while sports fans were put on the civilized road to the game in Sonora. The ride by rail and jump from Jimtown to Angels is undoubtedly the steepest, crookedest, hair-raising jaunt in

Engine No. 30 with Angels Camp mixed meeting Engine No. 32, Tuolumne-Oakdale passenger, at Jamestown, 7:15 a.m. Summer of 1927. This is the only known picture of the star on Engine No. 30. It was called "Old Star" for many years. The train was known as "Gus's Special" because Gus Swanson was almost always its engineer.

Part of Jamestown showing station and general offices in center. Roundhouse at right and top of water tank in foreground. Angels Branch veers off to the left at center of picture.

Table Mountain cut. This cut enabled the railroad to go from Jamestown to Rawhide Flat at a reasonable elevation. Machine drills were used to make this cut, the first such application to be used by this railroad.

Tuttletown. When this picture was taken in 1920, Tuttletown was reduced to a mere handful of houses. Highway passes under trestle in center of picture.

Marble spur. Workmen are unloading truck load of marble from Columbia quarries. For a time these quarries were a source of considerable revenue for the railroad.

FOUR PICTURES: SIERRA RAILROAD

4.15% grade on Angels Branch at Milepost 50 between Patterson Mine and switchback No. 1.

Mormon Gulch trestle as seen from the Patterson Mine.

Switchback No. 1 on Angels Branch.

Switchback No. 2. The necessity for this type of construction is obvious.

RALPH KERCHUM

Typical daily mixed crossing Stanislaus River Bridge at Melones in the summer of 1936.

J. AZEVEDA

Gus' Special on the Stanislaus River Bridge.

A rare occurrence: No. 30 running *extra* from Jamestown to Angels in mid-day. Special load of logs and cement for Pacific Gas & Electric Co. at Angels. Summer of 1930.

RALPH KERCHUM

Boomed steam shovel used in construction of the Angels Branch. Wood for this machine was cut along the line and burned in the donkey boiler on the rear. It was quite a novelty in its time. Later some 20 of these shovels were sent to the Panama Canal construction project.

SIERRA RAILROAD

Irvine was located at the top grade of the Stanislaus River canyon. Glory hole of Carson Hill mine at right was mined from below at near river level.

Mixed daily leaving Carson Hill station on way to Angels. Note Sierra Railway boxcar and Standard Oil tanker.

RALPH KERCHUM

Switchback No. 3 between mileposts 51 and 52.

Switchback No. 4.

Train and shovel crew of the construction train headed by Shay No. 10 on Angels Branch. Mose Baker is sitting on coupler.

RALPH KERCHUM

Afternoon train from Jamestown crossing trestle between Carson Hill and Angels. Summer of 1927.

Near Milepost 55. Stanislaus River below with Table Mountain in upper background.

Trestle between Carson Hill and Melones. Summer of 1928. Afternoon train headed by locomotive No. 30.

Carson Hill section foreman in front of company-owned house, Carson Hill, summer of 1928. Note rail bender, track bar and gunnysack wrapped water barrel on section car.

A rare picture of engine No. 32 pinch hitting for No. 30 on the Angels Branch. This was taken near Greenstone spur, which was the last new stretch of track ever built on the Angels Branch, and the best piece of track constructed. It was located a half mile east of Angels Camp.

Jamestown mixed daily arriving near Greenstone spur, summer, 1929. Had this unusually heavy consist been normal, the branch would be in operation today.

TWO PICTURES: RALPH KERCHUM

Afternoon train crossing trestle in dry creek pass one mile from Angels in the summer of 1926.

Engine No. 30 on turntable at end of line near Big Trees highway in Angels Camp.

Engine No. 30 taking on water at end of day. Engineer Gus Swanson is standing in the gangway.

Late afternoon switching in Angels yards.

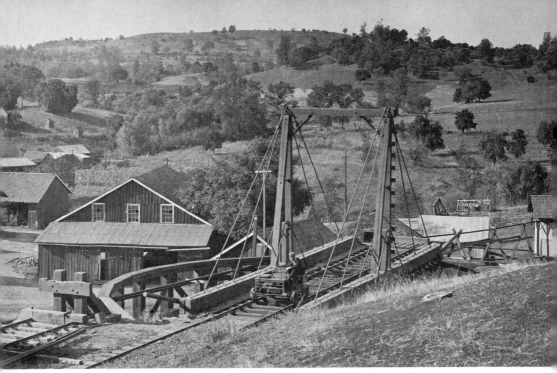

Track car on turntable of Angels Camp.

Main Street of Angels Camp in 1923.

SIERRA RAILROAD

Looking toward end-of-track at Angels.

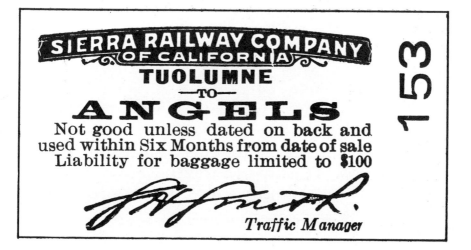

ONE DOLLAR
ROUND TRIP
EXCURSION TO ANGELS
Sunday, JUNE 19
BASE-BALL GAME
BETWEEN
ANGELS
And SONORA

Don't miss this cheap rate as you may not get
another such chance for this fine scenic trip.
Train leaves Tuolumne 7:20 A. M., Sonora 8
A. M.   Returning leaves Angels 7 P. M.

TUOL. INDEPENDENT PRINT, SONORA

Combine No. 5 and its accompanying coach No. 6 were made for the tight curves of the Angeles Branch. They are the most unusual railroad cars still in use in this country.

So unusual are the two little cars that they are avidly sought by model railroaders everywhere. Here is a picture of a car built from a kit by Binkley Models of Englewood, California.

THREE PICTURES: ARCHIE STEVENOT

Empire City engine house. Engine at left is a Shay; the other two are the Porters from the Yosemite Short Line. The Porters were the first oil burners ordered by the Sierra.

At left: Lumber train on Empire City railroad heading for Lyon's Dam incline. The gauge of this railroad was 30″. This is one of the Porter locomotives purchased for the Yosemite Short Line Railway, but not used by them.

Empire City railroad locomotive with long train at Empire Mill. Man sitting with back to cab is Roland Binder. Bill McCallom is leaning out of cab window.

MRS. WILLIAM WENNESON

Sugar Pine Shay with heavy log train.

At left: This picture would seem to be promoting Smith Premier typewriters, but was taken on the Sugar Pine Railway line.

PICKERING LUMBER COMPANY

Heisler No. 2 with water car.

PICKERING LUMBER COMPANY

Wrecks were frequent, but the ingenuity of the lumber railroaders always seemed to be able to save the situation.

ARTHUR RONTEN

During the years prior to the flooding of Beardsley Flat the Pickering log train traveled the winding track down from the surrounding mountains, crossing the middle fork of the Stanislaus River on a steel and concrete bridge, then climbing the south canyon wall again. An approximate three miles of track was dismantled to make way for the dam, and was relocated to run across the dam itself. With the addition of a horseshoe curve it now rejoins the former alignment to the north. In this picture a log train headed by a Shay may be seen crossing the top of the dam.

West Side No. 2 just above Camp 8 in 1907.

At left: First excursion of the West Side railroad. Railfan photographers of the day had either to steady their cameras on a fence post or use tripods and black hoods.

Annual excursion outing of West Side Lumber Company to the now extinct Camp Nash.

West Side officials inspecting the line in 1900. Left to right, Mr. Nash, G. H. Wendling, Mr. Coggins, D. H. Steinmetz, Mr. Mullins, Henry Crocker. Engine was either Fido or Star.

On page opposite, construction crew about to be taken to railhead on West Side line. The two little engines used on this construction were saddle tankers named Fido and Star. They had no numbers and were, of course, fired with wood. The home made tender was built to enable these locomotives to carry enough slabs to operate for a long time without refueling. (Picture courtesy Donald Segerstrom.)

West Side No. 1. Nos. 2 and 3 of same series are still on hand.

West Side railroaders of 1905. Man in derby hat was locomotive Engineer Ketcham.

TWO PICTURES: FRED ELLIS

West Side Shay No. 6 with log train.

Group in foreground, right to left, G. W. Johnson, W. J. Hanlon, J. R. Prince.

No. 5 after being rebuilt.

The West Side sported this narrow gauge Locomobile for an inspection and hunting car.

West Side No. 5 appears to be completely demolished, but was rebuilt (page opposite) and used for many years.

No. 5 being rescued.

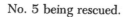

Clavey Creek Bridge.

Page opposite. Large picnic excursion. (Picture courtesy Sonora Museum.)

Train crew standing beside one of the Shays.

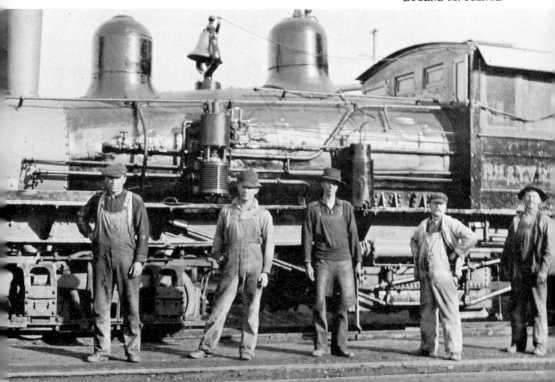

Home made cabooses like the one above are in every day use on the West Side. They may not be pretty, but they afford a good view of the train and provide shelter for the crew against the mountain thunder storms.

West Side No. 12 at Camp 45 in 1958. This is one of the engines in regular use on this line. These engines are equipped with straight air as well as regular air brakes due to the heavy grades in favor of the loads.

Yosemite Short Line

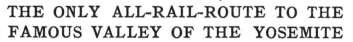

THE ONLY ALL-RAIL-ROUTE TO THE
FAMOUS VALLEY OF THE YOSEMITE

The Yosemite Short Line Railway, in conjunction with the Sierra Railway, makes close connections with both the Southern Pacific and Santa Fe railways. Are you contemplating the trip? Information furnished for the asking.

Address, S. H. SMITH, Gen. Pass. Agt. Sierra Railway
JAMESTOWN, CALIFORNIA.

No pictures have been found of equipment on the Yosemite Short Line Railway. Although many advertisements were run and almost all of them illustrated, it was always a piece of Sierra equipment shown. The line sported a much fancier insignia than the current company. Its life was short, and it never came near reaching its destination, the Yosemite Valley.

California. There is not 100 feet of straight or level track anywhere on the ninety minutes run at an average of twelve miles
an hour. The engineers who surveyed the line were indeed
fortunate that they came out at such a pretty and thriving town
as Angels. The road is full of switchbacks, swaybacks and
hunchbacks, trestles, torrents and terror, and the right of way
is disputed by cows and goats, cliffs and chasms. The line
passes three sides of the old schoolhouse in which Mark Twain
taught in early days and on three sides of Table Mountain made
famous by Bret Harte."

Thus, Sierra tracks kept busy with regular and special trains
while the struggle to lay rails into Yosemite Park continued. Jay
Gould had a survey made for a railroad to cross the Sierra Nevada
mountains to the south of the park before it became Federal
property in 1898. Charles Crocker, Sr., had also projected a railroad into Yosemite via Wawona, which was built to the town of
Raymond's where the granite quarries were located. Stetson, of
Holbrook, Merril and Stetson, had surveys made up the Merced
River for an electric road in 1902; since then surveyors for the
Crocker Estate Company had resurveyed this route. Since the
upper part of these areas were now in the Federal Park, surveys
were made there in winter while patrols were lax, for the edict
had been issued that no railroad would enter park boundaries.
The owners of many private land titles in Yosemite Park, acquired
before Federal boundaries were defined, however, claimed the
right in 1902 to give private rights of way. At that time the
Crockers had agreed to again financially back Bullock provided
he could secure a practical rail route into the park area. It was
Bullock's aim that such a route would enter the park from the
north side in order also to touch timberland to which he had title
on the border between Tuolumne and Mariposa counties. He had
conferred with Newell about this but reconnaissance work was
postponed in January, 1903, by a surprise petition presented to
Tuolumne county supervisors by Hershel F. La Motte requesting
a franchise for a standard gauge electric line to run from Chinese
Camp to Yosemite National Park.

Backed by Stockton and Eastern capital, La Motte was promoting his line as a passenger and freight service to use S.P.
tracks Stockton to Oakdale, Sierra tracks Oakdale to Chinese
and his electric line from there to the North Rim of Yosemite

Valley, passing 46,000 acres of La Motte's patented timberland inside the park boundary. This projection coincided with Bullock's aim sufficiently for him to await developments.

Meanwhile, in March, 1903, the following article appeared in a San Francisco paper:

> "Virgil G. Bogne of New York, formerly chief engineer of the Union Pacific and now consulting engineer for J. Pierpont Morgan, John D. Rockefeller, and other railroad owners, has been gathering data relative to three proposed electric roads into Yosemite Valley. He got soaking wet out from Merced and went to bed. He left for Mexico City refusing to discuss the matter."

Then in July, 1903, a group of La Motte's Eastern capitalists received a franchise for an electric line to run all the way from Stockton via Chinese, Big Oak Flat and Crocker, touching sawmills and timberlands before reaching the park. Some rights-of-way for such a road which ignored the Sierra Railway actually were secured, though the exact location of it had not been determined.

In 1904, Congress had before it a bill providing for cutting off a section of the National Park on the north side, nine miles wide, which would permit the building of a railroad much nearer to Yosemite Valley. It was also rumored that the government would make an appropriation to assist the building of a railroad up the Merced River. Late in 1904, the National Park Commission selected the Merced River route as the only one which the government would consider for a railroad over national park territory to Yosemite Valley.

Reconnaissances on frozen ground were made early in that year for a feasible railroad location which would accomplish Bullock's desires and also bring Sierra tracks to the north Park boundary. Of this proposed line Bullock said:

> "This road is designed to reach the mines south of the Tuolumne River, miscellaneous traffic between these and Mariposa County, and to and from Yosemite Park. Preliminary surveys have been made and work will be rushed as far as the park where Congressional permission must be obtained for further work."

Articles were filed in August naming this proposed railroad the Yosemite Short Line Railroad Company with a capitalization of $1,250,000, of which $125,000 had been subscribed principally by a board of directors that established the following officers: F. J. Solinsky of Berkeley, president; Frank R. Whehe, Berkeley, vice-president; John Hancock, San Francisco, secretary; and L. B. Doe, San Mateo, treasurer. This was to be a 30 inch gauged steam railroad branching from the Sierra Railway two miles below Jamestown, to carry passengers and freight by a practicable route to Yosemite Park with an intermediate branch to run from Crocker's station on the Big Oak Flat road to the Hetch Hetchy Valley. Estimated length of the main line was sixty miles and branch line ten miles.

In September, 1905, this new company issued and sold its Forty Year First Mortgage, sinking 4½% Gold Bonds guaranteed as to principal and interest by the Sierra Railway Company of California to help finance costs of construction and equipment.

Rights-of-way for the Yosemite Short Line were obtained as far as Groveland. Bullock, general manager of the short line as well as the Sierra, ordered two special 30 inch gauge locomotives from the H. K. Porter Company of Pittsburgh, and enough 30 pound steel rails from the East for the first 20 miles of track. Word went out that a 250 room log cabin style hotel with electric lights and modern plumbing was to be built at the rail terminus in the Big Trees. Also, that Newell had promised to cut straight through one huge sugar pine in the right-of-way which Bullock considered too majestic for felling. A tuberculosis sanitarium was planned for the line east of Chinese. In October, an order from Washington, D.C., gave less approval than had been expected. "Yo Semite line cannot enter Yo Semite Park but can cross the Sierra forest reserve up to the park line," was the heart of the order as it appeared in the Sacramento *Bee*. But nothing could stop the Yosemite Short Line now.

A subsidiary company to build it was incorporated in Nevada and called the Tuolumne Construction Company, with Bullock as president. On October 9, 1905, the construction company entered into a contract with the Japanese American Industrial Corporation represented by K. Abiko, by which the J. A. I. C. agreed to furnish at their own expense the necessary tools and men to do the grading from the point where the right-of-way began at Woods Creek crossing to Moccasin Creek on the south side of the

Tuolumne River, a distance of about ten miles. The work started on October 15, it being further agreed that immediately at least 100 men, and six weeks later not less than 300 men, work continuously until the job was finished. By contract:

"All the work is to be done under Newell's direction, control and supervision, as Chief Engineer of the Yosemite Short Line Railway Company. Any and all of his decisions as to the work are to be conclusive, even to such changes in direction or grade as he might consider expedient. Foremen in charge of men, animals or materials are to act on Newell's orders. All material taken from cuts is to be placed in embankment free of charge for a distance of fifty feet from the mouth of the cut with 2 and ½ cents per cubic yard to be paid for each fifty feet of material placed in embankment beyond the fifty foot limit. The work to be paid for at the rate of 40 cents per cubic yard with no claim for extra work allowed other than the overhaul just mentioned."

Grading work proceeded smoothly down the west bank of Woods Creek toward the Tuolumne River. Track layers followed the graders for a mile or so with old rails locally bought and spiked to ties so that two Porter locomotives which had arrived on flat cars at the Sierra Railway junction could carry supplies to the head of rails. In December, when ten miles had been graded and trestles built across Woods and Sullivans creeks, the new rails still had not arrived. Supplies supposed to have been hauled over them were being forwarded along the finished grade by teams at additional cost.

Steel and concrete caissons and piers had by then been planted in the gold-rich gravel of the Tuolumne River a half mile below Jacksonville where the railroad was to cross on a long bridge. On the south side of the river the road turned eastward on an almost level bench and then followed up Moccasin Creek canyon to the mining settlement of Moccasin. From there it snaked its way to Priests and Groveland up the steepest grade on the projected line. Above Big Oak Flat just beyond Groveland, the right-of-way wound through magnificent forests all the way to Yosemite Park.

Although the Tuolumne River canyon is tremendous, it is fortunately wider and less steep at the point of crossing than the Stanislaus River canyon at the point bridged with standard gauge track on the Angels Branch line. But the granite and grades to be surmounted on the south side of the river by a "practicable freight and passenger railroad," even though 30 inch gauge, made the engineering challenge of the Yosemite Short Line equal to its Angels' standard gauge predecessor. As soon as contact with Oriental laborers and their bosses was established on a mutually friendly and understanding basis, the survey crew mapped and staked out the route up Priests grade and then proceeded to locate the line as far as possible before winter set in. Racing the weather, the engineering corps were at the 5,000 foot elevation that December and fifty miles ahead of grading. One morning the survey crew left their quarters at Crane Flat by horseback to ride to location work. They pushed their luck too far. The men and seven horses were forced by a sudden snow storm to huddle for two days in the hollow trunk of a huge, fallen Sequoia gigantea. This arbitrarily ended location work in 1905.

The survey crew then returned to Jacksonville at the 800 foot level where the Japanese graders were encamped. That town's population had diminished since booming placer mining days to about ninety permanent residents, but the Big Oak Flat road from Chinese and two back roads from Jamestown and Sonora merged at the nearby toll bridge over the Tuolumne as they did in '49'er days. A new, wider bridge and new road from Coulterville to it had increased traffic enough for the town to remain a busy crossroads where animals were watered and passengers fed. The town had a novel Oriental atmosphere, since more than 200 Japanese graders were camped at its back door.

In those days before its later control by dams, the Tuolumne River was deep and strong, and regardless of season never carried less than 5,000 miner's inches of water. Already it had risen six inches on the new railroad bridge piers, which would have to withstand a possible six foot crest when the river lashed at them in the spring. But as yet, the piers stood starkly unsupported by any superstructure because there were no rails to lay across it. Non-arrival of the steel rails ordered from the East had necessitated the purchase of ten miles of used track from the West Side Lumber Company on which the two little Porter engines were plying back and forth with cement, structural materials, tools and camp supplies. A flat car excursion had brought 100 visitors to this area of old placer settlements on the north bank of the

Tuolumne River, but until the railroad bridge was complete this was the end of train operation.

The Japanese graders crossed the Tuolumne River each morning that winter on wagons loaded with tools and supplies to complete the level section of the Yosemite Short Line on the south bank and to continue grading up Priests canyon. At this same time construction work was completed to the snow line on the Sugar Pine railroad and, in the spring, grading continued on both these extensions. A survey crew was encamped at Big Oak Flat to continue location work toward Yosemite Park. This meant three construction and engineering crews working over fifty miles apart on Sierra railroad branches in early 1906.

While construction crews on the Yosemite Short Line were crossing the river each day to cut and fill into Moccasin, Groveland and the Cavagnero ranch above there, strapping young Joe Cavagnero rode down Priests grade each day to keep a date with a little Porters locomotive at the Jacksonville end of the tracks. This was the start of a lifetime affair between Joe and steam locomotives, for he spent the best part of thirty-six years as one of the Sierra's most capable engineers. Most of that time he sat at the controls of bigger locomotives on the main line because his first love, the little Porter engines, were doomed to curtailed narrow gauge operations. But for Joe, at least, 1906 was a pleasurable year.

On New Years Day in 1906, the Sonora *Union Democrat* carried an editorial:

"Tuolumne County enters the New Year as auspiciously as any other interior county in the West. Cold weather keeps mining at a standstill but this is temporary and, as there is no crop to spoil in a gold mine, it is only a delay. Soulsbyville, Confidence, Carters, Big Oak Flat and Groveland will again make good. The pocket claims near Sonora and Columbia look splendid so bumper crops from gold-spot quartz are expected. Our lumber interests are an important factor in the state's greatness. Ranchers, stockmen and businessmen are prospering and our banks are gaining in deposits and business."

While this sounded somewhat like barking in the dark, the first and last statements in it were essentially truthful and were reflected in the activity of the Sierra Railway. Freight and passengers were profitably carried over its seventy-nine miles making connections with two great western railroad systems at Oakdale. The Southern Pacific's freight yards there switched full merchandise cars and carload lots to and from Sierra tracks while passenger coaches went through to Stockton or San Francisco. The Santa Fe's "dinky" (two coaches and a locomotive) shuttled passengers from Oakdale to Riverbank to join luxurious main line trains consisting of dining and pullman cars as well as regular and second class coaches. "Go Sierra and Santa Fe to San Francisco arriving at 2:30 p.m." was the Sierra Railroad's stepped up schedule which led the Oakdale *Leader* to report:

"The Santa Fe took forty-five passengers yesterday [March 7, 1906] with tickets to Los Angeles. People are learning the advantage of this line. The S.P. sent their usual coach loads of passengers into the hills and picked up an extra coach load of passengers coming from the hills to a production of *Ben Hur* showing in Stockton. Our Sierra is a popular line."

Passenger train Conductor Long had resigned and Jim Burgess, who had worked for Bullock previously in the south, filled Long's post at the tempting pay of $125.00 a month. Jim, like Engineer George Wright, was to hold this position to the end of the Sierra's passenger service. Walter Baker was then fireman on the *No. 6* and George York, brakeman. The latter would be replaced first by T. Mercer and then by Elmer Bonquist, who also became a fixture on this train. Two daily westbound freight trains were hauling a preponderance of lumber and ores with occasionally other sizeable shipments, such as three boxcar loads of California redberries that were shipped Sonora to San Francisco for the past holidays. Eastbound freight was largely oil, machinery and merchants' supplies. Recently 6000 poles were cut, peeled and shipped by the Standard Lumber Company to Calaveras County mines over the Angels Branch. But mine supplies were not being hauled as regularly as in the past, and the railroad, like everyone else, hoped for an upswing in mining.

The most read column in a Sonora paper, "Tuolumne's Gold Fields" reported such bits of news in 1906 as the following:

"T. A. Fisher, mining and railroad capitalist, bought a one-sixth interest in the Black Oak Mine for $50,000. Twenty-two dollar rock is being taken from the Lady Washington's tunnel near Carters. Fred Sutton has bonded the Atlas Mine on Jackass Hill (now called Burro Heights), and is unwatering the main shaft. — The Harvard Mine at Jamestown is virtually shut down but with pumps running to keep it free of water. It is too valuable to lay idle for long.— The once prolific Omega Mine, north of Rawhide, sold for $25,000. The Swerer Mine at Tuttletown was bought by a Los Angeles company and will be reopened. The body of Will Liddle, foreman of the Rawhide Mine killed 950 feet below the surface, was taken to Sonora by Coroner Burden. The Grizzley Mine in the East Belt picked up the old vein and rushed into the blue ribbon class.— The north shaft of the Soulsby Mine was pumped out but it is difficult to get crews to do driftwork in this dangerous mine."

The Cornish miners not only saw the dangers of the Soulsby Mine at this time, but also the handwriting on the wall that foretold the not too distant closing of this mine. Around 1906, many of them began hijacking in earnest. Thousands of dollars worth of gold was stored in tobacco cans, buried under trees and otherwise hidden as future insurance for these men and their children, now rooted in foreign soil.

Another local resource pertinent to railroad interests at this time was water for power. In February, 1906, the following sarcastic item appeared in a Sonora newspaper:

"At last San Francisco supervisors acknowledge they dismally failed to win their fight for a water supply from this county. They only wanted the Hetch Hetchy system which meant the Tuolumne River. They admit the thousands of dollars spent trying to get Tuolumne County water has been thrown away. It is suggested that they flim-flam some other mountain county out of its greatest asset."

Sonorans who thought they could not be flim-flammed by city slickers would soon have to admit that San Francisco had the county's Tuolumne River watershed and that the prior sale of the Tuolumne County Water and Electric Power Company's vast holdings for $500,000 to the Stanislaus Electric Power Company was one in a series of steps by which the county's water power ultimately became a part of the Pacific Gas and Electric Company's system.

Due to productive East Belt mines, Carters was still a going mining town. The Tuolumne *Prospector*, previously of Groveland, had set up its printing press there in 1904, and reported that rivalry between Carters and Tuolumne City still kept peaceful citizens off the streets at night. However, there was no interruption to the productivity of the West Side mill or that company's little *No. 1* and *No. 2* Heislers bringing logs to it from ever deeper in the woods.

Jamestown still claimed to be Queen of the Mines. Nearby mills continued to glow and pound day and night as elusive gold veins in rich old mines were worked wider and deeper. Businesses related to the mine were still active on Main Street side by side with saloons and "Back-of-Town." The Willows and National hotels were busier than the austere Nevills Hotel overlooking weed-grown lots in the Pereira addition, but the Nevills still maintained its lavish service and table.

Along the Angels Branch, Tuttletown was reduced to a dozen old homes with Swerer's old-time store still selling goods to employees of nearby mines, such as the Rawhide and Patterson.

The Melones Mine was the wonder of constancy in production among Mother Lode mines, but as that mining spread grew, the straggling barns and farm houses on Carson Hill faced a silent glory hole.

Angels Camp citizens in 1906 were rebuilding with limited income from the mines, after fires had almost destroyed first one side of town and then the other. When both newspaper offices had been burned, such papers as were salvaged were taken with other local records to San Andreas and stored in a barn, there to be sorted and kept in the County Courthouse. Meanwhile the barn went up in smoke, along with most of the historical data of Angels Camp in its fabulously gold-producing prime.

Back along Sierra's main line, Chinese Camp was holding its own due to the still operating Eagle Shawmut Mine, but was concerned over its future as a stage and teaming town when the Yosemite Short Line would go into operation paralleling the Big Oak Flat road stages.

Oakdale, a community of rich farmers, was ready for incorporation and planned to have the town's streets resurveyed, named and systematized. At this busy time, Civil Engineer Newell was asked and had to refuse, temporarily, their proposal that he do this work. Also, there was talk of forming an Oakdale Irrigation District to alleviate the shortage of water for irrigation. The generally poor economy in 1906 was reflected in agricultural Oakdale by produce prices. At that time a carload of "gilt edge" wheat hay could bring $16.50 and the choicest oat hay $14.50 to $12.00 per ton.

This, then, is a partial picture of the communities the Sierra Railway was serving in the spring of 1906, when a tea party of considerable importance was given by Mr. Abiko of the Japanese American Industrial Corporation at Jacksonville. The principal guests were T. S. Bullock and W. H. Newell, both of whom were presented with handsome Japanese tea sets. Abiko advised that his company would fail and could not continue grading the Yosemite Short Line roadbed under the terms of the present contract. Newell considered the work done by these Japanese bosses and laborers on the Yosemite Short Line to have been satisfactorily pursued. He therefore agreed with Abiko that due to the delayed rails and unfortunately heavy winter just past, the contract should be amended and payments increased unless more and bigger equipment could be procured to augment manual labor. Since the Sierra Railway was committed to see the Yosemite Short Line built at the least possible expense, Bullock agreed to call an emergency meeting of the Sierra directors in San Francisco to sanction increased costs. The date for this meeting was set for April 17th, 1906.

In that meeting the pros and cons of the limited finances of the Yosemite Short Line Railway and its bonded dependence on the Sierra Railway were discussed at length. Mr. William Crocker tipped the balance in favor of continued and increased financial backing of the Sierra Railway in such commitments as were deemed necessary. Bullock, having recently bought Prince Poniatowski's interest in the Sierra Railway, was the largest single stockholder, as well as the most determined to build the Yosemite Short Line into forests owned by him and F. J. Solinsky. Therefore, at great personal risk, he seconded the motion to increase the financial responsibilities of the Sierra Railway Company in backing Yosemite Short Line bonds.

Having been present by request at the above directors' meeting, Newell returned to the Palace Hotel that night intending to leave for Jamestown the next day with signed agreements for the more liberal construction contract on the Yosemite Short Line railroad. The completion of this project would not only be an engineering achievement in itself, but held possibilities of future associated engineering work such as the extension of the Yosemite Short Line to the Hetch Hetchy Valley with its great water power potential. Such a possibility, expressed before the board, had carried considerable weight as a deciding factor in the costly continuance of the project. With these hopeful thoughts in his mind and the contracts in his valise, Newell slept soundly until the world turned over under him at 5:00 a.m. on the morning of April 18, 1906.

April 18, 1906, was a day of inestimable disaster in San Francisco, chiefly remembered as "The Fire." But the earthquake alone played villainous tricks up and down the whole central California coast, including damage to railroads. Tracks were shifted, locomotives upset, one engine dumped onto a turntable pit, water tanks toppled and tunnels caved in. Such damage was possible to repair, but the San Francisco earthquake and fire put the Yosemite Short Line to eternal death, although its tracks were hundreds of miles away.

Newell himself had narrowly escaped with his life that morning when a marble mantle crashed beside his bed. Hurriedly dressing, he set out with the intention of depositing his papers in the Sierra Railway Company safe at 229 Crocker Building until he knew the extent of the damage. On the hotel stairs he met an elderly Englishman in bare feet and a long night shirt who dazedly kept repeating, "What's up? I say, what's up?" Finding the old gentleman's room where everything, including clothes, were hopelessly buried under fallen plaster, he turned over his own valise and only change of suit to this stranger before hurrying on with his papers. At the Crocker Building he joined a crew of porters, bankers and others removing all valuables from the bank, which was in the line of fire, and then set out to find Bullock.

Among those outside of San Francisco to whom sparse news of the disaster had filtered through, were Prince Poniatowski and Mr. George Crocker, both of whom happened to be in New York City at the time. Piecing together conflicting accounts received from the West, their concern, next to the safety of family and friends, was for the welfare of the Crocker Bank. This was almost as important to Prince Poniatowski as to Crocker himself, since his own and his entrusted British and French capital were largely in, or involved in, the Crocker Bank and its investments. In an alternate two man vigil on the telephone, they learned first that the bank's securities had been transferred from its downtown location to a safer section of the city, and then that that location was also in the line of fire. As soon as possible, Crocker had his private car put on the fastest train to California. Prince Poniatowski, however, seems to have concluded that San Francisco and all of the West had become a poor financial risk and would so remain for some time to come. Consequently, he requested the Crockers to conclude and close out his remaining investments and commitments in California as expeditiously as possible. Among these were his investments with his old friend Bullock in timberland to be reached by the Yosemite Short Line and in the railroad itself. Recoverable funds were returned to France to satisfy French capitalists whose money had been so heavily promoted by Prince Poniatowski for the Yosemite Short Line Railway Company that it had been necessary to print the bonds in both English and French. (All these bonds were carried and ultimately paid out by the Sierra Railway Company.)

A week after the earthquake Newell left San Francisco with the disheartening word from Bullock and the Crocker interests that, due to financial losses in San Francisco, no further expansion was possible and the two day old agreement with the Yosemite Short Line was temporarily canceled. This was the end of the Yosemite Short Line since, during its construction, time had been of the essence.

The Merced and Yosemite Railroad, promoted in 1904, had begun construction on its eighty mile roadbed up the Merced River to El Portal with a projected side line into the forests of the Mariposa Big Tree area. This shorter line of simpler construction and almost identical objectives had been a competitive threat to the Yosemite Short Line for some time. Now, the Merced and Yosemite Railroad, unaffected by disrupted San Francisco capital, promised the public it would be open for business in May of 1906, (which in fact, it was, with tickets on sale at all Santa Fe stations.) The uninterrupted progress of this line made further thought of the Yosemite Short Line mere folly, although a hard pill for promoters, investors and its chief engineer to swallow.

After returning to Oakdale, Newell told the fathers of that newly incorporated city that he would be available to lay out their modern townsite after all. While there, he met the young engineer for the newly organized Oakdale Irrigation District, R. E. Hartley, whose company desired to utilize Tuolumne County's water and power potential. Since the upper Tuolumne River water sources were still being contended for by the city and county of San Francisco, and since the Stanislaus Electric Power Company already controlled much of Tuolumne County's lower water resources, these engineers discussed possible upper Stanislaus canyon dam sites. One such site was highly recommended by Newell who had seen it as a natural for dam construction during reconnaissance done for the Sugar Pine Railroad when it hoped to become a trans-Sierra Nevada line.

Boarding the Sierra train at Oakdale, Newell rode to Rosasco Junction where he climbed in the cab of one of the little Porters and continued down the doomed Yosemite Short Line to Jacksonville while giving the engineer and fireman the bad news. At Jacksonville, arrangements were made for the Japanese graders to break camp and complete their contract working on a two mile long, 30" roadbed to be used by the Standard Lumber Company's logging operations near Saint's Rest at the 5,000 foot elevation in the Sierra mountains. The Yosemite Short Line locomotives were also to be put onto this piece of roadbed as soon as the first rails were laid. Then riding horseback across the Tuolumne River to the Cavagnero ranch and continuing up Deer Creek along the graded right-of-way toward Big Oak Flat, he turned onto the Defarari ranch and canceled previous arrangements for a summer construction camp which was to have been set up there. After marking material and equipment for re-use, resale or transfer, he arrived back at Rosasco Junction by dusk only to be met with the news that a nearby bridge, named Quigley #2, was on fire. Before the bridge crew arrived, a handful of fire fighters put out the disastrous fire, but for the rest of that night Newell sat on the creek slope advising and hurrying the bridge crew so sustaining timbers would be replaced and other damage repaired in time for the safe passage of early freight and passenger trains out of Jamestown.

The Sierra main line and the Angels Branch continued to ply their routine trade but not without further disaster in that inauspicious year. At 11:00 a.m. on June 26th, the Sierra Railway train dispatcher at Jamestown dispatched an extra freight on the Angels Branch destined for Angels Camp. It was headed by the Sierra's *No. 9* Heisler pulling an oil car next to the tender, followed by a flat car loaded with a traction engine, another flat car loaded with two cords of sawmill slabs, a box car loaded with fifteen tons of giant powder and a flat car carrying machinery and three men. Two of the men were recently employed brakemen, one having been with the Sierra for three months and the other for three days. The third man was a stranger who had bought a ticket to Angels Camp the day before but had missed the daily passenger train. This morning, seeing the extra freight pulling out, he had climbed aboard unsuspecting that he was going closer to the angels of heaven than the Angels to which his ticket read.

Locomotive engineer N. Barton let his dangerous load carefully down the McArdle switchback, crossed over Stanislaus River bridge and, passing Melones without a stop, held his head of steam for a steady climb up Pendola Switch. At Gee Whiz Point, or the top of the grade, Engineer Barton shut off his steam to make a sharp curve and there the dynamite exploded. Though the engine and first three cars of the train stayed on the track, the powder car and empty flat disappeared leaving nothing beneath them but a hole in the ground. The two cars were blown into toothpicks and the two brakemen killed, while the uninvited passenger was thrown forty feet down the bank, miraculously escaping with slight injuries. Engineer Barton and Fireman E. R. Corey were stunned but unhurt, as was Conductor F. A. Hawkins, although he was checking the traction engine for possible slippage at the moment of the explosion and the concussion had literally blown his pants off. One car wheel crashed through the roof of an abandoned building at the Jones Mine across the canyon. Parts of other wheels were imbedded two feet in the bank on one side of the tracks or thrown a half a mile down the ravine. Three ovens in a chlorination plant at the intersection of the railroad with Angels Creek fell in. Owners of this plant later sued the Sierra, bringing the number of damage suits against the railroad, in this case, to four, including $5,760 paid to the man who bought a ticket to Angels, and never quite got there.

The flash of fire, volume of smoke and concussion seen, heard and felt as far away as Stockton, made the accident known long before details were sent to Jamestown by wire from Irvine, where the dead and injured were taken by the *No. 9* engine, in spite of a shattered cab. A wrecking train brought Superintendent Blanton and Dr. C. E. Congdon of Jamestown to the scene two hours later, but meanwhile Newell, who happened to be at Tuttletown, arrived by track car with section boss Azeveda and his crew. The hole was filled in and the roadbed made safe in time for the evening passenger train dispatched two hours late from Jamestown.

In investigating the cause of the accident, it was found that the cars did not jump the track or turn over. The dynamite, consigned to the Angels Iron Works had been five days enroute from the shipping point in Contra Costa County, and evidently had been sidetracked in the hot San Joaquin Valley, which could have caused glycerine to leak from the dynamite boxes and drip down onto the track to spark the explosion. At any rate, carelessness by the train crew was excluded and a positive accident cause not proven.

On the afternoon of this accident a railroad crew at Rosasco's Junction *was* loading one of the Yosemite Short Line engines (Porters) onto a flat car for transportation to the new two-mile long logging railroad at Empire Mills. The engine was hoisted aboard by use of a derrick and hauled, with derrick, up grade to Ralph's Station where a double-header took the load up the steep Sugar Pine railroad to Middle Camp, or the end of that then ten-mile long road. There the Porter was reloaded onto a freight wagon and pulled by eight-horse team over the logging road to Stoddard Springs where it was re-derricked onto Empire City's thirty-inch track which was soon to connect with extended Sugar Pine rails by an incline railroad just above Lyon's Dam. A Porter engine was a comparatively large object to move in the days when an 85 ton Heisler for instance, was a big locomotive, but also since locomotives were the last word in work power then, the success of this move could have led the way for a like undertaking several years later when a locomotive was somehow hauled from the Tuolumne West Side operation to isolated narrow gauge tracks during construction of Relief Dam which is almost at the summit of the Sonora Pass.

The business recession in California after the San Francisco fire was called temporary, but conditions had not improved in mid-1906 when the Sierra tried to coax people in the San Joaquin Valley to use their line by advertisements such as the following:

"Lots of folks will be going to Tuolumne for the Fourth. The train pulls out at 8:00 a.m. with cars full of patriotic throngs off to enjoy the sports and feasts that Tuolumne knows how to offer. It is a delightful ride over the Sierra rails to the high Sierras and a grand barbecue of fresh Tuolumne beef on arrival. Amusements will be log-rolling, rock-drilling contests, Indian races, burro races and a windup at the free dance. No firecrackers, but there will be a hot time in the old town."

At a hearing before the State Board of Equalization, Treasurer Freshman and Auditor Hamblin represented the Sierra Railway regarding the Tax Commission's plan to impose a 4% state tax on the gross earnings of corporations. In the Sierra's case, these men said, this would raise their taxes from $9,000 to $14,000, which they could not afford while the lines' antiquated depots and equipments reduced earnings. The Sierra reported a $20,038.46 net income before betterments and additions on 84.40 miles of track with sidings. This report and that of other short line railroads were taken under advisement, but the tax was later imposed.

As the year 1906 came to a close, the Sierra was to suffer another calamity. On the evening before Christmas Eve, the Sugar Pine railroad construction crews had been paid off as had lumberjacks up in the woods, and all work discontinued until the following spring. As a final clean-up job and to bring usable parts back to the shop, the Sierra's *No. 9* Heisler went to the end of the line at Middle Camp heading a wrecking train. Returning down grade, the train stopped to pick up two wrecked lumber cars and an oil car which had been abandoned after jumping the tracks two weeks before in a snowstorm. The *No. 9* was the engine which had let two freight cars get away on the Angels Branch to crash into the passenger train. Also, two years later, the *No. 9* headed the freight on which a load of dynamite exploded. A new crew under Conductor Ordway, were Engineer Grummet, Fireman Currier and George Condron, who as brakeman, had found all brakes in good shape except those on the oil car. Besides the wrecking crew, consisting of five car repairmen and ten assistants, the Sierra's Superintendent Blanton, two Japanese construction hands and a Chinese camp cook rode as passengers. The train descended five miles without incident, then reached the steep grade above Newell Station, five miles from the Sierra mainline, where the whole train began to roll uncontrolled down the mountain. It was later presumed that oil slushing forward in the oil car on the steep curving grade had given extra momentum to the train running on wet tracks. In any case, Grummet lost control of his engine and became so scared he and the fireman jumped to safety. While the train hurtled on down the grade at increasing speed, two members of the wrecking crew, A. Cholez and J. A. Whitesides, jumped to their death on the rocky canyon side. James Gallagher of Jamestown, who until recently had been night boss at the Dutch Mine, was preparing to jump from the rear door of the wrecking car, when he was struck over the heart by a 4 x 4 car stake which killed him. Sixty feet further down this Horse Shoe Curve, the engine jumped the track and was turned completely around and stripped as it crashed into the bank. Two flatcars and the oil car also jumped the track, but all those aboard who stayed in the wrecking car were unhurt, as those who died would have been had they done likewise.

Glaring and inaccurate accounts of this wreck were printed in all local papers, even to the Stockton *Record* reporting that, "Civil Engineer Newell was so badly injured he was expected to die." Emphasis was put on the record of the *No. 9* Heisler with three wrecks involving seven fatalities, and on the steepness of the grade. On this unchanged roadbed, however, capacity loads were successfully handled over the Sugar Pine (later the Pickering) railroad for thirty-five years afterwards.

"DASTARDLY ATTEMPT TO WRECK SIERRA RAILWAY TRAIN." The above headline appeared in the *Sierra Daily Times* of Sonora on January 8, 1907, only two weeks after the last wreck of *No. 9*. On that Sunday evening as the up passenger train approached Sullivan Creek bridge, Engineer Wright suddenly applied the emergency brake, the air brakes and reversed his engine. The train stopped within inches of a 400 pound steel rail, one end of which was stuck against a main support to the bridge and extended lengthwise between the tracks so the other end of the rail would have struck the *No. 6* engine just above the cow-catcher. Since one man could not have handled a 400 pound rail, more than one fiend was presumed to be involved. In the past five years, three similar attempts had been made to wreck Sierra trains near Cooperstown. In those instances the railroad management had thought the less publicity the better, but in this instance $1,000 was offered for any information leading to the arrest of the criminals. No one collected and no arrests were made.

An accident to a freight train was averted later that year by Miss Josephine Fassler of Sonora, who flagged down the train just ahead of a burned out bridge on Curtis Creek not far from the lime plant. For her heroic act, Mr. Anthony Arnold, on behalf of the Sierra railroad, presented Miss Fassler with a gold watch.

The year 1907 had come in like a lion, bringing heavy snows to areas in Tuolumne County which normally saw only a few flurries. Two feet of snow on Buck Horn Mountain disrupted schedules on the Sierra railroad. Mines stayed full of water and lumbering was late to start in the mountains. The resulting delays in wages and bill paying in Mother Lode towns brought hard times to the area even before such conditions became nation wide. Among industries hardest hit were the railroads, and 1907 became known as the year of financial crises and railroad receiverships. Hundreds of short lines comparable in size to the Sierra Railway were dissolved never to operate again, while the largest railroads reduced expenditures to a minimum. In his *Centennial Story of the Pacific Gas and Electric Company of California,* C. M. Coleman said:

"In 1907, San Francisco was pulling itself out of the ruins. The problem of financing was universal and the leaders of P.G. and E. in serious condition. The company was reorganized and the new president encouraged to gain time by means of receivership. Instead, an assessment was levied on common and preferred stock to raise cash for immediate needs. Directors assessed themselves ten dollars a share, which assessments were all paid before the unhealthy economic condition of the year reached a climax in the market crash of October, 1907."

As the financial ships of big companies were kept afloat by every possible device, the Sierra's financial ship rocked in its smaller way on the rough waters of that time and was kept afloat by strict economy. The Sierra's *No. 18,* a Baldwin of 2-8-0 wheel arrangement, purchased new in 1906, was the last locomotive purchased by the company for nine years. All rolling stock was maintained, repaired and often rebuilt in the Jamestown shops under Master Mechanic Ben Stein. To minimize accidents and reduce road maintenance costs, sixty-pound rails were spiked down on the entire mainline and the growing Sugar Pine Railroad. It was anticipated that this heavier rail would be partially paid for by consecutive shipments following a block of rough marble weighing eight tons which was hauled by fourteen mules to the Sonora depot and consigned to San Diego, California. Additional shipments did not materialize and the rails were long carried on the red side of the company ledger.

Besides supervising maintenance of the Sierra railroad during this static period, Newell laid out the streets, sewer and water systems of Oakdale and located the Stockton and Jenny Lind interurban railroad. The promoters had hopes of ultimately extending this road to Oakdale to become another paying outlet for the Sierra. This line was built to Jenny Lind but never reached Oakdale.

Regardless of the times, warehousemen Hales and Symons opened a large ice plant in Sonora, and Standard Lumber Company enlarged their Sonora box factory to fill a contract with the California Fruit Growers Association for 1,000,000 orange boxes annually, all to be shipped out by the Sierra.

While Bullock was involved in the million dollar promotion of a Northern California Lumber Company with an allied railroad to work his timberland in Tuolumne and Mariposa counties in 1907 and 1908, the Sierra railroad was involved in a war over freight and passenger rates. Hard times in Tuolumne County were blamed on the Sierra's "exorbitant" rates and it was said that no new business could afford to come into the area at existing transportation costs. "Think," one paper said, "of paying one dollar for the privilege of riding from Sonora to Tuolumne,— or $2.75 to Oakdale. This is nine and one-ninth cents per mile. Other states and parts of this state have a three cents a mile rate for passengers and are prospering."

Another paper said:

"Rate on Sheep Mighty Steep.— An importer of sheep shipped sixty bucks Modesto to Stockton for $6.48. From Stockton to Sonora $53.76. He wanted to ship them to Middle Camp over the Sugar Pine but instead of paying $30 freight decided to walk them. And did. The Sierra lists itself in the red for over 30,000 bonds due to pecuniary obligation such as interest on funded debt and interest bearing bonds. Why should this excuse exorbitant freight and passenger rates? Rather than see the line go into receivership we suggest it be sold to some real railroad men."

True, Sierra freight rates were higher than those on the Southern Pacific and Santa Fe for transportation reasons understandable to the Railroad Commission, which investigated and sanctioned its charges. And true, the Sierra was encumbered by obligations due on the aborted Yosemite Short Line as well as on loans from the Crocker Bank. Luckily, the supply of timber outside of national forests appeared limitless in Tuolumne County where lumbermen were giving more regard to second growth trees, and the Forestry Service was insisting that trees be felled with less abandon to decrease fire hazards due to discarded trunks and trimmings. The West Side Lumber Company would cut at its peak into 6000 feet elevations near Lake Eleanor, and the Standard Lumber Company was milling 100,000 feet of lumber a day at their Cold Springs mill alone since its rebuilding after a fire. This lumber freight hauled out of the county by the Sierra Railroad kept the line going.

Important contributory freight came from the Sonora Lime and Cement Works now directed by the Knowles brothers of Sonora whose rebricked kilns turned out 500 barrels a day. F. J. Ralph brought 1200 more apple trees to his twenty-six acre orchard at Ralph's Station, which were shipped in free; but the apples were shipped out at usual rates to points as far away as New York's Central Station.

The Hetch Hetchy water project for the city and county of San Francisco, which had been controversial for five years, was now up before Congress to approve the impounding of water in a national forest. In San Francisco the people's intention to own their own water was contested not only by the Spring Valley Water Company in its attempt to continue serving the city, but by other private and public interests. When Mr. William Hammond Hall of San Francisco had located three reservoir sites with thousands of inches of water originating above Lake Eleanor and Hetch Hetchy Valley for irrigational purposes, the Tuolumne *Independent* concluded:

"The companies represented by Wm. Ham. Hall and the City of San Francisco both claim the head waters of our Tuolumne River. San Francisco wants the water to drink. Hall wants it for power, agriculture and mining. If Hall wins out, San Francisco will be compelled to go back to steam beer or Spring Valley water."

Meanwhile, an eminent mining engineer, John Hays Hammond, tied up several Tuolumne County water and power companies for mining purposes, while his associate, E. A. Wiltsee, put a half million dollar gold dredge to work on the Tuolumne River. Also, the Sierra Club of California brought an injunction against San Francisco for plans to destroy one of California's greatest scenic assets, the "sublime Hetch Hetchy Valley."

Such divergent interests were impeding San Francisco's Hetch Hetchy project when U. S. Government engineers came to California in 1909 to ascertain whether San Francisco was, in fact, dependent on the distant Hetch Hetchy water supply.

While this immense project hung in the balance, F. S. McGovern, and G. B. and W. L. Price of Sonora instigated a small irrigation project with intent to build a reservoir at Don Pedro Bar in the lower Tuolumne River to impound 24,000 inches of floodwater during May and June to benefit ranchers between Cooperstown and Warnerville. Work was simultaneously begun by the Oakdale Irrigation District with $1,000,000 promoted to flume and tunnel water to the Knights Ferry and Oakdale farmers by use of a dam on the Stanislaus River below Melones. And to cap the climax in water development, D. H. Steinmetz and T. S. Bullock filed on 40,000 inches of water in the North Fork of the Tuolumne River to be used for irrigation between Cooperstown, Paulsell and Oakdale, by a diverting dam at Cold Springs millsite. This promotion grew to such proportions, in print, that orchardists and ranchers from Middle Camp and Confidence to Paulsell and Warnerville expected to convert their dry land into blooming gardens. Bullock and the Sierra had Newell make an engineering study of this proposition. The Sierra's primary interest was in freight revenues. This promotion was not intended to interfere with the Don Pedro damsite project or the water desires of the city of San Francisco on the main fork of the Tuolumne River.

Realizing the financial risk in over-extending himself at this time, Bullock sold his timberland to the south and returned to enlarge his holdings in the prosperous Standard Lumber Company. By quiet negotiations between that lumber company and the California Forestry Department, 600,000,000 feet of timber was purchased in the Cow Creek section (above Cold Springs) of the reserve. The area was to be cut, logged and cleared according to laws laid down by the Forest Service, with rangers in attendance. This was reported to be the largest sale of standing timber ever made in the state.

In December, 1909, the Sierra Railway Company celebrated its tenth anniversary. The weekly *New Era* of Tuolumne reported:

"Ten years ago the last spike was driven on the main Sierra track in our town. Gorges and peaks then reverberated with the shriek of the first locomotive seen here. It was the quickening spirit of labor and capital laid over our chaotic expanse of resources. An achievement opening the vistas of future progress. Old timers may still regret the passing of the twenty-mule team but all will admit a larger population thrives today than could have been possible under the old regime. Our Sierra railroad not only supplies our needs but covers the varied aspects of our foothill country. Beginning at this end with a hundred mile view from Buck Horn Summit across the great San Joaquin Valley to Mt. Diablo and even Tamalpais, then through mine and cattle land to the rolling wheat fields surrounding Oakdale at the other end."

Yes, the Sierra railroad had friends as well as enemies. This was proven at such times as that of the 1909 flood when severe storms not only washed out roadbed and culverts, but, also, the Woods and Sullivan Creek trestles on the active mainline. On these occasions, local people offered teams and other free assistance in transporting people and needed freight between sections of washed out track. At this time, a well-known man of Tuolumne named Fipps had died in Stockton and his body was being shipped back home. The casket had been transferred across Woods Creek to a train waiting on the other side, but an impasse was reached at Sullivans Creek where not only the railroad bridge but the wagon road was completely destroyed. Three days passed before it was possible to "take Fipps home," by which time, it was admitted, without rancor, that "a body can get to smelling pretty bad in four days."

In 1910, at midnight the roundhouse in Jamestown burned to the ground. When the fire was discovered, flames were bursting from every part of the structure. Engines *No. 4* and *No. 9*, dismantled in the roundhouse, were badly damaged. The *No. 2*, *No. 3*, and *No. 7* standing outside were saved as were other buildings by employees and every male of the area who contributed his fire-fighting best. Bullock's Thomas Flyer was pulled to safety but one track car burned and six machinists lost all their tools. It was estimated that $10,000 would cover the cost of destruction, but this fire, started by spontaneous combustion in oily rags left in the heat of that October night, was not without benefit. An electrically wired round house with eight stalls, two of them 70 feet long with 4 x 28 foot drop pits 5½ feet deep, replaced the old one. The *No. 9* which had had more than its share of bad luck, was rebuilt in the Jamestown shops and used as a switch engine in the Tuolumne yards. The old *No. 4* also was rebuilt for the same service at Jamestown.

The recently enforced sale of the Rawhide and App mines had left only a half dozen big mines in full operation in the area served by Sierra tracks. Some carloads of Columbia marble were hauled to the Jeffersonville spur by Holt 75 Caterpillars and consigned to the San Francisco Ferry Building to replace old wooden floors. Lumber shipments remained high but it was doubtful that the railroad could survive on them alone.

High hopes were raised in 1910 in Oakdale and Knights Ferry by reports of oil discovery in those areas. Several wells were sunk and some gas produced but no oil. Groveland townspeople anxiously watched the Hetch Hetchy project believing it would bring them prosperity if passed. At a mass meeting there two hundred people agreed to build a wagon road from Stevens Bar (Jacksonville Bridge) to the mouth of the Hetch Hetchy Valley and maintain it during construction if such action would facilitate the project. For them, like the Sierra Railway, activity on proposed water power projects in Tuolumne County was the only bright spot on the gloomy horizon.

CHAPTER NINE

The years 1910 to 1920 continued depressed in the area served by the Sierra Railway Company although trains operated without interruption. World War I had little effect on this area's enterprises except to render the coup de grâce to the mines, already staggering under government regulations and union demands.

Locomotives numbered *2, 4, 6, 7, 11, 12* and *18* were equipped with electric headlights during these years, and *7* and *18* with an air pump for brakes. The little bobtailed combination coach on the Angels Branch was entirely rebuilt and electric lights and steam heat added to passenger and mail cars. These improvements, plus additional equipment bought for the carpenter shop, roundhouse, blacksmith shop and machine shop, cost the Sierra Railway Company almost $22,000. That little old lady, the *No. 3* Rogers, was overhauled with new headlights and air brakes costing another $2,000. One of the Sierra's electricians changed many old acetylene lights along the line to electricity.

A young machinist employed for Sierra work in 1910, John Keagy, had learned his trade with an eastern hometown friend, Walter Chrysler, later to become famous in automobile design and development. Like his friend, Keagy was an enthusiast of the gasoline motor. Though adept in the shop repairing steam equipment, he enjoyed caring for Hamblin's Maxwell, Bullock's Thomas Flyer, the old Winton and other track automobiles. Every two weeks, Keagy drove Harry Guilds, the Sierra's paymaster, in a converted Model T Ford over the whole line. This familiar and welcome pair stopped at each station and section house as well as at the boxcar home of the bridge crew, which was shunted from trestle to culvert to bridge while repairs were being made.

In the long dry summertime, when all of California was apprehensive about fires, the lumber companies observed the strictest fire prevention rules possible. Nevertheless, Standard Lumber Company suffered a major forest fire and the loss of their Empire Mill in 1913. This was costly not only to them but to the Sierra railroad in reduced freight. In that year also the Sierra's Jamestown depot burned down with all the company's office records, including Newell's location notes, profiles, alignments and realignments. With the best of intentions, typewriters and furniture were tossed from second story windows to become rubble on the ground. The depot was rebuilt with its original two stories but without the oriental upcurling corners that had united it architecturally with the Nevills Hotel.

By late 1914, Bullock's name appeared on the company roster as both president and manager. He was in his San Francisco home on the summer weekend in 1915 when the Nevills Hotel, symbol of past extravagance, burned to the ground. Everyone in the hotel escaped the conflagration although one drunk had to be carried to safety from the third floor. All available Sierra employees as well as many townspeople joined volunteer fire brigades with hose carts, hook and ladders, and other fire fighting equipment from the surrounding towns in attempts to smother the flames. Even Cassie, long time head of the hotel's housekeeping department, was seen frantically pouring chamber pots of water onto the fire while the hotel bartender neatly stacked his best liquor on the railroad tracks. But all efforts proved futile. The result was not a direct Sierra Railway Company loss, but as a housing unit, a passenger convenience and an aesthetic attraction the destruction of the hotel was a blow to the company and the community. Within an hour after the blaze started a dozen or so quartz pillars, some marble flooring and a few singed palm and walnut trees near the unburned tank house were all that was left of the famous Nevills. The new Sierra depot looked small and starkly alone beside the blackened area where once had been elegance, gardens and throngs of fashionable people.

During the summer and fall of 1915, when automobile drivers were bravely experimenting with this method of transportation, cars carrying extra gasoline and plenty of spare tires traveled the Oakdale to Sonora road with increasing frequency. Mr. Charlie

Ellinwood, a dashing cattleman with a Stutz Bearcat, had to cross Sierra tracks to get to his ranch below Cooperstown. After a day of business, tire changing and other thirst causing delays in Oakdale, Ellinwood was apt to cross the Sierra tracks without waiting to open the barbed-wire fence gate. The next day the Sierra Railway would get the scribbled message to send him the bill.

The stages into Yosemite Valley were still horse drawn, although, in 1913, the Forestry Service permitted automobiles to enter the park via the Coulterville and Wawona roads, and in 1915, largely due to the efforts of Senator John B. Curtin, they were allowed to enter from the Big Oak Flat road. It was difficult to say in those days on such roads whether a chauffeur, or the driver of frightened horses, was the worse off when they met.

Needed revisions were being made on the Sierra's mainline such as filling in small bridges and replacing the Woods Creek trestle with a concrete arch 107 feet long and 22 feet high, necessitating 1800 feet of realignment. After eight bridged culverts were filled in, only the Sullivan Creek trestle and the 100 feet high Rock River bridge were left on the main line. Before it was filled in, the Quigley #2 bridge was the scene of a near accident. Whenever eastbound freight was extra heavy, cars were usually set out on the siding at Cooperstown to reduce the load going up Canyon Tank grade. Early next morning the freight engine would return down grade to pick them up. One such morning *No. 20*, a brand new "2-8-0" Baldwin, with Frank Miller at the controls and Jim Baker firing, was making good time running ahead of the passenger train when they rounded the curve below Rosasco Junction. Lo! There ahead of them, glistening with dew, were two shining streaks of rails, all intact except that there was nothing underneath. The Quigley bridge had burned to ashes, leaving these bare rails like a trap in an engineer's nightmare. Fortunately, the locomotive was able to come to a grinding stop before the phantom crossing and remain there as a bulwark while signals were set out and whistle warnings sounded to alert the oncoming passenger train. In all probability the faster moving passenger train would not have been as fortunate as the lone engine in spite of Engineer Wright's usual alertness.

While improvements were made along the Sierra's line, work was resumed and advanced on the Sugar Pine railroad, which now ran twenty miles into the woods and was graded to Jenesse's Flat at milepost 22. Work within the snow line was done in the summers when construction camps took on a happy atmosphere of vacation-land resorts. The Mono wagon road at that time of year was often blinding with dust from hundreds of head of cattle driven to summer feeding in the high altitudes of government land. But logging work and railroad construction camps were now far back from that road. Evening fires burning in forest clearings near construction tents induced song and laughter from hearty young men whose energies had not been spent by the day's surveying, grading, track laying or timbering.

The Rushing Meadows construction camp at about 4,000 feet elevation was too prettily and healthfully located to be enjoyed by men alone. Or so the prostitutes of Jamestown and Sonora must have decided, for a group of the girls moved into a vacant cabin not far from camp. It was not long before the superintendent decisively ended their stay. A little party was arranged one evening with refreshments at the cook tent and music by two young men who harmonized with guitar and harmonica. The camp boss made sure all the girls were present and the party in full swing before a stick of dynamite was set off in their cabin. With their "house" demolished, the homeless females had no recourse but to return to town.

In his supervision of construction on the Sugar Pine railroad Newell was keeping in mind Bullock's original scheme when he asked to have the first surveys made. For Bullock still hinted that this logging road might some day form a continuation of the Sierra mainline reaching across the Sierra Nevada Mountains to a connection with the Virginia and Truckee Railroad in the state of Nevada.

In those optimistic days some twelve years past, Newell had made such surveys and inspected the route chosen by Theodore D. Judah, the only man ever to have engineered a railroad across those peaks. After reviewing "Crazy" Judah's 7,000 foot high Donner Pass section of the Central Pacific railroad requiring thirty-seven miles of snowsheds at $25,000 a mile, then adding the enormous operating and maintenance costs to construction costs, he had put his mind to a different type of railroad crossing over the 9,000 foot high Sonora Pass. This was to be a four mile tunnel at the 6,000 foot elevation through rocky crags just north of Mono Road, which would cost little more than Judah's location and be much cheaper in the long run because it would be practically snow free. It was a daring plan. The chances for such ambitious schemes ever to mature had admittedly dwindled, by 1915, to the vanishing point.

In 1913, Congress had given San Francisco the right to impound water in magnificent Hetch Hetchy Valley. And in 1914, an agreement had been made between the Sierra Railway Company and the city and county of San Francisco whereby a projection to be named the Hetch Hetchy Railroad would branch from the Sierra tracks and use part of the defunct Yosemite Short Line grade as its right-of-way to Groveland. From there the Hetch Hetchy Railroad was to turn a little north of easterly to the lower end of Hetch Hetchy Valley where a dam was to be built. This 68 mile standard gauged railroad for dam and aqueduct construction was approved in 1915.

Construction began on the Hetch Hetchy Railroad at milepost 26 on the Sierra main line in 1916. The eight mile descent from there to the Tuolumne River was more gradual than that of the higher Yosemite Short Line route, but the two lines met before crossing the river and climbing up Priests grade to Groveland on the old right-of-way. From there the new line ascended steeply to Poopenaut Pass at 5064 feet elevation and then sloped down six miles to the O'Shaughnessy Dam site in Hetch Hetchy Valley. Tracks were at last laid over the old short line bridge piers when this railroad crossed the Tuolumne River that year, bringing construction men and materials as far as Moccasin Creek where a huge power plant was being built. The six locomotives used belonged to the Hetch Hetchy Railroad, although the Sierra's geared Shay engines were rented and many Sierra cars used.

Before the Hetch Hetchy Railroad reached the dam site, work was slowed by U.S.A.'s declared participation in World War I. Quicksilver used in the recovery of gold went from $70 to $225 a flask. This and other increased costs shut down the few big mines that had managed to continue day and night operation until then. Among these were the Harvard and Shawmut mines whose closing stopped pay checks for hundreds of families. Even the Melones Mines became inactive after taking twenty million dollars from their Stanislaus Canyon operations, although work was resumed in 1918, when the Carson Hill Mines Company reworked the old Morgan Mine from underground. The awesome glory hole at Carson Hill was then extended as ore was pulled out through the Melones tunnel. But very few mines were re-opened in Tuolumne or Calaveras counties. When most of them sold their equipment to the wartime government for junk, it marked the end of that spectacular and fascinating era called "Golden Days on the California Mother Lode." Such an era may never again occur in the world. Such careless indifference to gold and the value of it by the very men giving their lives in the search for it. Such exciting conditions with inexplicable risks and personal independence would be impossible in today's era of re-strictions and regimentations."

During the war, Bullock's activities in Tuolumne County were curtailed. His position as general manager of the Sierra Railway was assumed in 1917 by C. N. Hamblin, previously auditor, secretary and treasurer. The railroad's routine activities continued un-interrupted, but, like those of its customers, greatly reduced. 1918 saw the last car overturn on their now well-ballasted, graded and heavily railed right-of-way, but by this time passenger service had been reduced to the regular one up (eastbound) and one down (westbound) daily trains.

In 1918, the Turn Back Inn at Tuolumne City suffered the same fate as had the Nevills Hotel. In spite of its wide green lawns and excellent water supply, this shingled building went up like a torch with nothing left within two hours to prove its past exist-ence. Again there was no loss of life, but as in Jamestown, the Sierra trains now pulled into another isolated depot without the hospitable surroundings that had charmed tourists and new-comers of the past.

Shortly afterward, the engine house in Tuolumne City was torn down and six engines sold by the Sierra railroad. Of these, the *Nos. 9, 10* and *11* were sold to the Sugar Pine railroad. But four other Baldwins were ordered. *Nos. 22* and *28,* bought new, worked on the line for at least twenty years. The *No. 24,* also a 2-8-0, was bought second hand and retained for over thirty years, but *No. 26,* the only 2-6-0 type ever operated by the Sierra railroad, was sold two years later.

In the winter of 1919, construction on the Hetch Hetchy Railroad was again slowed at high elevations by snow. Work on the Moccasin Powerhouse, however, was completed at its low elevation near the Tuolumne River which was to become the site of a yearly production of $2,000,000 worth of electricity by San Francisco's Hetch Hetchy plant.

In 1919, the Standard Lumber Company and its Sugar Pine Railroad were saved from foreclosure by a loan from a Suisun banker, but Bullock's investment in it ceased at that time. Shortly afterward, in 1920, this lumber company had a fourth serious setback when another mountain mill burned down. Insurance companies would no longer insure mountain sawmills, so a new mill was built only three miles from Sonora. The site on the Sierra railroad was named Standard City, where construction began on a new box factory and employees' homes in addition to the mill.

Bullock's severance from this lumber company ended Newell's connection with the Sugar Pine Railroad, and its future extensions zigzagged through the forests with the sole object of logging. The sale of the Standard Lumber Company and the Sugar Pine Railroad was negotiated in 1921 to eastern interests and became the Pickering Lumber Company and the Pickering Railroad.

The 1920's started on a very sad note among Sierra Railway employees, executives and many men of distinction all over the West. In that year T. S. Bullock, heart and head of the railroad, as well as the prime mover in so many other Tuolumne County promotions, passed away. His death came at the end of that era when men of daring enterprise, in the West, indulged in free-wheeling business tactics which spurred them on to do or die, independently.

The Hetch Hetchy Railroad was completed at a cost of $3,000,-000 in 1918. It was operated as a common carrier by the city and county of San Francisco, and the town of Groveland had a spurt of new life while railroad shops and construction workers' homes were located there. Even after the railroad discontinued service and sold its rolling stock, considerable activity continued in Groveland while nine miles of track from Mather to the dam were torn up and the grade made into a scenic highway.

By then the Sierra's main line stations — Arnold, Paulsell, Keystone and Black Oak — were retired as passenger stops and later used as freight sidings. Still struggling under its bonded indebtedness, and facing severe freight reductions in the 1920's, the Sierra railroad made continued effort by excursions and improved service to maintain sufficient passenger patronage to keep that department self-supporting. The Angels Branch had been low in power units since the *No. 9* Heisler and *No. 11* Shay had been sold, but two Prairie type Baldwin 2-6-2's had been ordered specially built for that run. One, the Sierra's *No. 30*, came onto the Angels Branch in 1922, and the *No. 32* followed in 1923. Of these 75 ton short engines whose rods connected to the piston rods and extended to rear driving wheels, the *No. 30* was to become the most colorful engine in Sierra railroad history. At first, it hauled a combined freight, mail and passenger train over to Angels Camp each evening and back the next morning. When the *No. 32* took over the freight trains on the Angels Branch, *No. 30* pulled only passengers and mail in the short coach and bobtailed combination that made up the Angels Branch passenger train. On Sundays in the summertime, excursions were pulled over this line by both engines.

Excursions continued to be big events in Tuolumne County, for the day of privately owned automobiles and regular bus lines had not yet arrived. Buses made regular summer trips into Yosemite Valley over the Big Oak Flat road and up to the P. G. and E. lake at Pine Crest, but such comparatively small carriers made uncertain schedules over bad roads, and "specials" were not available.

The railroad was still the best way to the ball games between teams from rival towns such as Sonora and Angels Camp. Young and old, rich and poor paid the dollar round-trip fare to ride in the Sierra's open picnic cars to these games where each home team was backed one hundred percent. The local band, the team, rooters and their best girls climbed aboard trains waving lunch boxes and parasols and calling out jokes and bets. As one fan recalled:

"Always a few would be liquored up and there would be a few Indians and Chinamen who joined the shouting, fighting, drinking, cussing, singing and the laughter of good humor prevailing through it all. At the switchbacks the clowns could always be depended upon to start walking up the track and defying the engineer to overtake them. The best and worst were all fans among whom hundreds of dollars were wagered, and the Sierra train ended by waiting an hour past departure time for those who could find the saloons in Angels Camp but not the train afterwards."

One local young man who started playing on the Sonora team and also had worked at fence building for the Sierra railroad was Earl "Hap" Collard. In the early 1920's, Hap was the idol of Big League fans and his popularity in Tuolumne and Calaveras County was to stand him in good stead years later when he took over the famous old Smoke Saloon in Jamestown, which he still owns and operates.

In 1921, the 18th Amendment brought Prohibition. This law was difficult enough to enforce among city people but among rugged foothill individuals of '49'er background, it was unthinkable and quite generally ignored, at least in the first years. Saloons and gambling ran wide open and were frequented by everyone including local sheriffs and peace officers until the "Feds" came on the scene. Even then, these activities were only temporarily closed down. When the situation became really tight, more ingenious methods of getting around this law were devised than the city speak-easy. In Angels Camp a shoe store became unusually popular. There a man could ask for a pair of boots, size nine, for instance, and be handed a shoe box containing a reasonably aged bottle of bourbon.

In 1926, during Prohibition, the first annual Jumping Frog Jubilee was held in Angels Camp. In those days the celebration was held on the main street where temperatures could rise to 104°. Dark saloons carpeted with beer-dampened sawdust set up other thirst quenchers besides beer. Excursions were run by the railroad from Tuolumne County to the Jubilee as well as to baseball games, but profits from them hardly made up for dwindling patronage on the regular Sierra trains. The Angels Branch had become a happy-go-lucky little line far removed from the busy quartz mining days for which it was intended.

The *No. 30*, ahead of the passenger unit, had by then become known as "Gus's Special." Gus Swanson had been at the controls for the past five years and had put his mark on it — a white star painted on the smoke box in front of the boiler. In that time, Waldo Bernard and Bill Scott had fired with Gus, with J. B. Harris and Charlie Smedley as consecutive conductors. It was rumored that when a cash fare was paid on the train, two-bits of it might be tossed up at the bell cord. If it stuck there the railroad got it, if not, it was pocketed. If such were the case, the company probably knew so; at that time a few dollars made or lost on this line were not worth checking.

Gus Swanson was affectionately conceded to be a good, dependable engineer as well as a comical character. Besides painting a white star on the *No. 30*'s smoke box, Gus wore little bells on his engineer's cap, which, he said, kept him from being bothered with balls of wax that he otherwise heard rolling around in his head. When the Jumping Frog Jubilee was on, however, Gus discarded his cap for a wide yellow hat and let the wax balls roll!

His cab was his house, in which no hot water went to waste. He kept a tub of it in the cab where he often washed and hung his clothes. At such times, the passenger train might be seen crossing the Melones trestle with Gus's wash flying in the breeze. Gus could even maneuver the switchbacks with his feet soaking in this tub of hot water. He also had a special talent with a steam whistle. His signals were varied and musical and understood by everyone along the line. Folks at the section house in Tuttletown, the mine foreman's children at Melones, the mayor of Angels Camp or Hamblin, manager of the Sierra railroad — all waved to the man in the cab of Gus's Special.

Gus had a fine record for safety and knew what his engine could do. In bad weather he would lean far out of the cab to judge the roadbed and sometimes left the cab to the fireman while he got out to walk along beside the engine to mark bad spots for the attention of the section crew. Once when he was hanging on the steps of the cab, intently watching the road, a cattle guard wiped him off and the little train went merrily off without him. Gus had to be a good judge of timing to meet schedules while slowing or even stopping on the grades and curves of the Angels Branch. On icy winter mornings coming down the Pendola Grade, the brakeman would sit over the cowcatcher sprinkling sand from a tomato can onto the sharply curved rails which the sand box of these rod engines could not reach. Barring slippage, however, the little passenger train had no trouble making the grades of the Stanislaus canyon crossing, and regular passengers relaxed while riding with Gus at the controls, whatever his eccentricities may have been.

Conditions on the Sierra's main line passenger train in the 1920's were about as relaxed as those on the Angels Branch. In the spring the east or westbound train might stop on wide sweeps of foothill country above Oakdale to allow passengers to get off and pick armloads of California poppies that turned the whole countryside bright orange in that season. Or Conductor Burgess might stop the train to stop a baby's crying, warming a bottle of milk in the cab and returning it to the mother. The train often came to a stop somewhere along the line to pick up a rancher or a rancher's daughter, such as one of the Gatzman girls, who could wave the engineer down with less than a handkerchief.

Fares in those days were sold on the train as well as at the depot. Tickets on the Angels Branch were white, those sold at Sierra main line depots were red, while Conductor Burgess sold blue ones on his train. Gold coins and silver cartwheels were the common means of exchange in the West, where most people had never seen paper money.

The 1920's were fortunately years of lifesaving additions to the freight status of the railroad. Sierra management dipped into its small capital for the construction of three spurs from the main line. The first, or Gravel spur, though only three miles long, necessitated a trestle over the highway out of Oakdale, which seemed to mean an excessive outlay of money to reach such a small business as the Atlas Rock Company. But it was a means to another end, for two irrigation districts intended to build local dams. One was the Turlock and Modesto Irrigation District planning a dam on the lower Tuolumne River at Don Pedro Bar, and the other, the Oakdale Irrigation District whose dam site on the Stanislaus River was to be below Melones. Both of these sites had been projected some years before. Now, with well-to-do farmers behind them, it was almost certain that both dams would be built and would need gravel in construction. Newell felt so sure of this, that before his company agreed to build the Gravel spur, he and three accomplices took up four "mining claims" on land adjacent to the Atlas Rock Company's property which would be needed for a right-of-way to it. This was done to forestall any activity there by a rival transportation company.

As soon as the bonds for the Don Pedro dam were voted in 1921, the Gravel spur was built over rescinded mining claims — no strings attached. By the time construction began in 1923, an eight mile spur had been added to the Sierra tracks reaching southeast from Rosasco Junction to the Don Pedro dam site. During this dam's construction Sierra railroad equipment carried men, supplies and machinery over this spur to the construction town of Don Pedro, as well as ten carloads of cement and forty carloads of gravel daily. All of this gravel was sluiced for gold at considerable profit before being dumped into Sierra hoppers.

While these spurs, or branches, to the Sierra main line were in operation, a complete re-evaluation of the whole line for the Interstate Commerce Commission was made. Complicated through the loss of many records by fire, the completed figures showed the Sierra Railway on the black side of the ledger, largely due to recent profitable dam-building freight. The railroad, meanwhile, installed tie plates, tightly cleating heavier rails to sounder ties, and with better ballast greatly reduced maintenance costs previously necessary to hold a true gauge. Guard rails were also added on curves where engines might still spread the gauge and drop through. These improvements nearly ended any use for that 150 pound tool which Sierra engines customarily carried for frogging wheel flanges back onto the track.

With unlimited water in Tuolumne County's back yard, local communities were little better supplied than in placer mining days until ten local utility companies were united by Pacific Gas and Electric in 1922. The supply, then increased by small dams such as the Pine Crest dam, still was not adequate for the demands of Stanislaus and San Joaquin counties. But being primarily a power company, the P. G. and E. was not prepared to develop Tuolumne County's water, but was willing to buy and distribute as much power as might be produced there. With such an understanding, the Oakdale Irrigation District had promoted a million dollars toward dam construction near Melones and had approached the Sierra Railway regarding transportation aspects.

The Melones Dam and Power Plant, a larger project than the Don Pedro and less accessible, was estimated to take two years to build. The Sierra's Melones Dam spur branched from the main line at McCormicks (or Jacks) siding below Jamestown and, crossing Table Mountain at its low Peroria Pass, followed down grade to Beckley, two miles above the dam site. From there to the Stanislaus River a steep roadbed was set aside for the use of one Shay engine. This was made possible by use of a switchyard at Beckley where regular freight engines left their loaded cars and turned, or at times backed all the way out with empties. During this activity, the Sierra bought its heaviest engine to date (175,000 lbs.), a new 2-8-2 Baldwin which became their *No. 34.* Eighty hoppers and side dump cars were also purchased in which to haul thousands of tons of gravel from the Gravel spur, which made the Sierra's profits from this operation very worthwhile. The Melones Dam was completed in 1926; the power house opened in 1927.

The West Side Lumber Company sold its properties to the Pickering Lumber Company in 1925. Four years later, due to the depression, the Pickering Company shut down its operations in Tuolumne. The day the mill closed was one of economic panic in that town so completely dependent on lumbering. That year many corporations succumbed financially, and the Sierra Railway almost became one of them after taking the enormous cut in lumber freight which resulted from the West Side closure.

In these depression years, the Sierra Railway Company led a hand-to-mouth existence in which fruitless efforts were made to encourage or develop new avenues of freight income. In pursuance of this policy, a lumber company reportedly willing to exploit a section of timberland in the Calaveras Big Tree area was shown the advantages of a sawmill site at Carson Hill where logs could be hauled down grade from the woods and lumber shipped out by rail. It looked as though this promotion might go through but the sale of the north grove of Big Trees to the State killed it. On another promotion the grade stakes were driven for a tie-in line to run from the Port Stockton Cement Company, near Columbia, to the Jeffersonville marble spur, but the company failed and the rails were never laid. After thirty years of talk about developing limestone deposits on Coyote Creek near the Angels Branch, the chances for a lime plant there looked good until the site was pronounced too steep for cheap operations.

A successful siding extension 750 feet long was put in at Rosasco Junction to facilitate the shipping of cattle from the Rosasco and Curtin ranches; a spur 300 feet long was added at the U.S. lime plant near Sonora; the Green Stone Mine near Angels Camp had increased its business in building materials sufficiently to warrant a short spur track laid with the only sixty pound rail on the Angels Branch. These and the dwindling Melones Mine were the only sizable shippers on the branch line and their employees about the only passengers.

The *No. 5* combination was the only coach needed on the Angels Branch and became locally known as Mose's Caboose because Brakeman Mose Baker so often rode it alone. When it was conceded that passenger service there should terminate and a petition to that effect submitted to the State Railway Commission, no one in the Sierra Railway Company saw anything humorous in the slap-happy Angels Branch riding to its doom.

During this struggle for existence, the Sierra Railway Company had to continue payment to Yosemite Short Line bondholders, though owners of Sierra Railway stock had long since ceased to receive dividends. The 1928 final payment to the railroad by the Oakdale and South San Joaquin Irrigation Districts for their spur-switch layouts had been a big factor in keeping the railroad's head above water. By then Highway 108 was widened into Tuolumne County, and to compete with trucking lines carrying storekeepers' freight the Sierra railroad bought two Fairbanks Morse roadway trucks for depot-to-consignee freight delivery instead of following the old come-and-get-it rule of railroad shipping.

Because the necessity of raising the O'Shaughnessy Dam was already apparent to the city and county of San Francisco, bonds for it were being sold. D. J. Murphy of the Crocker Bank, who was then chairman of the Sierra's board of directors, procured a life saving agreement with city and county engineers to the effect that at the time the dam was raised, the Sierra railroad would reactivate and operate the Hetch Hetchy Railroad to it. This was the one hopeful prospect on the Sierra's main line when passenger losses had made it necessary to petition for discontinuance of that service.

Half of the railroad's 250 employees lived in Jamestown during the 1920's, but the loss of the mining element had left its mark.

The earlier boisterous town had become a drowsy community which had lost its bank, its *Mother Lode* newspaper, its little motion picture hall, its dance pavilion and the many saloons of this prohibition era. The long boardwalk up to the Protestant and Catholic churches had rotted and been torn up, revealing $28 in silver and gold coins which had fallen through its cracks. False-fronted buildings still proclaimed it a '49'er town, but the cotton-wood trees and hitching posts had been removed to widen Main Street for automobile travel from Yosemite Junction or Highway 120 to Sonora Pass on the Mono Road. Other towns along the line weathered that period without the support of railroad pay checks, and Sonora kept the old rivalry alive with a sewer system using septic tanks on Woods Creek, which promoted placards tacked in public toilets to read: "Pull the chain. Jamestown needs the water."

CHAPTER TEN

SIERRA RAILWAY

Repercussions from the financial crash continuing through the early 1930's directly and indirectly brought the Sierra Railway Company to its knees. The increasing power of regulatory governmental groups caused such a flurry of activity by Interstate Commerce and California State Railroad Commissions that the Sierra Railway's petition to discontinue passenger service was either slowed by red tape or was comparatively too small to be heard until the delay almost killed the line.

In 1930, the Pickering Lumber Company went into bankruptcy and closed for reorganization. With the West Side Lumber Company already closed down, this was almost an end to the Sierra's biggest freight item. At this same time competitive trucking lines, using free highways improved and paid for by the State, could afford to contract at a cheaper rate than the railroad for all the small lots of freight coming in and going out of the hills. These losses and the prevalence of local passenger travel by private automobiles reduced the Sierra's main line and Angels Branch service to one mixed freight and passenger train daily. Though a reduction in operating personnel followed, it was still impossible to make both ends meet on the accounting ledger.

When T. S. Bullock passed away in 1920, he was rather heavily indebted to the Sierra Railway Company and its bankers. An agreement made in 1926 between the heirs of the Bullock estate and the railway, whereby the indebtedness of the former, with interest, would be cleared within five years, was about to reach maturity. In 1930, Bullock's heirs offered a compromise to be accepted by the Sierra Railway Company within six months. Among trustees appointed at the time of the compromise agreement to administer the first and second party's interests was

C. N. Hamblin, then general manager of the railroad. Due to these conflicting problems and personal complications and losses unrelated to his position, Hamblin committed suicide in December of that year. John T. (Jack) Bullock, son of T. S. Bullock, then moved in as general manager of the railroad. William H. Crocker and D. J. (Dan) Murphy, vice-president of the Sierra Railway Company, agreed to this appointment as a means of giving Jack every opportunity to justify his claim that the Sierra Railway Company should accept the compromise offer. At the same time, the directorate appointed W. H. Newell as assistant or acting manager of the Sierra Railway. It was understandable how Bullock's son, who with his mother and sister were controlling stockholders, might contend that the Sierra Railroad was a rightful inheritance. However, it was an inauspicious time in which to take this stand when the railway was in arrears on interest payment on its own bonds and the bonds of the Yosemite Short Line, which it had guaranteed. Nevertheless, Newell assisted the son of his former friend and employer in every way possible while also endeavoring to keep the railroad alive and operating.

Passenger stations at Warnerville and Cooperstown were retired as were numerous old friends whose faithful service to the railroad had to be dispensed with. But in spite of these and other curtailments, traffic and income were not sufficient to prevent bankruptcy. Carrying out managerial duties under such circumstances was increasingly hard for a sixty-nine year old man torn by divergent loyalties. In May, 1932, the bondholders forced the Sierra Railway Company into receivership and the trustees foreclosed on the note owed by the Bullock heirs. With the Bullock interest in the railroad concluded and the management of it to pass into the hands of bankers, Civil Engineer Newell knew he was expendable and tendered his resignation before it was asked of him.

Mr. C. H. Segerstrom, Sr., of Sonora was appointed receiver of the Sierra railroad by the Bond Holder's Committee and Mr. J. E. Taylor, of Nevada City, made general manager for the new regime.

At receivership, the railroad was allowed a temporary freight increase which was of doubtful benefit to the line since ranchers, who had to pay more to ship a carload of cattle Oakdale to Warnerville than from Idaho to Oakdale, simply bought trucks and gave up Sierra shipping. Mr. Albyn Rydberg, whose clay from deposits at Cooperstown had been shipped out by Sierra, closed down operations because the profits were lost in freight. Efforts to revive some of the mines when the United States went off the gold standard failed in part due to freight costs. Many small businesses scrimped to purchase their own motor trucks because of these freight rates and yet the Sierra was hauling half full cars.

The repeal of Prohibition in 1933 channeled considerable money gained through bootlegging and undercover liquor agents into legitimate business. Saloons and liquor dealers began importing large quantities of their commodities into old Mother Lode towns such as Angels Camp. But due to rail-versus-truck freight rates, none of this traffic fell to the little one car Angels Branch. In that same year, when gold coins were called in by the U. S. Government, the Angels Branch carried one shipment worthy of note. This was $24,440 in gold pieces hidden under water in the locomotive's tender. It can be imagined what a day of conspiracy this was on Gus's Special!

The Sierra railroad's motor trucks, on the other hand, had become a rather good source of revenue from local deliveries and highway freight. Sierra trucks then operated from Sierra rail points to Stockton with an interchange of equipment and drivers under an agreement with the Pacific Motor Transport Company. This revenue was welcome but to main line operating crews it was not railroading. Meanwhile, train operators complained that maintenance of the railroad was so neglected that half the equipment was off the tracks all the time. Track gangs were accused of removing every other good tie and selling them without the profit going into the Sierra's accounts. When three boxcars of lime spilled all over the hill near Fassler station, the crew was accused of too much speed, but engineer Joe Cavagnero found two loose bolts on the switch which had turned the cars loose. In fact, old time train crews, whose union status kept them working, insisted that their jobs were increasingly hazardous because creepers, or horseshoe clamps between rails and ties were also regularly missing. Such accusations between train operators and maintenance men resulted in poor cooperation all along the line. Meanwhile, the Sierra's old *No. 7* engine and their *No. 3* Rogers were relegated to rust and weeds. To all appearances the railroad was being run into the discard.

There is no doubt that influence was brought to bear on this new management by owners of Yosemite Short Line and Sierra Railway bonds who were more interested in getting some refund on their investments by dissolving the company than in saving the railroad for a doubtful future. But the Sierra Railway Company refused to die and life was slowly pumped back into it by improved economy throughout the country.

In 1934, the West Side Lumber Company bought its idle plant back from the Pickering Company. Thorsen, who was the only member of the earlier management left, became president again and Fred Ellis became manager. Ellis had been the company's surveyor and then engineer, and had built their Hetch Hetchy and Yosemite logging railroad from the first miles where Newell left off, to its by then sixty-three mile length covering thirteen airline miles. This railroad, with its original Shays and Heislers, as well as the entire lumber plant, went back into operation in 1935.

The day the West Side Lumber Company blew a blast on their sawmill whistle signaling to loggers and mill hands that their four year unemployment was at an end will long be remembered in Tuolumne. The resulting spree lasted a week and became an annual commemorative event. The railroad was benefited although some of the old inter-company good will was lost by increased freight rates which the logging company had no alternative but to pay. Also, the railroad had no alternative but to haul, whether it was agreeable to the receivership regime or not. The Sierra railroad was again in the big lumber hauling business.

Also, in 1934 San Francisco's bond issue for more water had passed and work began on raising the O'Shaughnessy Dam. The remaining fifty-nine miles of the Hetch Hetchy Railroad from Sierra tracks to Mather were restored to proper condition for heavy hauling during dam raising, and the lifesaving agreement made years ago by Dan Murphy went into effect. Per agreement, Sierra Railway equipment and personnel activated these railroad miles as a division of the line, and in so doing the Sierra reached its peak of linear operations, over one hundred and forty miles. At this time a local paper reported:

"... the Sierra may now be termed long, lean and narrow-minded in that the tracks are long, the economy lean and the management narrow-minded." True or false, the railroad could hardly fail now.

With a maximum elevation on its own line of 2,900 feet, the Sierra Railroad had had only minor experience with snow. Now however, supplies, passengers and mail were delivered summer and winter over Poopenaut Pass above the 5,000 feet elevation. The Sierra's *No. 22* and *No. 24* engines did most of the heavy hauling over Hetch Hetchy tracks, augmented as needed by their *No. 36*, a Schenectady.

The winter of 1937 was a record-breaker for snow. Wedge or semi-rotary snowplows were attached to the *No. 24* with its 200 pound boiler pressure to keep the Hetch Hetchy line clear. In February, two engines and snowplows worked a week to open the snow pack. But train crews were happy to be hard at it again, and the whole operation was carried out without interruption or major casualty until the huge Hetch Hetchy dam was completed.

In 1935, when dam construction and increased lumber hauling were bolstering the Sierra Railroad, the Sonora *Banner* Press printed a booklet sponsored by Tuolumne county supervisors to boost local business. The foreword, by Edward M. Jasper of Jamestown, said:

"Tuolumne County offers opportunities to the pleasure seeker and to the investor." To enlarge on this theme in the good old-fashioned way, the romantic past and hopeful future of gold mining was the most lengthily stressed subject. Descriptions of local sports and scenery were aided by a county map showing highways and byways usable, supposedly, by cars. The Sierra Railway was not shown on the map nor mentioned in the text as a means of transportation. Nor was hydro-power although this was the biggest current development in the county with a history contemporaneous with the most exciting phase of Mother Lode mining.

Charles Coleman did not ignore this in his *Centennial Story of Pacific Gas and Electric Company:*

"Progress in hydro-construction was aided by devices developed by hydraulic miners to handle water under high pressures and by water wheel improvements, begun by men like Pelton, to more efficiently produce power for hoists and machinery of the deep mines of the Sierras. The gold miners of Tuolumne County left vast water systems and legal rights to water sources — tunnels, canals, flumes, rivers, lakes — which were bought by contending local companies none of which had the capital or promotional genius necessary for progressive development."

Now, however, since this natural resource had been exposed to progressive development, thousands of employees of Pacific Gas and Electric had come to Tuolumne County power sites and points on its distributional system which, combined, made P. G. and E. its biggest taxpayer. Other thousands, who had never before heard of Tuolumne, were now visiting the enormous Hetch Hetchy reservoir. These projects alone accounted for an increase of about one hundred registered voters a year in Tuolumne County between 1920 and 1935.

In 1937, the Pickering Lumber Company was studied by the Reconstruction Finance Corporation, which brought about a $2,500,000 loan that year. At that time the reorganized company became The Pickering Lumber Corporation, and the old Sugar Pine logging road became the Pickering Lumber Corporation Railroad with over fifty miles of track. Operations were resumed full force as logs were cut from a billion feet of Pickering timber holdings backed up by U. S. Forests in Tuolumne County. The lumber milled and dried at Standard City was shipped out by Sierra rails. Extra freight trains were again needed.

In March of this same year the Sierra Railway Company was sold at public auction and bought in by the company stock and bondholders. The Bondholders' Committee arranged for Yosemite Short Line bonds to be paid off at face value and the remaining interests were reorganized and renamed the Sierra Railroad Company. D. J. Murphy, representing the largest stockholder, the Crocker interests, became president of the railroad. J. E. Taylor was retained as acting manager.

The following year permission was at last granted by the California Railroad Commission to discontinue all Sierra passenger service. On March 12, 1939, the main line passenger train left Tuolumne on regular schedule in care of Conductor Burgess, Engineer Wright, Fireman Baker and Brakeman Boquist. Among the handful of passengers on the train was a young woman who had grown up in Tuolumne watching folks scurry at her father's stentorian "All-a-b-ooo-rd!" Through the past nearly thirty years no one dead-heading it down and up the Sierra line was more welcome by the crew than Vivian Burgess, who had now chosen to ride her father's last down train before he and the coaches were retired.

As this train pulled into Oakdale, things looked strangely quiet. There was no hustle of people at the depot and no trains to transfer to. For on this same date the Southern Pacific and Santa Fe railroads had also discontinued passenger service into Oakdale. The Sierra railroad's representative in the Oakdale S. P. depot had been retired in the economy measures of 1929. Since then, S. P. Station Agent W. B. Reynolds had acted jointly for both lines. While continuing as freight agent in Oakdale for the next ten years, Reynolds was so active in progressive measures in his community that he was elected mayor of Oakdale. Highway approaches to this town from three directions were even then being improved, so this one-time big wagon freighting town and one-time busy exchange point for three railroads would not long remain a mere junction for freight rails.

Service, such as it was, had meanwhile been operating on the Angels Branch. Each evening Gus's Special had waited, steamed up and softly panting, for the Sierra's main line train to pull into Jamestown with a possible transfering passenger. Then, whistling bravely, it had set out with its short *No. 5* combination to climb to Table Mountain cut on its way to Angels Camp, and each morning the usual two long and two short whistles again were heard as the *No. 30* crossed the Rawhide road on its way back to Jamestown. If sometimes Gus made his run without passengers, mail or baggage, who then was to care if on his last regular run into Jamestown a few snipers rode in style in Mose's Caboose?

On March, 1939, Gus made his very last run over the Angels Branch without even one coach. Instead, he pulled two flatcars and a wrecking crew. When this train pulled into Angels Camp, most of the town went on about its business, which was already being done ninety per cent by auto trucks. The grass had grown through the cleats of Hard Scrabble Street because few horses were left to use it and automobiles could not. A gasoline service station operated on the site of the Cross shaft on Main Street. The old Utica shaft was the central feature of the town park. The power wheel used long ago to regrind the tailings on the old Angelus, Stickle and Utica dumps stood idly on the west side. Movable relics of local mines were even then being collected to form the nucleus of Dan Daniels's museum which twenty years later had grown into Angels Camp's biggest tourist attraction. An unmovable relic was reported by George Ross of the Oakland *Tribune* in February, 1959.

> "Up in Angels Camp, once one of the richest and most riotous of gold camps, there's a move afoot to get owners of worked-out mines to fill 'em or fence 'em. A citizen kicked a couple of rotting boards up there the other day and uncovered a shaft 900 feet deep. Thar's holes in them thar hills!"

In Angels Camp in 1939, another service station was being installed on the site of the razed Calaveras Hotel. Some new homes were plotted on Democrat Hill although rutted roads to them were hardly usable by car. Surveys for a needed sewer system had recently been made by W. H. Newell but the project had been delayed by World War II and as yet chick-sales and creeks were the town's disposal units. In short, Angels Camp was holding its own as one of the most romantic sites on the golden chain of Mother Lode mining towns, but it was not affluent in March, 1939, when a few people came out to the Sierra depot to say good-bye to train service in Calaveras County.

On that day the turntable was torn out, and the property, depot included, was turned back to the Tryon family. Gus then started slowly back toward Jamestown, while the crew of wreckers pulled up the tracks behind and loaded them on to the flat cars. Progress was slow down to Melones where a few habitable houses were scattered around the silent millsite. The sixteen miles of wooden flume which had brought water to the powerhouse for thirty-one years was now replaced by eleven miles of tunnel bored for Stanislaus Electric Power Company use at the Melones dam. A stone bridge which had finally been built over the Stanislaus River parallel to the Sierra Railroad trestle in 1909, was already old, mossy and narrow for trucks and cars. Proceeding across the river with mounting loads of steel rails, Gus chugged up the McArdle switch and on to Tuttletown. The bare ballast being left behind would become tomorrow's faint trail of a past era in railroads. So Gus's star-trimmed little *No. 30* left the Mother Lode country like a genial smoker leaving a ghostly wisp of smoke, the scent of good tobacco and pleasant talk behind him.

The passing of the Angels Branch did not go unmourned by the few old timers who remembered the days when full trains ran in and out of Calaveras County as well as making daily calls at eighteen Mother Lode mines. But no one seemed to remember the man who had built it, though he was still active in their midst. One early day passenger, Elizabeth Kaler, waxed poetic for the Calaveras Historical Society many years later when she wrote:

> "Oh you little railway of the yesterdays
> We keep your memory clear.
> Though we often smiled at your oddities
> Yet in our hearts we hold you dear."

At the time the Angels Branch was torn up, a Sonora paper printed the following:

> "Stories of little railroads which came as a blessing, flourished for awhile and gave up the ghost to gasoline and concrete, are numerous in our mining West. They have in them a romantic tragedy that sets old tongues to wagging; they built so much before they were scrapped. In a letter, R. Kerchum calls attention to the fact that on the first of this March the Angels Branch of the Sierra Railway passed into history after thirty years of continuous service. It seems only yesterday, he observed, that Angels Camp was celebrating the completion of the branch on a hot September day in 1902, with one of the wildest celebrations ever held there. W. A. Wenneson, traffic manager for the Sierra, comments that the next generation will enjoy telling about the train that chugged to the Jumping Frog community for thirty-three years. The construction of the railroad over rugged mountains was considered an engineering feat thirty-five years ago. The switchbacks necessary on hairpin turns were unusual in railroad construction and few instances of this type of construction are recorded."

The Sierra Railroad's *No. 30* was immediately sold to the Howard Terminal Company. The sister Baldwin, or *No. 32*, was sold to the Tidewater Southern Railway. The short *No. 6* passenger coach had been traded to the Hetch Hetchy Railroad when passengers were hauled on that line and the *No. 5* combination was now used as a crummie on Sierra freight trains. When this caboose

SIERRA RAILROAD

Excursions have always been popular on the Sierra. Here in 1934 is a 17-car passenger train being pulled by three beautifully kept Sierra locomotives.

Extra train just out of Standard. Combine No. 5, which saw service for many years on the Angels Branch, serves as waycar.

JIM BAKER

Excursion train headed by No. 3. Location is south of Keystone Station.

Left, No. 3 with fake headlight pulling special passenger train through Red Hills area. Track parallels highway.

Excursion special. Rail fans hanging out of baggage car and vestibules are the bane of photographers.

No. 28 with excursion train east of Paulsell.

Train at Paulsell, October 1957.

THREE PICTURES: DONALD DUKE

Sierra No. 3 at Quartz Junction. Table Mountain may be seen in background.

On page opposite: No. 38 with eastbound freight entering Jamestown yards.

Excursion train leaving Oakdale.

Extra freight near Ralph.

No. 30 at Baldwin Locomotive Works prior to delivery.

SIERRA RAILROAD

One of the many special passenger trains.

Climbing grade east of Sonora.

On page opposite: No. 28 heading train out of Sonora.

Two engines having a hard time with a heavy train.

East of Sonora the curves get tight.

Not a sign of modern civilization mars these scenes from the movie "Man of the West," filmed in February, 1958.

Sierra backshop crew doubling as makeup men. False headlight and stack are being installed on No. 18 prior to a movie assignment.

SIERRA RAILROAD

Movie train at rest in yards at Jamestown.

No. 18 sitting outside of roundhouse at Jamestown.

DONALD DUKE

was no longer used, Mose Baker is said to have cried bitterly, but was somewhat appeased when it was added to the Sierra's Movie Train.

After passenger service between Tuolumne and Oakdale was discontinued, the Sierra Railroad ran a motor bus service over the highway between those towns. But with the now extensive use of private automobiles this became an unprofitable investment which was retired.

World War II was a sleepy time in all the Sierra Nevada foothills and especially Tuolumne County. Lumber and cattlemen, being in essential industries, were exempted from the draft and those businesses proceeded as usual. But other young men were inducted into the service and older ones left the area by the hundreds to work in factories and shipyards. Unessential expenses and expansions were shelved for the duration and it was not until after the war ended that these men returned bringing back new ideas of change and progress.

During those years Newell was living in his home above Jamestown's Main Street as he expressed it "on borrowed time," due to a faltering heart which was laboring to keep up with an active body and mind. On one of his frequent trips to San Francisco he visited with directors of the Sierra Railroad Company in the Crocker Building. At that time a successor to Taylor for manager of the railroad was being considered. When asked whether he thought Bill Cheney would be "good enough," Newell smiled in reminiscence of many things.

"Bill is one of my boys whom I see often. It's hard for me to think of him as old enough," he said, "but 'good enough?' Bill is a railroader, born and bred, and the best man you could pick."

Twenty-five years before, Bill Cheney was a young married man working as a brakeman in Sparks, Nevada, where his father was in charge of Southern Pacific shops. At that time, Mr. Cheney, Sr. addressed a letter to W. H. Newell asking if there might be an opening with the Sierra railroad for a young man who thought his chances of becoming more than a brakeman would be better with a small company. Newell consequently hired Bill into his own department which then meant anything from surveying to office work, to trips over the line in a track car while inspecting maintenance. In the tight years that followed when Bill came onto the

list of expendables, Newell insisted that Bill had shown an apti-
tude for office work which he, himself, despised, and could take
over the accounting department. Having filled this office successfully up to the reorganization, Bill was then a natural for the
position of auditor. In 1946, W. C. Cheney was made manager of
the Sierra Railroad, and Ferol "Pat" Egan was promoted to the
position of freight agent.

The first thing Manager Cheney did was to reorganize the
maintenance department. Under carefully chosen section bosses,
the whole line was re-laid with new 90 pound rail. On difficult
curves and grades, 100 pound steel was used to make the line
safe for the heavier engines which Cheney intended to try out
on this line. The twenty-odd hoppers left on the line after Melones
dam construction were loaded with ballasting material from an
old mine dump near Jamestown and placed where needed on
grades and curves. Six new 70-ton boxcars were bought to replace
old wooden ones. The depot at Chinese Station was retired but
sidings were added at Ralphs Station where the Pickering line
branched. The logging roads of both the Pickering and the West
Side lumber companies now reached over 70 miles back into the
Sierra Nevada's seemingly unending forests.

All but six of the Sierra Railroad's locomotives were sold or
scrapped. The *No. 24, No. 28, No. 34* and *No. 36* engines were
then the work horses of the line. Two of the units, retaining numbers *3* and *18*, were like fancy old ladies living in luxurious idle-
ness, for these were the Sierra's moving picture stars. This motion
picture phase of the railroad's activity has been somewhat
neglected here partly because it was spotty and because at first
it was embarrassing. In the early 1920's, when Fatty Arbuckle
and Mabel Normand were making slapstick comedies, their producers were looking for comical settings and pounced on the
Sierra Railroad as one of these. At first, the railroad barely tol-
erated the use of its engines and coaches for arrivals and de-
partures of flossy and sinister comedy characters wearing bloomers
and whiskers. In those less detail-conscious days producers
began taking pictures of the early West using the *No. 3* Rogers
on routine duty. When this little engine was laid up for repairs
and later retired, the Sierra Railroad allowed the *No. 18* or
No. 30 to be half disguised as old timers, with cordwood piled

on top of the water tank in the tender and a tin cabbagehead tacked to the stack. But such occasions were rare and the money made on rental equipment comparatively small. However, it was not only the equipment which led the Sierra Railroad into the moving picture business as a serious sideline. It was the locale in which its tracks ran. There were bridges, cuts and above all, plains and rolling hills without fences or telephone poles. And for such terrain 400 cowboys and other extras could be hired, locally, on twenty-four hour notice.

More pretentious Western productions attracted larger and more critical audiences that noticed every flaw and anachronism in settings. In the 1930's, rail fans as well as members of historical societies became enthusiastic critics of early day motion pictures, insisting on seeing the real thing or a reasonable facsimile. Productions,therefore, became more authentic and more expensive. The price moving picture companies were willing to pay per day for the use of Sierra's equipment in that setting soared from $100 to $500 a day, which not only removed the stigma previously felt by Sierra Railroad operators that theirs was an antiquated little old short line but made the movie business a profitable side line.

A backlog of material for movies was retained by the railroad, as were the *No. 3* and *No. 18* locomotives. The original tender on the latter engine was replaced by a wood burner type. A diamond stack, kerosene head lamps and gold filigree were also added. In this disguise the *No. 18* was star performer in a dozen pictures, notably *Duel in the Sun* in which she was "wrecked" on a curve near Cooperstown. For *Go West* the Sierra laid a whole circle of track on the Gurney ranch near the old town of Stent so the Marx Brothers could "go nowhere fast." When the *No. 3* was restored and back on the tracks in 1949, she also was reflued and given a permanent diamond stack to re-enter show business.

This little Rogers became the queen of many later movies in spectacular roles such as she portrayed in *Dodge City*, filmed at Cooperstown with cattle rustlers racing after the little train chugging across the prairie; also, a part in *High Noon* in 1951, and *Rage at Dawn* in 1954. From then until 1959, or the time of this writing, the *No. 3* comes chugging around a turn on the Sierra tracks to introduce every televised showing of "Tales of Wells Fargo."

In 1949, the *No. 6* passenger coach, left to rust down in Tuolumne River Canyon by the Hetch Hetchy Railroad, was discovered and bought for $100 by the Pacific Coast Chapter of the Railway and Locomotive Historical Society, who reclaimed it for display purposes. By then an important and sizable storage space had been set aside in the Jamestown yards for old cowcatchers, wheels, stairs, railings, tall, short and fat smoke stacks and a cord or so of wood, all props for the Sierra's Movie Train with two engines and three coaches. While the total book value of this unit is less than $25,000, it is priceless to Hollywood because such a train on the Sierra Railroad with thirty-seven of its fifty-seven miles of tracks in curves laid in California's true gold-mining hills, is more authentic of the early West than can be found anywhere else.

When the Sonora depot caught fire in 1946, the Sonora fire department came to the town limits about two hundred feet distant, and watched it burn down to the marble foundations. It was rebuilt as a freight station only, with a longer loading platform for handling freight in carload lots. Thereafter, there were many times when Sierra freight trains whistled at the road crossing as they came around the bend into Sonora, but, without stopping, continued up the grade with oil cars and box cars of machinery for the Pickering and West Side lumber companies at Standard and Tuolumne. On the way down just after leaving Sonora, these trains made regular stops at the U. S. Lime Products plant to pick up their shipments.

In the summer of 1948, Jamestown held a centennial celebration of gold discovery there. For this celebration the whole town was bedecked in bunting and the local people dressed up in '49'er outfits complete with beards, boots, pompadours and high-topped shoes. When the parade and speeches were held on the main street, Bill Cheney and Jess Fowler drove up to Newell's house and insisted upon taking him to the speaker's stand. This occasion, as it happened, was to mark Newell's last appearance in public and his last look at the town in the shadow of Table Mountain, which he had chosen to be his home. Two months later, in this early day house, built with square nails over an outcropping of the Mother Lode, Newell passed away.

Several changes took place among the Sierra's operating forces in 1949 due to the retirement of men like Frank Miller and Gus Swanson, who had been at the controls of Sierra locomotives for so many years. Jim Baker, who had grown up in Jamestown with Sierra smoke and steam whistles, had progressed from grease jobs to fireman and now became one of the Sierra's top locomotive engineers. In contrast to Jim, who might be called a born rail-roader, was Clay Waterhouse who had previously been a buck-aroo cowpuncher and now became a fireman. At this time there were four locomotives in regular freight service with Bill McCallom, Jim Baker and Joe Cavagnero at the controls.

Ore and sulphurets were not the only big freight items lost to rails in these days. Though marble at the Columbia quarry was not exhausted, the works had been closed down and the marble spur inactivated even before the Angels Branch was torn up. To a large extent marble had been supplanted by cheaper building materials, some made from colorful aggregates of crushed rocks native to this part of the Sierra Nevada foothill country. No more cattle were being rail-shipped out of Tuolumne County, or even driven in large herds to mountain grazing, as cattle ranchers were moving their stock entirely by truck. The Sierra Railroad's mail contracts had been canceled with passenger service. In short, freight on this short line was now ninety per cent carload lots of lumber, fuel oil, oil products and lime or lime products. Four trains a day were sufficient to handle these shipments. Train dispatcher Jess Fowler was not too busy. The line telephone jangled on his desk at regular intervals but he, too, looked back nostalgically to the busy clickety-clack of telegraph keys in the days of eight or ten east- and westbound trains a day with an occasional derailment thrown in. His telegraph keys were still in the office. They were not hooked up and the batteries were dead but they might be essential equipment when the next Western movie was made.

One of the most spectacular and sadly devastating fires ever to take place in Tuolumne County was started by lightning in 1950 on Duckwall Mountain. Beginning on Labor Day, this fire burned for eight days over ten miles east and west of the mountain. The California Forestry Service spent $800,000 in fire fighting with chemicals and manpower while endeavoring to save timber belonging to the West Side Lumber Company. But before these efforts could produce results, the fire dropped off all sides of Duckwall Mountain to blacken what had been 50,000 acres of virgin and second growth forest.

The West Side Lumber Company had endured more than its share of loss by sickening and costly forest fires. On the other hand, the Pickering Lumber Corporation had recently lost its Standard mill due to fire. Notwithstanding these losses, these two companies shipped out a steady 165 million board feet of lumber a year which constituted 80% of the Sierra Railroad's westbound freight.

In 1952, the Sierra Railroad bought its last "steamer." Dan Murphy, Paul Newell and Bill Cheney picked out a Baldwin 2-6-6-2 with the help of Master Mechanic Bill Tremewan. This true Mallet with 1,500 H.P. was the Sierra's *No. 38* and the heaviest locomotive ever used on the line. It was not a thing of pride to some of the shop mechanics who knew it was bought secondhand, and had been rolled several times. Its trucks were so out of line that one set would spring as fast as the others were lined up. But Tremewan had said he could "put the Mallet right" and he did. When properly aligned, *No. 38* handled most of the freight on the line. It was a spectacular sight to see it high-balling through Cooperstown with the throttle wide open as it made a run for the Canyon Tank grade with twenty cars and a half mile of smoke trailing behind it.

Almost as soon as the Melones dam and power plant had been completed it was apparent that more water and power were needed in Stanislaus County as well as in the adjoining south San Joaquin County area. Stanislaus County farmers were planting Ladino clover as a grazing crop and soil benefactor, but clover demanded more water than was available even though the Melones dam had been raised in 1950. Now, after World War II, there was talk of combining the financial capabilities of both the Oakdale and the South San Joaquin districts in one concerted effort to raise funds for a really adequate water project. With this aim in view, the engineering data offered twenty-six years before by W. H. Newell to Oakdale's engineer, R. Hartley, regarding reservoir sites on the upper reaches of the South Fork Stanislaus River were reviewed. This time dam construction of such magnitude was seen as a profitable long-term investment, and surveys for it were accepted subject to financing.

The project became economically possible when the Pacific Gas and Electric Company agreed to buy the electric power produced at the dam site and so became a partner with the irrigation districts. When the Sierra Railroad was approached on the transportation problem, the freight potential involved was, of course, seen as a most profitable one, and the railroad contracted to do all the heavy hauling between Oakdale and Jamestown. From there into the mountains construction essentials were to be hauled by truck.

With this transportation prospect in view, the Sierra Railroad moved into the modern age, or that of diesel engines. It was a tremendous turnover undertaking, involving equipment, shops and personnel. Though diesel engines are no heavier than the Sierra's steam Mallet, their more compact weight tended to spread the rails. Therefore, even seldom used sidings had to carry 90 and 110 pound rail. The roundhouse and turntable in Jamestown, too small and poorly situated for the anticipated new schedule of one freight east and one freight west each day, were abandoned. A new enginehouse was built at Oakdale at a cost of $30,000 and two diesels, Baldwin-Westinghouse, Type BB, Model S-12, were ordered. These two-truck locomotives, 1200 H.P. with automatic air brakes, multiple unit operation and a 65 mile per hour speed, were judged adequate for the Sierra's expected use. They were built to the same specification as similar Baldwin units of the Southern Pacific Company from whom additional diesel units might be leased in case of emergency.

When these two diesels arrived on the Sierra's tracks, the railroad joined in a "Farewell to Steam" celebration in which the Pacific Coast Chapter of the Railway and Locomotive Historical Society sponsored a thirteen car excursion from the San Francisco Bay area pulled by the Sierra's steamers *No. 36* and *No. 38* as a double-header from Oakdale to Jamestown. A special edition of the *Western Railroader* was published in anticipation of this occasion and almost every newspaper in the West noted the passing of the most romantic existing short line from the steam to the diesel age.

The Oakland *Tribune* printed:

"The steam locomotive that conquered the West and pushed the Frontier to the Pacific Ocean will suffer a fatal blow when operators of the Sierra Railroad abandon steam and introduce diesels to the fifty-seven year old railroad. Taking the place of the old timers will be two brand new 1200 H.P. diesel engines resembling switchers, though more highly powered. The Sierra's famous Picture Train, recently used in *Seven Bad Men* starring Randolph Scott, will be retained for movie use . . ."

The *Territorial Enterprise* (Mark Twain's old newspaper of Virginia City, Nevada) presently owned and published by railroad fan Lucius Beebe printed the following:

"HETCH HETCHY JUNCTION: Scourge! One more fatality among steam operated railroads dating from the old West was suffered when the management of picturesque and often photographed Sierra Railroad announced that the blight of diesel will supplant steam power after fifty-seven years of internal expansion motive power."

The *Union Democrat* of Sonora put out an extra edition devoted to pictures and articles relating to the old and the new power units of the Sierra Railroad. In it William C. Cheney, vice-president and general manager of the Sierra Railroad Company, was quoted as saying:

"We have spent over a half million dollars in the past four years to build for Tuolumne County a new Sierra. The railroad needs your patronage — the community needs the railroad."

The Sierra's agent, Pat Egan, explained how, beginning April 4, 1955, carload freight loaded before 6:00 p.m. would be delivered to and on its way by Southern Pacific and Santa Fe railroads the same day from and to all points.

On a rainy Sunday, April 17, 1955, six hundred passengers in undampened spirits arrived at Jamestown on this steam powered excursion. At the dreary depot with no shelter from the rain except that afforded by the freight platform, a handful of Jamestown people and the visiting rail fans watched Mrs. Marjorie Wenneson, widow of Sierra Agent William Wenneson, place a wreath on that "good engine" *No. 36* in tribute to the past glory of steam. Three young ladies of Sonora, Jamestown and Stent, bespoke the present while the diesels were christened. Seated on the platform were Sierra Railroad Company officers: D. J. Murphy, president; Frentress Hill, secretary and treasurer; and Directors E. Solomon, C. Kreis, Charles H. Segerstrom and Paul C. Newell, the latter two second generation representatives of fathers who had aided and abetted the Sierra Railroad through its more trying days. With Bill Cheney were his operating force: Ferol (Pat) Egan, Jess Fowler, J. E. Condon, master mechanic for the diesel age, and John Dossi, roadmaster. Also present on the speaker's stand was Mr. Fred Stindt, chairman of the Pacific Coast Chapter of the Railway and Locomotive Historical Society, who has done so much to glorify the steam engine age and had been to so many of their wakes.

While rail fans took pictures of steam locomotives spotted about the yard, and climbed all over the Movie Train, consisting of the *No. 3* and two coaches upholstered in red plush standing on a siding, someone took the time to tack this poem by Vaun Arnold onto the depot door:

> "A Farewell To Steam:
> They have taken the wild horse from the rail
> And the flying mane and the whipping tail
> Of the fast express and the midnight mail
> Are gone beyond redeeming.
>
> Now a streamlined steed with a swivel eye
> And a Diesel's docile humming
> With a streetcar clang and a cowlike cry
> Inspires no heart at coming.
>
> Gone is the high iron cannon ball
> On smoking drivers six feet tall
> With a blast of steam and a farewell call
> And a distant hoofbeat drumming."

With personal feeling, Mr. Joseph Azeveda, long-time authority on the Sierra's mechanical equipment, said:

"You could pound a good old steam engine to pieces but not a diesel. Of course diesels are cheaper in manpower, like when the Sierra can run a double-header up the canyon with two men in the cabs instead of four."

About this time the Oakland *Tribune* carried a sad little note:

"To many a passerby the steam locomotive about to be junked at the Seventh Street yard of the National Iron and Metal Company is just an outmoded relic of the past. To railroad aficionados it's another matter. This Prairie-type "2-6-2" to be cut up for junk is Tidewater Southern's *No. 132* built originally as the *No. 32* for the Sierra Railway in 1923."

Four of the Sierra's twenty-two steam locomotives still are held in the Jamestown roundhouse as extra work horses, while Jim Condon has charge of diesels only in the new Oakdale shop where he maintains them. The daily eastbound freight train pulls out of Oakdale at 11:30 a.m. six days a week with Conductor Al Moreno and Brakeman Louis Antone in a green caboose behind about twenty cars pulled upgrade usually by both diesels, with engineers Bill McCallum and Jim Baker and Brakeman Art Cullers in the cab. Both of these engineers might have been sorry to see steam go, but admitted preferring diesels with cooler cabs than those behind a steam boiler, especially in July when the foothill heat often tops 100°.

The joint venture called the Tri Dam project was to cost the lowland irrigation districts $52,000,000 with Pacific Gas and Electric power contracts to support their financial requirements. The intention was to build three dams, three power houses, clear three reservoirs and bring in a seven mile power tunnel. The project was divided into what were called the upper and lower works. The lower works involved the raising of the existing earthen Melones dam with power plant, to be renamed the Goodwin Dam after completion. The transportation aspect of this lower work was chiefly carried out by truck. The upper works consisted of an earthen (Beardsley) dam, power plant and afterbay forty-five miles upstream on the Middle Fork of the Stanislaus River, and twelve miles above that a concrete dam (Donnels), a power house and the tunnel. Transportation to and from these upper dams was to be carried out by truck augmented by Sierra rails. The Donnels dam was to be a five hundred foot high concrete arch requiring 207,000 cubic yards of concrete, the cement for which was to be hauled by rail to Jamestown and from there by trucks up the Mono Road to newly built roads branching down to the dam sites. For this construction a $30,000 cement silo was built on a Sierra siding in Jamestown. Also, enlarged freight sheds were used as depositories for heavy construction equipment not allowed on the Oakdale-Sonora section of Highway 108, and therefore shipped to that point by rail.

Begun in 1955, the 2½ years spent in construction of these dams continued through the winter snows, which many sceptics had maintained would be impossible. Through that period the Sierra Railroad brought eight to ten 70 ton carloads of bulk cement a day, or about 75,000 tons total, to the Jamestown silo for reshipment chiefly to the Donnels dam. Many tons of machinery were also delivered to this and the Beardsley dam, which was a 320 foot high earth embankment. Even without Federal or State aid this private development was completed ahead of schedule. On June 15, 1957, a dedication ceremony was held at the Beardsley powerhouse at the foot of huge Beardsley dam. Dwarfed by the dam and mountain bluffs rising thousands of feet above it, nine hundred visitors watched the presentation of a bronze plaque to Engineer Russell E. Hartley, then a white-haired man, in recognition of his untiring efforts to obtain an adequate water supply for the Oakdale and South San Joaquin irrigation districts. In reporting the event the Modesto *Bee* said in part:

"Russell E. Hartley was a surprised man during the Tri Dam ceremony when he was honored by the dedication of a bronze plaque officially naming the lake created by the Beardsley dam as Hartley Lake. Mr. Hartley made his first reconnaissance survey of this reservoir site in 1924. He had learned about the site through W. H. Newell, who was civil engineer for the Sierra Railway and the Sugar Pine road. Since that time, Hartley had made a study of many proposed sites, but the Tri-Dam project fulfilled his early dreams and stands as a monument to his faith and vision."

This extensive engineering project more than vindicated Newell's fifty years of obsession with the natural advantages of these dam sites in the narrows of the Stanislaus Middle Fork, although it is unlikely that he envisioned two dams there or a railroad crossing that gorge on one of them. Yet, by laying tracks across the broad top of Beardsley dam, the Pickering logging road is saved miles of tortuous grades now inundated but previously necessary in order to reach the magnificently forested area northward across the river.

In an earlier day, the Sierra Railroad would have reactivated its spur to the Goodwin (Melones) dam and benefited by freight contracts to it, but in the 1950's the company could not compete with trucks able to haul construction material directly to such a comparatively low level site. The same may be true at the time of raising the Don Pedro dam which is part of a projected 200 million dollar expansion of the Hetch Hetchy hydroelectric facilities to occur in 1960, though today's modernized Sierra short line can easily be expected to be in nearby operation through such construction. However, people are increasingly objecting to heavy trucking on their expensive highways. The most progressive step in recent railroading, the piggy-back flatcar, has been put to use in answer to this problem by the Southern Pacific, Santa Fe, and other railroads. This method of transporting truck trailers (with refrigeration units attached when necessary) on long hauls may considerably reduce highway trucking and highway maintenance costs to the benefit of railroads. Who can say then, with astronomical amounts being spent on California resources, and some limit being placed on auto trucking, what future expansions or inventions may take place to expand the Sierra Railroad. Meanwhile, her story closes with a peek at the towns she currently serves.

Progressive Oakdale sprawls over twice the city area surveyed in 1907. Supermarkets and every other type of modern business are represented in its commercial district at the intersection of Highway 120 or North Yosemite Avenue and the Sierra Railroad tracks. Public progress, education and recreation are ably and popularly administered by Mayor W. B. Reynolds, the past Sierra agent there. Trucks load and unload before the busy Gilbert warehouse built beside Sierra tracks by one of Oakdale's most prominent founders with money made in wagon freighting..

The routine eastbound *No. 4* starts out of Oakdale slowly pulling twenty cars and gathers speed as she rolls over nineteen miles of sweeping curves. At Cooperstown siding the train slows and stops to sidetrack two cars. Outside of a few cattle there is little sign of life, for travelers seldom pass that way and even rattlesnakes are few. As the train starts ahead up the six mile grade to Rosasco, the double-header moves along without much apparent effort, and no smoke. Between Rosasco Junction and old Chinese Station, the yellow diesels and long train comes in sight of Highway 120 as it snakes past Keystone and then turns back behind the hills. Without stopping at Chinese, the train sounds its mournful air-blown horn as it comes around the bend into Jamestown. In sight of the Sierra depot and freight shed she slows and then stops in the yards. The old steamers, *No. 28, No. 34* and *No. 36* are at home in the roundhouse. There the *No. 3* stands outside where she is being groomed with different lettering and numbers from those recently worn in *Man of the West,* starring Julie London and Gary Cooper, when she rolled onto the screen in a red cowcatcher, cap stack and lots of smoke veiling.

In the Jamestown office the dispatcher's telephone has become obsolete with the installation of radio communications all along the line. Within sight of the depot are quite a few new homes and the second largest grammar school in the county. The old Pereira Addition like all of Jamestown now has improved streets, direct telephones and a modern sewer system.

But there is not a single new building down on Main Street, and oddly enough the most drastic change there accounts for the fact that Jamestown is one of the most intact old mining towns in the Mother Lode area today. By tearing down or removing shacks and houses between Main Street and Woods Creek, the new State Highway 108 bypasses Jamestown to the west. Automobile drivers bent on getting to Sonora in five minutes on this four lane road speed past, seeing only the rear of Jamestown's Main Street homes and stores and a few trailers parked in what is left of Back-of-Town. But on quiet Main street many homes and business buildings remain as in mining days even to occupancy by descendants of original owners. Names of mail sorted by postmaster "Teenie" Madrid are largely those of old-timers including families of his own brothers, Morris, Jack and ...., who were all long-time Sierra employees. In "Hap" Collard's saloon, descendants of early day Chinese prepare their native dishes. Indians from dwindling Chicken Ranch under Table Mountain come into town in battered cars, but fullbloods like respected old Jesse Falls, who walked into Jamestown every day for forty years are seldom seen.

Up at the depot, the eastbound train has dropped off three more cars and is sliding over the hills toward Sonora. She slows and stops to drop off two empties at the U. S. Lime Products plant. Then with her diesels blasting she makes the turn into Sonora where two full cars are spotted at the freight shed.

Just across the ravine a steady stream of automobiles move along Mono, or 108, Highway which is almost solidly built up for five miles out of Sonora. On the brow of the hill above the road where a blast of dynamite was set off almost sixty years ago to celebrate the coming of Sierra's Iron Horse to town, stands Sonora's youth center. Just off the road is radio station KROG over which the Sierra Railroad sponsors broadcasts of local sports. On up Highway 108 is Twain Harte, newest and second largest town in the county, built on mining claims. Then Sugar Pine, Long Barn and Pine Crest — these and dozens of other vacation resorts on are magnificent Mono Road winding past forested summits from which lumberjacks are still hacking freight for the Sierra Railroad.

Up Washington Street, at the intersection of Highway 108, is Sonora Inn, or "Captain" Nevills old Hotel "Vic" in modern disguise. Ten minutes north of Washington Street by car is the State's memorial to '49'ers, or gold-famous Columbia. That old town's fleeting rebirth, when marble was hewn there by such men as the Sierra Railway's Prince Poniatowski, is a forgotten interim. A careful observer driving twenty minutes further on Highway 49 could detect the remnants of the abandoned Angels Branch grade which is almost followed as the road dips down to Melones Lake, crosses the Stanislaus River on a spacious new bridge and climbs into Calaveras County by sharp S turns. Few drivers today realize that this backwater behind the Goodwin dam submerges a town, two bridges, a fabulous tunnel and a mill which beat like a pulse for sixty years in the bottom of that canyon. Or that such were the fabulously rich mine operations which brought a railroad to this crossing of the Stanislaus River canyon.

The dieselized Sierra's eastbound freight train leaves Sonora, passing the county hospital where locomotive Engineers McCallum and Baker remember to wave at the old man who always sits on the porch waiting to wave back because he is old time Bridge Crewman Esteban Castan. Rumbling around curving Sullivan's Creek bridge, the *No. 4* train speeds up and easily pulls eleven cars over Buck Horn Hill. At Ralph's Station she grinds to a stop to drop off three loaded cars, two oilers and three empties.

Toward the west, sawmill smoke marks the town of Standard where the Pickering lumber empire puts out approximately

400,000 feet of lumber daily. Logs brought to this sawmill by the Pickering Lumber Corporation railroad over seventy-two miles of track are now hauled by diesels *No. 101* and *No. 102*. These were bought by new Manager F. F. Momeyer, succeeding the venerable manager and vice-president, Jack Rassenfuss. Pickering's old Heisler, their *No. 3*, bought from the Sierra Railroad, has been donated to California's Travel Town in Southern California. Their *No. 2*, a Shay, also once an Angels Branch locomotive, stands in silent dignity on a cement platform at Standard City. Sierra's eastbound train now pulling an oiler and a few box cars leaves Ralph's Station and slides down Buck Horn Hill into Tuolumne where she slows past drying yards and box factory to stop at the freight sheds. Across the park are Tuolumne's World War II memorial buildings on the site of Bullock's spacious Turn Back Inn.

Tuolumne, the lumber town, now faces a possible repeat of those depression years when its mill lay idle. In March, 1958, the Pickering Lumber Corporation took over the entire West Side Lumber Company. That month the *Western Railroader* magazine said:

> "The fate of the West Side's narrow gauge railroad is very much in doubt and speculation is that the West Side mill will be abandoned and logs diverted to the more modern Pickering mill at Standard."

However, as the March, 1960, Sierra diesel train comes into Tuolumne, such is not the case. Having escaped the hazards of fire, the West Side mill, oldest in California's pine region, is still operating. One of the company's little Shays comes smoking and puffing up out of the Tuolumne River canyon at this time, and as usual stops at the brow of the hill just outside of town to let off steam before chugging on to the millsite pulling four cars of mammoth sugar pine logs.

Carters is a forgotten town without mining or miners, but partially rebuilt as part of Tuolumne. A few local prospectors looking more for fun than profit sometimes dive for pay dirt in the Tuolumne River or work a backyard sluice box. High grade ores worked in this small way are reduced to amalgam with quicksilver, then melted and sent to the mint. Mining families in Soulsbyville now live to the tune of a small but active private lumber industry. A half dozen Indian families live on the site of a disbanded reservation since the death, in 1958, of picturesque Chief Fuller.

After a little switching, the *No. 4* westbound is made up with carloads of lumber. Locomotive operators and trainmen have a spell of railroad jargon over an early supper before starting back down the grade. As they pick up full cars and empties spotted at Mother Lode stations and sidings, the train grows. By dusk it is winding back onto level plains with the diesel's brake control slipped into running position. The strong yellow lights of the westbound illuminate the whole countryside as she comes home for the night to Oakdale.

In 1959, the Sierra Railroad moved an average of nine million tons of freight per year to and from two private lumber railroads at its eastern terminus and two major main lines at its western terminus. With over a million dollars in assets, it pays regular dividends to common and preferred stockholders, chief of whom are its "grandparents," the Crocker interests. The Sierra Railroad was born with money from Charles Crocker's Crocker-Woolworth Bank; was nurtured by son William H. Crocker of the Crocker National Bank and is now guided by grandson W. W. Crocker, 1959 Chairman of the Board of the Crocker-Anglo Bank.

When Joaquin Miller said, "There is more poetry in the rush of a single railroad train across the continent than in all the glory story of burning Troy," he was lauding construction versus destruction and the steam engine as dramatic builder of the West. The Sierra Railroad is a little short line that never crossed the continent nor grew beyond one hundred and forty-four miles, but no other railroad even came that far into the Mother Lode country of California or could have stayed longer. Her snorting wood burners came to those hills in the days when many a man would rather have his hand on the throttle of an Iron Horse than be a Bonanza King. These were some of the men who took Sierra Railroad trains through the coal and oil burning days of her peak of activity when her two long and two short were life-bringing whistles at every Tuolumne crossroad. Men who stood by as she abandoned 85 miles of branches, which made her too long, and who maintain her today, on 57 miles of dieselized track which might one day be too short.

BIOGRAPHICAL SKETCHES

A few sidelights on Thomas S. Bullock and Prince Andre Poniatowski, not previously touched on, are here included.

T. S. Bullock was born in Indiana in 1853, and came to California when he was only eighteen years of age. After a few weeks spent unprofitably in Los Angeles he set out to walk from there to Arizona. There he became so successful with an Arizona contractor that he was able to go into his own contracting business in New York City, where he made considerable money building street railways. After a trip abroad, he returned to Arizona and promoted his Prescott Central Arizona Railroad. The next nine years were spent promoting a railroad from Monterrey to Tampico, in Mexico, after which he returned to California and became engaged in the promotion of the Sierra Railway with coincidental branches and lumber companies now known.

Prince Andre Poniatowski, of noble Polish family, came to California in 1893 from France as a promoter of French and English capital. While associating in high social circles in Europe and America he was a known sportsman, soldier, composer, banker, promoter and diplomat. His career as a promoter in California was coincidental with his marriage to Elizabeth Sperry, niece of the grain magnate of that name and sister-in-law to Mr. William Crocker. When the California Exploration Company was first promoted with English capital in the sum of $300,000, and Western (principally Crocker) capital in a like sum, Poniatowski was President, W. H. Crocker, Treasurer and Mr. Richard Parker, an American mining engineer previously employed by Consolidated Goldfield in Africa, was General Manager. Working for C.E.C., Poniatowski and Parker marked some twenty mining claims, principally in Calaveras County, with the letters C.E.C. for option or purchase. Returning from this trip, Poniatowski joined with Bullock as before explained in railroad promotion.

Bullock was then a vigorous capitalist with no pretense of being other than a self made man. With great self confidence while joining in the grand manner of speculation open to Americans of his day, he was prepared to invest his own money in his promotional enterprises. On the other hand the legitimate social prestige of Poniatowski was an admitted asset in the promotion of other men's capital. In this respect Bullock was more of a gambler and sportsman than Poniatowski though the Prince was better known as both in the ethical sense here implied. These men of opposing personalities were bonded in ambitious friendship as they planted the seed that grew into the Sierra Railroad.

While men associated with Bullock for over thirty years in California considered him a man of inspired ability it was also known that his enthusiasm, at times, carried him beyond the realm of engineering practicability. Such an instance was the forming of his first company to build a branch line from the Sierra Railroad to Yosemite Valley which was to run from Tuolumne to Hetch Hetchy Valley with a spur shooting off to Yosemite across a canyon one mile wide and 1,000 feet deep. His plan was to stretch a cable across that canyon and run cars back and forth on it loaded with passengers. The cars were designed, details worked out and the cable actually bought. This cable still lay curled up in a heap in Jamestown on December 20, 1905, when Bullock's brother-in-law, S. D. Freshman said, "It was Bullock's scheme and he was very enthusiastic about his aerial tramway. Newell talked him out of it but he still thinks that is the best way to reach Yosemite. If you want to get a beautiful rise out of him just ask about that cable he wanted to stretch across a canyon one mile wide and 1,000 feet deep."

Bullock's courageous ideas were reflected in his personality. His pretty nine year old daughter, Louise, remembers her father's composure when a gun was pointed at him by Captain Nevills who threatened to shoot him for misrepresentation of their fifty-fifty venture in the Nevills Hotel. Nevills desisted when Bullock meaningfully nodded toward his daughter who was riding with him, and suggested that a more suitable place in which to commit murder or dissolve a partnership would be in his office the next day.

Bullock's courage in financial speculation was being carried to the hilt at the time of his death in 1920, when his controlling interest in the Sierra Railway had become a liability instead of an asset. Years later, when his son, Jack Bullock, sold the last of the Tuolumne County property previously owned by T. S. Bullock, the books of a memorable entity in the era of Cavalier Financiers in that area were regretfully closed. That memory has been revived from time to time in print.

While Bullock was still living, California Congressman S. D. Woods wrote a flowery biography of his legal client in his book titled "Lights and Shadows of Life on the Pacific Coast." In part, Woods wrote; "In 1897, when the Prescott line was transplanted to the Sierra Railway location the country there had to be quickened. To this Bullock applied himself. He was a tireless genius who wrought a change in the whole country in fifteen years. There is always breadth in what Bullock does. His dollars must work and along large lines. With the instinct of a seer, in 1893, Bullock bought 550,000 acres in West Virginia and Kentucky which was clouded by the hostility of settlers and uncertain land claims. In wisdom and friendliness Bullock took only the coal, or under surface rights, and deeded homes to all the settlers after twenty years of conflict with the law over legality of title. Bullock is a kind gentleman, poised, patient, winning, charming and simple. He is as full of integrity as capacity. A man whose generous charities are quietly done. Bullock is a resourceful man who rarely asks for advice outside of technical matters. The year following the disaster of 1906, those who had launched new ventures requiring large sums of money were perilously near the verge of financial ruin. Bullock was among those for he was always loaded to the guards with such ventures but he rolled up his sleeves, shut his jaws together tight and fought the peril to a finish. And though it took off some of the flesh from his ribs, paled his cheeks a little and added white to his hair, he won out. As an example of what a poor boy may become and do with an honest heart and an heroic will in the 'Wild West' Tom Bullock stands out in fine relief."

This eulogy of T. S. Bullock was parodied in January, 1955, by California's humorist Idwal Jones, in his "Vague Sketch of a Railroad Builder Gone with the Wind," published in *Westways* magazine. Careless of names and facts, this sketch pictured "Tom" Bullock as a legendary character whom few people in the region of his "Sugar Pine" railroad had ever beheld and continued, in part, as follows: "Tom had no traffic with swank. He was a New York capitalist but that does not describe him. He came and went without notice by the press, a quiet man, immersed, even on the train, in figures. The list of his private charities was long and known only to himself although his attorney and friend, Congressman Samuel D. Woods, seemed aware of it. In 1871, Tom Bullock came to Los Angeles at age nineteen but left in a few days to take a tramp over the desert to Arizona where he arrived shoeless. After working in a mine for a year, he had his savings of eight dollars made into a ring. An hour later he was robbed of it in the first stage hold-up recorded in Arizona. He clerked to scrape fare to New York and soon found himself creating a street railway. In 1886, he returned to Arizona to build a railroad of his own from Seligmann to Prescott. His next exploit was to build four hundred miles of railroad from Tampico to Monterrey which he sold to a French Syndicate. His profit of two millions was halved by the drop of the price of silver in the U.S.A. That Tampico route is now part of the Mexican Central Railway system. His Sierra Railway was a rather minor enterprise. It is unlikely that he visited it more than twice and court business prevented him from attending the last luncheon of consequence along the Sugar Pine." The setting for this "luncheon of consequence" as described by author Idwal Jones was a box car. The menu including grouse, rabbit, grapes, crêpes and a jug of red wine from the Willows Hotel in Jamestown.

Sidelights on Thomas Bullock and the origins of the Sierra Railway are included by Prince Andre Poniatowski in his fascinating memoirs titled "D'Une Siecle A l'Autre." According to these memoirs, the Prince was on the point of backing Bullock's proposition alone, when Mr. William Crocker joined him and the Sierra Railway Company formed. Poniatowski then relates how he set out with Bullock to find the "ideal road within the limits of our possibilities," which would reach the mines marked by C.E.C. and timber in the Calaveras Big Trees area which had awed and economically enthused the Prince on his first buckboard trip there with his wife. When Oakdale was chosen as the gateway to these immediate objectives Prince Poniatowski placed his last C.E.C. mark on the Bellview Mine for which his syndicate paid $150,000.

Six months later, when Bullock's construction company had completed the second ten mile section of the Sierra Railway, Poniatowski writes that Mr. Henry Crocker relieved him of his outstanding stock in that line amounting to around $655,000 worth, leaving a profit of $350,000 in shares which had cost the Prince nothing except time spent in promotion. Turning then to the second essential for more modern mining operations, or electric power, Poniatowski reviewed the six hundred miles of old mining flumes and ditches with lake and river sources in Calaveras County. While inspecting these possible sources of power, Poniatowski asked Bullock to make a trip with him to the Blue Lakes on the North Fork of the Mokelumne River to ascertain the extent to which that area was suited to his enterprise. In spring of 1897, the by now, two old traveling companions set out only to find those lakes inaccessible from the California side of the Sierra Nevada Mountains, due to snow. Undaunted, they crossed the mountains by Central Pacific rails and approached the lakes from the Nevada side. At the 8,000 foot elevation in Alpine County, Bullock became too ill to proceed but the determined Polish Frenchman continued by horseback trail to the lakes. The result of this trip was an agreement with the Blue Lakes Water Company to build a power plant where the water was let down to the Mokelumne River. A small plant was in operation by October, 1897, but planned only to be used in building a desired, larger hydro-electric plant. Due to the high estimated cost of this next enterprise, the California Exploration Company was reformed in January of 1898 to become the California Exploration Limited, for which Prince Poniatowski promoted new English capital. The then completed hydro-electric power plant, known as the Standard Electric Company's "Electra," was again taken over by banker W. H. Crocker, for completion of the job, at which time Prince Poniatowski resigned his Presidency. In 1902, the "Electra" furnished Oakland, and later San Francisco, with their first electric power and continued in operation for fifty years. However successful this project became, it did not succeed in its original intent, however, which was to revive the mining industry in the Southern Mother Lode.

Though not a partner in this power promotion, Bullock continued to be associated with Prince Poniatowski in many ventures besides the Sierra Railway. In July, 1901, they met in Chicago with Mr. Ripley, President of the Atchison Railway Company, whose California representative had sounded them out on the possibility of the Atchison acquiring possession of the Sierra Railway. They then agreed to sell their controlling interest in the line for fifty dollars a share which would return the Prince $175,000 and Bullock three times as much. One week after this agreement, they were stunned by a letter from Ripley regretting his inability to go on with the offer. Six weeks later, when they suggested to Mr. Harriman, the railroad magnate, that the Southern Pacific might benefit by a controlling interest in the Sierra Railway, Harriman admitted that it was he who had stopped their sale to Ripley by conceding and arranging advantages to their larger paralleling lines which precluded an investment in the Sierra Railroad by him, also.

To quote from "D'une Siecle A l'Autre" in which Prince Poniatowski wrote many years later to his three grown sons; "I learned, thus, from Harriman, how two great California financiers made a pact, under our very noses, whereby neither one nor the other would control the Sierra Railway . . . and it was not until two years later that I sold my shares, for a considerably less price, to my old associate. In the course of my fifteen years spent with Americans of all kinds and sorts, I never met another Bullock. A practical man, of quick decisions, I never heard him raise his voice. In cases of controversy he merely smiled and listened imperturbably for events to turn in his favor which they usually did. At an early age this eastern farm boy went to Arizona, which was his idea of the wild and woolly West. In three years of hard labor, he barely made a living but acquired enough business acumen to negotiate a contract for his boss which netted him eighteen thousand dollars while still in his twenties. He then put six thousand dollars in the bank for a new start at a later date and spent a year traveling in Europe like a king, spending one thousand dollars a month. Returning to Arizona, he went into partnership with his old employer and both became wealthy in a few years. This background no doubt gave Bullock his apparent intellectual distinction, although found in a man who obviously lacked the least rudiments of a primary education. Since he could not spell, he avoided writing and always asked me to read aloud the documents on which I wanted his signature. Contracts made by us in January might not correspond exactly with the changes made in May and it was our practice to have our respective lawyers make the changes and months and years went by without our signing anew. So, for seven years, 1896 to 1903, our numerous operations undertaken together were in the form of verbal agreements which never once gave rise to the least question between us. Affairs carried on in this way, achieve, by the nature of their handling, a flavor of elegance, almost of chivalry, which relegates the usual methods to second class by the rather sordid under-currents that they suggest.

The inspection trips taken by Bullock and me always necessitated our spending the night where it overtook us. We rode mountain horses accustomed to steep ravines and cliffs and Bullock would let his reins drop on the pommel of his saddle, his eyes fixed on the contours of the land while he mechanically jiggled a tiny valise fastened with steel buttons which was his only baggage. He was the only American who wore buttoned boots because, on his trip to Europe he had accumulated an unusual collection. An unforgettable man."

While the above paragraphs taken from Prince Poniatowski's memoirs give us flashes of insight into the character of his well remembered associate, so also, do they give us a glimpse at the man the writer himself was. An amazingly adventurous European gentleman accustomed to wealth and luxury, yet abstemious of liquor and adaptable to whatever hardships his persistent and courageous forays into new countries and undertakings might incur. After reestablishing his residence in France, this voyager to adventures all over the world lived to be ninety years of age. Having been called by W. H. Crocker and others—"The Prince of Bankers and Banker of Princes" his touch at the roots of the Sierra Railway Company lent it a distinction that once again sets it apart from the average American shortline railroad.

LOCOMOTIVES OF THE SIERRA RAILROAD

When the general offices of the Sierra were destroyed by fire on May 1, 1913, the original records were lost. Since many of the original engines were second hand, there is no tracing of them from the builders' records.

It is known that there were several strange engines on the line in its early days either rented or on trial for possible later purchase. Most of these were returned to the owners or as in the case of the supposed Heisler No. 2, were left to rust in the yards at Jamestown. World War I saw most of the scrap cleared out and no mention made of what was sold.

D. S. Richter and G. M. Best made a thorough study of the motive power by going over what records were available and consulting retired Sierra personnel. The resulting roster was published in "A Brief History of the Sierra Railroad," by *The Western Railroader* and is herewith reproduced with their permission.

NO.	YEAR BUILT	BUILDER AND NO.	TYPE	DIAM. OF DRIVERS	CYLINDERS	WEIGHT
1		No data available	4-4-0			
2	1889	New York (506)	0-6-0	44	18x26	94500
3	1891	Rogers (4493)	4-6-0	56	17x24	100000
		in service for movie and TV work				
4	1882	Baldwin (5851)	4-4-0	62	17x24	80000
5	1899	Schenectady (5177)	0-6-0			
6	1883	Baldwin (6113)	4-4-0	62	17x24	80000
7	1882	Baldwin (5674)	4-4-0	62	17x24	80000
9	1899	Heisler (1036)	2 truck	40	16¾x14	104000
10	1902	Shay, Lima (718)	2 truck	36	12x12	120000
11	1903	Shay, Lima (788)	2 truck	36	12x12	120000
12	1903	Shay, Lima (789)	3 truck	36	14½x15	180000
18	1906	Baldwin (29790)	2-8-0	42	18x22	111850
20	1916	Baldwin (43344)	2-8-0	42	18x22	118850
22	1920	Baldwin (53205)	2-8-0	42	18x22	121000
24	1912	Baldwin (39577)	2-8-0	50	20x26	163000
26	1908	Baldwin (32646)	2-6-0	48	18x24	124000
28	1922	Baldwin (55246)	2-8-0	48	19x26	142000
		in service for excursions				
30	1922	Baldwin (55412)	2-6-2	42	15x24	98000
32	1923	Baldwin (57010)	2-6-2	46	16x24	106200
34	1925	Baldwin (58679)	2-8-2	46	19x26	175000
		in Jamestown roundhouse				
36	1930	Schenectady (68278)	2-8-2	50	21x28	207000
		in Jamestown roundhouse				
38	1934	Baldwin (61781)	2-6-6-2	51	31-20x28	293000
40	1955	Baldwin-Lima-Hamilton (76092)		40	1200 HP	240000
		in service				
42	1955	Baldwin-Lima-Hamilton (76093)		40	1200 HP	240000
		in service				

INDEX

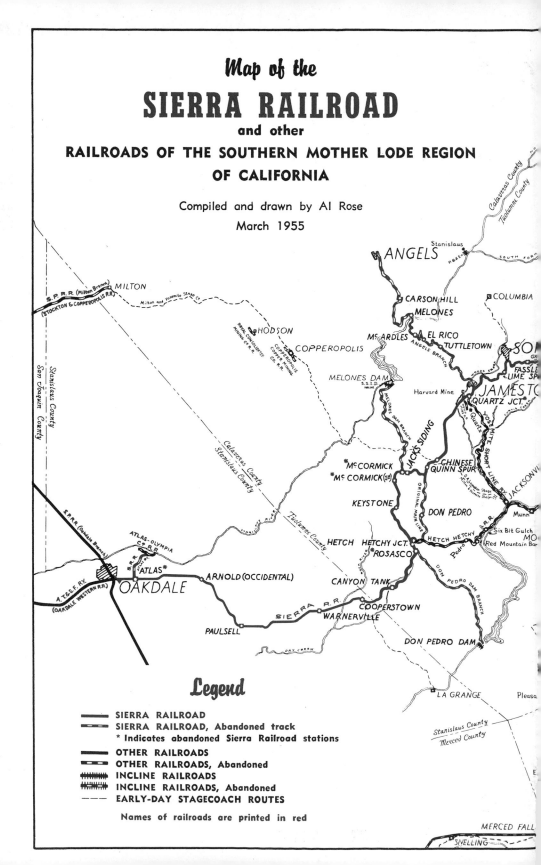

Map of the
SIERRA RAILROAD
and other
RAILROADS OF THE SOUTHERN MOTHER LODE REGION
OF CALIFORNIA

Compiled and drawn by Al Rose

March 1955

Legend

— SIERRA RAILROAD
‑ ‑ SIERRA RAILROAD, Abandoned track
* Indicates abandoned Sierra Railroad stations

━ OTHER RAILROADS
■━■ OTHER RAILROADS, Abandoned
╫╫╫ INCLINE RAILROADS
╫╫╫ INCLINE RAILROADS, Abandoned
‑‑‑ EARLY-DAY STAGECOACH ROUTES

Names of railroads are printed in red